Harlem Renaissance

Harlem Renaissance

NATHAN IRVIN HUGGINS

OXFORD UNIVERSITY PRESS
LONDON OXFORD NEW YORK

The page following constitutes an extension of the copyright page.

POEMS BY CLAUDE MCKAY
"Africa," "After the Winter," "America," "Baptism," "If We Must Die,"
and "To the White Fiends," from *Selected Poems of Claude McKay*
(copyright 1953 by Bookman Associates, Inc.) are reprinted by permission
of Twayne Publishers, Inc.

For Sue Bailey Thurman

Acknowledgments

I was helped in this book, in one way or another, by many people. I cannot thank them all on these pages, but I shall list a few with the briefest explanation of their assistance to me.

Henry F. May taught me a lot about the 1920s and American intellectual history. Kenneth M. Stampp first inspired me to do work in what is now called Afro-American history. Oscar Handlin opened my mind to social and cultural history. Howard Mumford Jones has been a friend to me in many ways, and he encouraged me to write this book when it was only a germ of an idea.

A summer's research was made possible by a faculty grant from Lake Forest College in Illinois. Ernest Kaiser of the Schomburg Collection of the New York Public Library, Wendell Wray of the Countee Cullen Branch of the New York Public Library, Helen Willard of the Harvard Theatrical Collection of the Harvard College Library, and Donald Gallup of the Yale University Library were very generous with their time and most helpful to me. I have no individual name, but the staff at the Theatre Collection of the New York Public Library at the Lincoln Center for the Performing Arts was of help to me too. Mary Beattie Brady talked to me for hours about some of the participants in the Harmon Foundation art competitions in the 1920s.

I was able to interview many whose names appear in the book: Regina Andrews, A. Philip Randolph, Louise Thompson Patterson, Aaron Douglas. I talked at length with the late Max Eastman at his Martha's Vineyard home in the summer of 1969. Of course, I am very grateful for the time and assistance of all of them. Two whom I interviewed, however, call for a special word. Meta Warrick Fuller, whose active years as a sculptress reached back into the nineteenth century, was in her ninety-first year when I talked with her. Her mind was alert and her perceptions were sharp in what was to be the last year of her life. Langston Hughes came to Boston one April day to read his poems. It was a cool afternoon, but there was a golden sun that came through the windows of the Charles Street Meeting House. And Hughes's ingenuousness warmed everybody as if he were a radiant sun. It was fitting that Langston Hughes should read his poetry from a pulpit that other great blacks had used: Frederick Douglass, Sojourner Truth. In the afterglow of that day—far into the night —he chainsmoked cigarettes and talked to me about the 1920s and all the people he thought wonderful (which was just about everybody). It could not have been more than ten days later that Langston Hughes was dead. I shall always regret that my mind and skills will not evoke in these pages the unrestricted gift of self that Hughes's April day was in Boston. But then, so too, all of his artistic life was such a free gift.

My research problems and questions engaged colleagues and friends. Bruce Kellner was of great help to me in locating photographs by Carl Van Vechten and securing for me permission to use them. Two colleagues at the University of Massachusetts at Boston were of particular help. Suzanne Gassner challenged and prodded me about my arguments from psychological assumptions. She helped me to see more clearly than I would have some of the questions I attempted to answer in Chapter 6. Thomas N. Brown brought to my attention some of Eugene O'Neill's thought on the use of masks in theater. Other colleagues read or listened sympathetically and made useful suggestions: Leon Litwack, Lawrence Levine, Samuel Haber, Jane Johnson Benardette, Henry F. May.

I mention Stephen Booth separately, because talks with him were always special to me. He always knew instantly what I was trying to get at. And he was generally able to ask the next question or to provoke associations and implications that would be fresh to me.

Ann Chiarenza read some chapters with a keen editor's eye. At different stages, Dorothy Hall and Dorothy Johnson typed the manuscript with care and attention to detail. Brenda Carlita Smith, who has become my wife, helped me check for final corrections, and I am very grateful for her help, love, and support.

My debt to the one this book is dedicated to goes beyond explanation. Her belief in me, when there was little to rest it on, was a profound influence on my spiritual and intellectual development. She reared me from the subjunctive to the declarative mood.

As with all things, the publication of this book depended on far more people than can be listed on a few pages. The ones that I have mentioned certainly must be acknowledged here. I trust that none, because his name appears on these pages, will be embarrassed because of the book I have written. All responsibility for what I have said is my own.

N.I.H.

Contents

Harlem Renaissance

Introduction

It is a rare and intriguing moment when a people decide that they are the instruments of history-making and race-building. It is common enough to think of oneself as part of some larger meaning in the sweep of history, a part of some grand design. But to presume to be an actor and creator in the special occurrence of a people's birth (or rebirth) requires a singular self-consciousness. In the opening decades of the twentieth century, down into the first years of the Great Depression, black intellectuals in Harlem had just such a self-concept. These Harlemites were so convinced that they were evoking their people's "Dusk of Dawn" that they believed that they marked a renaissance.

Historians have liked to use that word to characterize some moment when a "culture," once dormant, has been reawakened. But even the most conventional of them will confess the concept is a historical fiction, a contrivance of imaginations steeped in resurrections and similar rites of spring. Seldom, however, have the people—tne subjects of such history— knowing their roles, inquired of themselves, "how goes the

Renaissance?" While not so exaggerated, that was what Harlem men of culture were doing in the 1920s.

Of course, our own moment of history has given us preoccupations of our own. Harlem now connotes violence, crime, and poverty. For many, it represents a source of militancy, radical social change, and black community culture. "Ghetto" and "Harlem" have become, to most, interchangeable words. Whether we see the ghetto as a center of despair or source of hope, we tend to read back into the past our assumptions, perceptions, and expectations. But the 1920s were almost a half-century ago, and we may miss more than we learn when we force upon that time our own frustrations. Recent histories of that "Black Metropolis" have tended to treat it as always having been a ghetto in the making. Because of our compelling interest in the morphology of the economically deprived, we are likely to be insensitive to the fact that to Harlemites in an earlier decade the concept of Harlem becoming a ghetto would have seemed absurd. James Weldon Johnson believed that Harlem promised a future of "greater and greater things" for the Afro-American; he wrote as much in *Black Manhattan*, notably published in 1930.[1] Johnson's optimism, and that of the renaissance generation, had not been soured by an economic depression which drove home the special vulnerability of Negroes, a war which informed the world of pathological racism, and promises and dreams which were glibly announced and rudely deferred. The generation which Johnson spoke to, which this book is about, was optimistic and progressive. It would take more defeat than they had yet known for them to believe that what they were building would, in time, imprison them.

All of the ingredients for ghetto-making were in evidence in the 1920s. Yet, in those years few Harlem intellectuals addressed themselves to issues related to tenements, crime, violence, and poverty. Even *Opportunity*, the magazine of the Urban League and social work among Negroes, did not discuss urban problems as much as it announced the Negro's coming of age. In part this was due, no doubt, to the desire of black leaders to stress black achievement rather than black problems. A positive self-image—there was cause for one—was considered the best starting point for a better chance. Inequities due to race might best be removed when reasonable men saw that black men were thinkers, strivers, doers, and were cultured, like themselves. Harlem intellectuals, with their progressive assumptions, saw themselves as the ones most likely to make this demonstration. They were on the threshold of a new day.

Present-day readers are likely to be annoyed with what they will see to be the naïveté of men like Johnson. Some would call them elitists when it comes to culture. With notable exceptions, like Langston Hughes, most Harlem intellectuals aspired to *high* culture as opposed to that of the common man, which they hoped to mine for novels, poems, plays, and symphonies. They saw art and letters as a bridge across the chasm between the races. Artists of both races, they thought, were more likely to be free of superstition, prejudice, and fear than ordinary men. They might meet on the common ground of shared beauty and artistic passion. It was thought that this alliance "at the top" would be the agency to bring the races together over the fissures of ignorance, suspicion, and fear. Despite a history that had divided them, art and culture would re-form the brotherhood in a common humanity.

This was an attitude of cultural elitism. But it is wrong to assume that these black intellectuals, because of it, were not related to the black common man in Harlem. I think that in the early decades of this century most Negroes were apt to agree that it was a good thing to have Negroes writing "good" novels, poems, plays, and symphonies. Not always because they could read, listen, and understand them, but because the fact that these works were written was a remarkable achievement. And such achievement, because it was elite in character, was a source of race pride and an argument against continued discrimination. While many Afro-Americans might call Harlem intellectuals "dicty niggers" and laugh at their pretensions, they would also glow in the reflection of their honor.

Many of our generation, alienated by what are thought to be corrupt middle-class values, may be impatient with the unquestioned bourgeois assumptions of these men, especially because they were black men. This, too, is more our problem than theirs. The people from affluent homes (white and black) who have come to maturity in the 1950s and 1960s have been disillusioned by the spiritual emptiness at the top of the up-ward-mobility escalator. And we have all been a bit inclined to romanticize the honesty and the relevancy of the man at the bottom. Again, we must remember, however, for Afro-Ameri-cans in the 1920s individual achievement connoted more than personal comfort and ease. The future of the race seemed to depend on men and women making it in America. Doctors, lawyers, judges, teachers, poets, writers, and actors were essen-tial, in their achievement, because they showed that it could be done, and they leveled barriers for others—so it was thought. So, what may appear to us to be attitudes of bour-geois naïveté were very often highly race-conscious and aggres-sive.

Our problem here, as in any history, is to see men and women of another era in their own terms and not our own. And that will require of us a humanism that will modulate our own egos and self-consciousness enough to perceive theirs. Their world was different from ours. We must start there.

Like others of that generation whose collective experience was World War I, Harlemites were caught up in its wake. Surely the ethnocentrism that generated self-determination as an Allied aim in that war informed a new racial awareness among blacks throughout the world. The war also forced a re-

evaluation of Western civilization and encouraged non-Euro-
peans to esteem their own cultures as being as valid and civilized as Europe's. War-disillusioned white men (American and
European), on the other hand, helped enhance a black self-
concept through their own search for valid, authentic experience. Even before the war, Freud and the new psychology
caused sophisticated people to deny the artifices of civility and
manner and to seek the true self through spontaneity and the
indulgence of impulse. In so far as Afro-Americans could see
their own lives as being more natural and immediate than
their countrymen's, they could be convinced that the mere ac-
centuation of their characteristic spontaneity would work toward the creation of a new Negro, a new man. Indeed, if anyone doubted that the black man's time had come, he needed
only look at the awakening of Mother Africa as evidenced in
the recent European discoveries and appreciation of African
culture and civilization. Such elements of the spirit of the age
contributed to the Harlemites' view of themselves and their
historic role.

While their world was different from ours—their attitudes
and assumptions different—it is nevertheless familiar to us. I
discovered, when I looked through the eyes of those men who
thought themselves the harbingers of the "New Negro," ana-
logues to our own age of black self-consciousness which were
compelling. Their assertion of the militant self, their search for
ethnic identity and heritage in folk and African culture, and
their promotion of the arts as the agent which was to define
and to fuse racial integrity resonate what we hear about us
now, fifty years later. Black men of the 1920s, as easily as our
own Afro-American contemporaries, talked of the end of Negro
accommodation, of the importance of ethnic identity, of the
new day a' dawning when black men would have and would
wield power. Such similarities between now and then suggest
fundamental characteristics of American racial life that have

provoked the same questions and responses time and again. For, as all who have studied the story of the African in America will know (and as those Harlemites seemed not to know), the formulations of racial identity and culture in the 1920s were variations on earlier themes which have persisted into our own time. What I have wanted to do in this book is to illuminate, through a searching look at this one instance of Negro self-consciousness, that essential condition of American life which has caused such periodic racial identity crises.

But even to speak of racial identity crisis is to distort, I have come to think. For, looking outside the confines of race, looking at the general American culture, one finds a no less persistent and recurrent demand to define American character and American culture. From Hector St. John Crevecoeur to Max Lerner, the effort to characterize "this American, this new man" has been an intense and serious national sport. Students of "American civilization" will also be familiar with the equally persistent (and compulsive) announcements of the "coming of age" of American culture. Such definitions of American character and trumpetings of cultural maturity seem necessarily repeated time after time, as if they had never occurred before. The simple matter is that Americans have been a provincial people, forever self-conscious of themselves and their society in the making, and pulled by the powerful gravity of the European civilization to which they are heir and, despite claims to independence, which they emulate. Negroes, no less than other Americans, have suffered this same condition. Even more so, in fact, for Afro-Americans have inhabited a special ethnic province within provincial America. They have been perplexed by the desire to emulate the European-entranced white American and by the equally appealing dream of self-definition through the claiming of their inheritance of African culture. But from the perspective of their ethnic province it has been impossible for black men to see how American their predicament is. White Americans and white American culture have had no more claim to self-confidence than black. The Negro has been unable to see the beam in the white man's eye for the mote in his own. For both black and white Americans, art has been the more problematic because of these provincial uncertainties.

It was commonly thought, in those decades around World War I, that culture (literature, art, music, etc.) was the true measure of civilization. Harlem intellectuals, sharing in that belief and seeing themselves as living out the moment of their race's rebirth, naturally marked off their achievement by such artistic production. Thus they promoted poetry, prose, painting, and music as if their lives depended on it. Most of us who have looked at this episode have merely accepted those same assumptions and applauded this self-styled Harlem Renaissance because it was a period of considerable artistic activity. I have chosen, rather, to probe into the pretensions of some of the artists and their works and by doing so place them within the context of American cultural history. Because this book does not simply remark and congratulate, some readers may be disappointed. For in questioning the quality of the works—the artistic achievement—I necessarily challenge the success of the "renaissance" in delivering what it claimed for itself. Some will argue that in our day of crisis of black identity it is harmful to question *any* Afro-American achievement; positive self-concept needs pure black poets as well as pure black heroes. I have chosen, however, to avoid that condescension which judges all Negro art as required evidence of a black cultural contribution. Who really needs such proof? I have preferred to use the works that I discuss to expose peculiarites of Afro-American expression. Such critical analysis is necessary to any true understanding of black identity in America.

Harlem intellectuals promoted Negro art, but one thing is very curious, except for Langston Hughes, none of them took jazz—the new music—seriously. Of course, they all mentioned it as background, as descriptive of Harlem life. All said it was important in the definition of the New Negro. But none thought enough about it to try and figure out what was happening. They tended to view it as a folk art—like the spirituals and the dance—the unrefined source for the new art. Men like James Weldon Johnson and Alain Locke expected some race genius to appear who would transform that source into *high* culture. That was, after all, the dream of Johnson's protagonist in *Autobiography of an Ex-Coloured Man* as he fancied symphonic scores based on ragtime. The same improbable will-o'-the-wisp entranced white musicians like Paul Whiteman and George Gershwin. It perplexed black musicians like James P. Johnson and Fats Waller. We now know better, but some would have said that Duke Ellington was mesmerised as well. Anyway, the promoters of the Harlem Renaissance were so fixed on a vision of *high* culture that they did not look very hard or well at jazz.

It is a real pity, because it would have been wonderful to have had contemporary accounts of jazz in the making from curious and intelligent non-musicians. We know that various versions of ragtime, New Orleans music, and the blues were being welded into a fresh musical idiom within earshot of all Harlemites. Louis Armstrong (occasionally in New York City), Jelly Roll Morton, James P. Johnson, etc., were at the prime of their creative lives. Duke Ellington, Fletcher Henderson, and Don Redman were already learning to give orchestral form to a music of improvisation and virtuosity. It is clear enough, now, that the blues were more than sad, bawdy, and entertaining songs. They were (not like spirituals) the ironic voice of free men, conscious of the unmitigating paradox of being free men and black men. Were it not for Langston Hughes, we would have almost no specific notice of that art from the Harlem writers. It is very ironic that a generation that was searching for a new Negro and his distinctive cultural expression would have passed up the only really creative thing that was going on. But then, it is not too surprising. The jazzmen were too busy creating a cultural renaissance to think about the implications of what they were doing.

The black intellectuals were searching for their own identity, but they were bound up in a more general American experience than a "Harlem Renaissance" would suggest. For black and white Americans have been so long and so intimately a part of one another's experience that, will it or not, they cannot be understood independently. Each has needed the other to help define himself. The creation of Harlem as a place of exotic culture was as much a service to white need as it was to black. So essential has been the Negro personality to the white American psyche that black theatrical masks had become, by the twentieth century, a standard way for whites to explore dimensions of themselves that seemed impossible through their own *personae*. The blackface minstrel show stylized a Negro character type that black men used to serve as a passport through white America. Yet, the mask demeaned them while it hid them. Thus the strands of identity for Afro-Americans in the 1920s were confounded in a tradition of white/black self-concept that could not be unraveled by simple proclamations of the birth of the New Negro. In order to trace out some of these lines into the American psychic past, I have ventured in the last chapter beyond the limits of Harlem in the 1920s and have looked into the origins of such cultural phenomena as the minstrel show. I hope that the reader is not impatient with such forays. I think that they are necessary to expose facets of the Negro self-concept. I think that the readers' indulgence will be rewarded with a fuller understanding of American character and the black man within it.

In such ways, I hope that this book demonstrates something that I firmly believe: the study of the interplay between white and black in American life, the illumination of the Afro-American experience *within* American culture will serve to expand and infinitely enrich our sense of that "civilization." I say this not merely to confess my bias, but to alert the reader to the kind of questions he should ask of this book as he reads it. For I have wanted Harlem in the 1920s not to be the focus of this book, but rather a lens through which one might see a new view: white men and black men unknowingly dependent in their work to shape American character and culture. Whenever Americans do come of age, they will have gained true insight into themselves by the claiming of that dependence.

1 ♟ Harlem: Capital of the Black World

What made Harlem special was not that it was bawdy and tended to epitomize the most sordid aspects of the Jazz Age. While that was true enough, so had numerous other "colored districts" of American cities. New York had similar black centers in earlier years. James Weldon Johnson recalled one such district on West 35th Street that thrived around the turn of the century. Ike Hines's place, which Johnson described, had all of the qualities of the cabaret and "sporting life" that were later to characterize Harlem for many. Ike Hines's had collected black musicians and entertainers, and they, in turn, attracted scores of white pleasure-seekers and white heirs of the minstrel tradition in search of material for their blackfaced theatrical acts. There seem always to have been "darktowns." They were a bit spicy because of community indulgence. The respectable white citizenry sought pleasure in their brothels and cabarets. And their patronage shielded the extra-legal life of Negroes from police harassment. Harlem, before World War I and the years following, had all of these features. But the time and the circumstances of its creation made Harlem symbolize the Afro-American's coming of age.[1]

It is easy enough to understand why people saw more in Harlem than was there. It was the historic moment, among other things. Half a century had passed since the emancipation of slaves when black Harlem came into existence. What better point at which to declare the past of slavery and servility dead and to proclaim the new day of the liberated and independent black man? It was the twentieth century now after all, a time for new beginnings. Black Americans, like white Americans, were becoming an urban rather than a rural people. Large numbers of blacks had streamed into the northern cities in the first years of the new century, forced out by the poverty of southern agriculture and the mean brutality of southern racial bigotry. Harlem gained from that migration, as shortly after, in World War I, it gained from the waves of blacks who came to fill the war industries' labor needs that had been aggravated by the war-severed European immigration. Great numbers of blacks seemed to mean new power. It was the power of numbers after all, and the astute, economic aggressiveness of black businessmen that had snatched Harlem's newly developed real estate from white middle-class hands and converted it into the biggest and most elegant black community in the Western world. Harlem had thus freshly become a great concentration of blacks—not peasant but urban—within the most urbane of American cities then just feeling its youthful strength and posturing in self-conscious sophistication. No wonder Harlemites felt that they and their community were something special; not just another darktown. And when black soldiers paraded up Lenox Avenue to a jazz step—returning from a war that had ended war and guaranteed to all men the right of self-determination—it is not surprising that black men's dreams would find in Harlem a capital for the race, a platform from which the new black voice would be heard around the world, and an intellectual center of the New Negro.[2]

Afro-Americans, of course, were not the only ones in the first decades of this century to be deceived by their dreams and their innocence. That was common with Americans. But Negroes—up from slavery—had more to hope for than others, more of a dream to be deferred and then denied. The flourishing of Harlem came at just the right moment to indulge innocence and make it all seem possible.

It was just that sense of possibility and power that persuaded many black men and women to come to Harlem in the years around the Great War. Blacks who wanted to be where they could reach the widest audience—to organize and inspire blacks throughout the world, to cajole whites to reform. Those Negroes who had pretensions of talent and intellect wanted to be where, to greatest effect, they might convert their skills and minds into personal and racial success. Many saw Harlem as the retort where the best achievement of colored people would be crystallized into the hard, permanent stuff of the race's positive future. And, of course, as more self-confident, sophisticated, and articulate Negroes came to Harlem, the more attractive it became for others who wanted to make their way. By the end of the 1920s there was a discernible old and new guard of black intellectuals in New York. But whether old or young, Harlem had pulled them all the same.

When James Weldon Johnson moved to Harlem in 1914, he was actually coming to New York for a second time, following a young manhood of wide experience. His decision to establish himself in Harlem was, in fact, a final commitment to a life's work as an intellectual (a writer and poet), and as an organizer and propagandist for the Afro-American cause. Johnson had been successful at almost everything he touched as a young man. He had been a high school principal as well as a lawyer in his native Jacksonville, Florida. With his brother, J. Rosamund Johnson, and Bob Cole he had had enormous success writing songs and plays for the New York musical stage in

the first years of the century. This team excited Tin Pan Alley
with such hits as "A Maiden with the Dreamy Eyes," "Nobody's Lookin' but the Owl and the Moon," "Under the Bamboo Tree," and "The Congo Love Song"; they were among the
most popular songwriters of the period. Because he had been
active in Republican party politics Johnson was appointed to
the consular service, serving during the Theodore Roosevelt
and William Howard Taft administrations in Puerto Cabello,
Venezuela, and Corinto, Nicaragua. A very high intelligence, a
strong command of Spanish, and a conciliatory temperament
served to make Johnson an excellent consul. It was mainly
through his intelligence and skill that the United States was
able to place troops in Corinto during an insurrection in 1912.
While in Latin America, Johnson extended his literary talent.
He published two poems, with excellent critical reception:
"After Fifty Years" and "O Black and Unknown Bards." In addition to poetry, Johnson anonymously published his novel,
Autobiography of an Ex-Coloured Man. So by the time Johnson came to Harlem, he had tasted success in several fields.[3]

Johnson's decision to leave the consular service was
prompted by the political change that brought Woodrow Wilson and the Democrats to Washington. A career in the foreign
service that would be severely limited for Negroes under the
Republicans would surely be even more circumscribed under a
southern-dominated Democratic administration. One suspects,
however, that even under liberal circumstances, the consular
service would not for long have satisfied a man of Johnson's
wide range of talents and interests.

But his decision to come to New York was not automatic
upon leaving the foreign service. He had at first thought of returning to Jacksonville. His father had died in the years he
was in the Caribbean, and his mother hoped that one of her
sons would remain home. But the deterioration of race relations in the town had gone so far as to make it impossible for

him to stay. Perhaps the deterioration had not been so great, but his long experience outside the South made Johnson see it differently. Also, he had married a Brooklyn girl and now he had to see Jacksonville through her eyes. White men whom he had known from his boyhood seemed different now. Trivialities were annoying. White men, who had been his friends, were now embarrassed to greet him on the street, frightened away from all the courtesies like tipping their hats to his wife as they passed. Jacksonville was not a large town, everyone knew everyone else by name and reputation; the little courtesies were important. The trivial slights stung, and Johnson could no longer find a common ground with men who could not treat him as a man.

The New York that Johnson moved to in 1914 was strangely different from the city he had known before. The center of Negro entertainment and night life had moved uptown from the old Marshall Hotel on West 53rd Street, the place that he remembered. The trek had already begun to Harlem. J. Rosamund Johnson had been one of the first Negroes to buy a home west of Lenox Avenue, on 136th Street; James Weldon followed his brother's move. In 1917, James Weldon Johnson was asked to be the first Negro executive secretary of the National Association for the Advancement of Colored People, and he accepted. He served in that position until 1931, just seven years before his accidental death. His appointment in 1931 to the Adam K. Spence Chair of Creative Literature at Fisk University made it possible for him to devote full time to lecturing and writing. But through the 1920s he contributed strongly to the intellectual life of Harlem. He wrote editorials for the *New York Age* and published many poems, including *God's Trombones* (1927). In addition, he and J. Rosamund edited a collection of Negro spirituals. The city encouraged creative work. He was, in his words, "materializing the intangible." He had "minted some rather inconsequential dreams, and the process

seemed to possess an element of magic." As an official of the
NAACP, he succeeded in giving national organization and
strength to the Association. He attacked the brutality of white
Americans, the crippling limitations on Negro opportunity imposed by a race-conscious society, and he lobbied forcefully and
effectively for federal legislation that would remedy these evils.

Johnson's establishment in Harlem, then, was really a part of
a final definition of his purpose and career. Harlem seemed to
provide the place and the opportunity for this black man of
talent and experience to have a real and broad-ranging impact
on his world. Actually a member of an older generation, Johnson in the 1920s was a compeer with what people began to call
the "New Negro."

The circumstances that made Harlem and New York appear
a viable center of Negro cultural, intellectual, and political life
were in part the result of the large migration of talented blacks
to the city in the years before the war. But, more important,
what distinguished Harlem from the several other burgeoning
black metropolises were changes, seemingly centered in Harlem, in the character of Negro protest and thought. These
changes resonated in the formation of the NAACP and resulted
in the migration of W. E. Burghardt DuBois to New York.

DuBois, like Johnson, was part of an older generation than
the one that was to personify the New Negro. He, like Johnson,
had grown up in the critical years of Reconstruction. Like
Johnson's, his family had not personally felt slavery. But Du-
Bois, unlike Johnson, was not to know the South until his adult
years. Born 1868 in Great Barrington, a small Massachusetts
town in the Berkshires on the Housatonic River, DuBois could
feel his family roots going down into this soil which was both
Hudson River Dutch and New England Puritan. Although he
was forced because of his race to make detours, DuBois received the kind of education that any exceptionally bright
Yankee would have taken: Great Barrington public school,

A.B. at Fisk University, A.B. and Ph.D. at Harvard, and post-doctoral study in Berlin. While at Fisk, he had taught in the rural schools of Tennessee, and after his return from Europe he took a position at Negro colleges—Wilberforce in Pennsylvania and then at Atlanta University.[4]

Atlanta had been James Weldon Johnson's college, and when Johnson returned, fresh from his success on the New York stage, for the tenth reunion of his class, he had in his hands *Souls of Black Folk,* just published by a brilliant Yankee Negro from Harvard and Europe. DuBois's book was enormously important, not merely because it dignified the Negro through some of the finest prose of the period, but because it laid bare a rift that had been widening between young Negro intellectuals like DuBois and the established Negro leadership under Booker T. Washington. Washington had stressed industrial and agricultural training for Negroes, thus he tended to be anti-intellectual and he saw problems from a rural and small town perspective. His counsel was for conciliation and patience on the part of Negroes; therefore in DuBois's eyes he was ignoring the reality of white force and violence against Negro citizenship. He depended on the white good will in the South and upon white philanthropy in the North; therefore his ability to be a spokesman for Negro aspirations could be doubted. He had built around him an efficient machine which channeled white good-will and philanthropy as well as Republican patronage to selected Negroes; thus he could stifle criticism, militancy, and threats to his power.

Militant black antagonism against Washington was very deep. DuBois's criticism in *Souls of Black Folk* was measured and respectful; nevertheless the book signaled the break, and DuBois thus became the leader and spokesman of the anti-Washington forces. DuBois brought the militants together in a conference held July 11–13, 1905, at Buffalo, New York. The "Niagara Movement" issued a direct challenge to the philosophy and leadership of Booker T. Washington. Having been subjected to the tyranny of the Washington machine, the conferees asked that free speech and the right to criticize be honored in the fact. In response to what they saw as Washington's sell-out of the Negro's political and social rights, they insisted on the principle of manhood suffrage and demanded the abolition of all caste distinctions based on race or color. While they were willing to concede to Washington's concern for the training of the Negro common man, the conferees rejected his anti-intellectual position against higher education for the Negro man of ability. *Souls of Black Folk* had anticipated all this, crystalizing inchoate Negro thought, creating a commanding argument against the black conservative establishment.

It was the glaring failure of Washington's model for black advancement that had galvanized blacks into action. Washington's notions were questionable and anachronistic on a number of grounds. He encouraged training in obsolete crafts, based the Negro's economic future on a sick and dying southern agriculture, ignored the future urban role of Afro-Americans, and relied completely on whites in the North and South. But nothing equaled his public blindness to the growing horror of racial violence against blacks. It was in response to this that blacks and whites organized, independent of him.

Indeed, in 1909, Mary White Ovington, observing the rise in violence against the Negro throughout the country, issued a call to whites and Negroes for a new conference. Along with Miss Ovington, Oswald Garrison Villard, Jane Addams, John Dewey, Florence Kelley, Rabbi Stephen Fine, and William Dean Howells answered the call. The conference in May 1910 brought together the Negroes of the Niagara Movement and these white reformers to form the National Association for the Advancement of Colored People.[5]

DuBois, who had given the initial nudge to this direction of

Negro protest, was appointed editor of the *Crisis*, a monthly publication of the Association. So he left Atlanta, moved to New York, and began to make his name almost synonymous with Negro militancy. And so, too, DuBois, the National Association for the Advancement of Colored People, and New York City became identified with the spirit of Negro protest and self-assertion in the minds of the magazine's wide national readership.

DuBois's editorials were trenchant—his language was often acid. He was aware that his mind was superior to most men's, and not tolerating fools gladly, he could not hide his contempt for whites simple enough to be condescending. With his high forehead—his head was bald except for a rim of short-cropped graying hair—trimmed mustache, pointed beard, and sharp features, this brown man was imperious. He personified a new manner. He did not hide his bitterness to whites and would fit no philanthropist's conception of a good Negro. It was through his prodding that James Weldon Johnson was appointed executive secretary of the Association after a succession of white administrators.

DuBois and Johnson, very different in training and temperament, became the active agents of the Association. By the 1920s when Negroes thought of the Association and Negro protest, it would be these two names that would come to mind. They were the old guard. By the time the 1920s had begun, Johnson and DuBois were well established in New York, and a new generation of Negroes considered them leaders. Without perhaps knowing it, they were attracting young Negroes to New York because they symbolized the new spirit that the postwar generation felt. They, New York, and Harlem had come to mean a future of great possibility to the Negro.

The same characteristics of Harlem that could cause men like James Weldon Johnson and W. E. B. DuBois to center

their lives and the Negro's future there would bring others
with different political messages. Marcus Garvey was tuned to
different chords in Booker T. Washington's message. Garvey
heard self-help and racial independence, and his mind transformed that into militancy and aggressive black nationalism. A
Jamaican, Marcus Garvey had an imagination that was captured by a fantastic dream: black men re-establishing themselves in Africa, being a real people, becoming a real nation.
His dream captured some reality after he based his Universal
Negro Improvement Association in Harlem, which he made his
temporary capital, and from there touched the hopes of
hundreds of thousands of black people throughout the world.

Garvey, who had come to New York in 1916, found in men
like DuBois and Johnson great antagonists; but he gave more
than he took in vitriolic rhetoric. He made their self-conscious
aggressiveness seem conservative. Even after Garvey's failure,
his conviction for fraud, and expulsion from the country, he
was still able to appeal to people who had never been so affected by any other political leader (or dreamer). Garvey's
coming to Harlem helped make it seem a capital for an international black race.[6]

Men like DuBois, Johnson, and Garvey made their head-
quarters in New York in the years before America's entry into
World War I. It did not matter that these political leaders and
intellectuals were often antagonistic; that merely suggested an
openness, variety, and sophistication that had never existed for
Afro-Americans before. What did matter was that these men
were in New York, their manner and style was forceful, and
they were being heard. It is not surprising, then, that Harlem
drew young black intellectuals who wanted to find themselves
and their own voices. The effect was cumulative: the more who
came, the more who followed in their wake.

With Louise Thompson, an identity quest, a desire for intellectual challenge, and a compelling urge to do something im-

portant were the motive forces behind migration. Louise Thomspon's family had moved as domestic help through numberless far western towns, each much like the last. Towns, even cities, in Oregon and California had few Negroes in those early years of the twentieth century. Afro-Americans there found jobs more available the more they were able to change, to become something else, to take on the coloration and ethnic identity that each white community found tolerable. Louise and her mother were sometimes white, sometimes Mexican, and sometimes it did not matter. What kind of ego could survive such effacement? Masks always, the constant denial of self. And, of course, one had to remember to forget Negro friends in public when it was necessary.[7]

But humiliation only fed a longing for race identity within Louise Thompson. She felt the quiver and exaltation of race pride when, as a student at the University of California, she heard and saw, from an audience filled with whites, a brilliant brown man named DuBois. No denial or self-effacement here. DuBois, *Crisis*, the NAACP, and Harlem—there was superiority and self-respect.

After taking her degree in business administration, Louise Thompson took a teaching position at Hampton Institute. There she supported a student strike against the school's philosophy of paternalism and "uplift," which reflected its white philanthropic control. She sensed here another kind of humiliation of race, and she wrote DuBois about it. Her letter was published anonymously in *Crisis*. She and Hampton agreed to part. The school's management thought that she did not fit, and she wanted something more womanly than a conservative, southern Negro college would allow. Of course, she went to Harlem to become a part of those young intellectuals who were asserting their race.

The new postwar generation of Negro intellectuals might have been attracted to Harlem by the lures of older greats, but they also brought with them the spirit of the Jazz Age. They, along with their white contemporaries, ushered in the liberation of the 1920s. Harlem for blacks, like New York for whites, was synonymous with opportunity, the release of the individual spirit. For some, it meant the possibility to write or to be near those who did. Not a few quickened to the excitement of the musical stage and the effervescence of sophisticated and ribald nightlife. For all—black and white—New York was the occasion for breaking away from small town life, the restrictions of family control, and for growing up.

Langston Hughes belonged to Harlem even before he came. In the June 1921 issue of *Crisis* there appeared Hughes's first published poem, "The Negro Speaks of Rivers." Hughes had been writing since his high school days in Cleveland, but his literary beginnings were in *Crisis*. After high school, Hughes lived in Mexico with his father, a wealthy rancher and miner who had little sympathy for the arts. What is more, the elder Hughes had a quite violent hatred of Negroes. It was perhaps in defiance of his father that Langston Hughes nurtured his warm and deep interest in the Negro common people and an art that would speak their spirit. Langston's father wanted him to go to Switzerland to be trained in engineering, but the young man had heard of the famous musical *Shuffle Along* and he wanted to go to Harlem. "More than Paris, or the Shakespeare country, or Berlin, or the Alps, I wanted to see Harlem, the greatest Negro city in the world." So he convinced his father that Columbia University could train him as well as any European school. He never liked Columbia, but Harlem made him glad.[8]

For Hughes, Harlem was to be the center of his life, the black people there the main source of his literary inspiration. Another poet, Claude McKay, used Harlem in a different way, but used it nonetheless. McKay had grown up in the rural hills of Jamaica, and worked in the constabulary as a young man in

Kingston. His first literary success was with poems written in the West Indian dialect. But his native island was too small a field for him. A traveling troupe of Negro theater people turned McKay's eyes to New York and Harlem. McKay spent a time working in railroad dining cars, but New York and the black city within New York continued to pull him. While much of his writing was intensely expressive of Harlem, he nevertheless managed to remain outside and independent of it. White intellectuals were his main support and his primary intellectual association. Frank Harris of *Pearson's* gave him his first real support in this country. During much of the 1920s he was on the editorial staff of Max Eastman's *Liberator*, where he worked with Crystal Eastman and clashed with Michael Gold. And, later, although he remained in Europe for much of the late 1920s and 1930s, Harlem continued to be an important focus for his writing. He was to be one of those who would try to describe the essentials of Harlem in a novel.[9]

Liberation was the magnet that drew Regina Andrews, a pert olive-skinned girl, who escaped from Chicago to discover her race and her womanhood. Her father was a lawyer in Chicago, and Regina found it difficult to fit into the comfortable and complacent middle-class society that was expected of Negro young ladies. It was not that New York was more congenial than Chicago to Negroes. A librarian with experience in the Chicago public libraries, she had found it even more difficult in New York until she was placed in the 135th Street branch of the New York City system. Not that New York was kinder; rather, Harlem was filled with young Negro men and women who were writing and singing and dancing and painting and acting, and she was in the midst of it all. Her place at the library put her in close touch with the young artists. She made her apartment an uptown salon where all of the intellectuals came. (Her apartment, indeed, was described in Carl Van Vechten's *Nigger Heaven*.) As to many a young girl, white or

black, New York offered womanhood to Regina Andrews. But
Harlem offered something more. While there, she was on the
crest of a creative wave that would surely define the New
Negro, and let her know her self through her race.[10]

Harlem meant still another kind of opportunity. With such a
large concentration of Negroes it provided a market for business and professional men. Negro lawyers, doctors, and den-
tists could anticipate for the first time a large potential clien-
tele. Of course, it was not easy for the professions. Negro
doctors found it impossible to use white hospitals until the
Harlem hospital was built on 135th Street and Lenox Avenue.
Lawyers' cases with Negro clients were not the most reward-
ing, and the field was too crowded for good business. Yet there
was the chance. Prohibition opened great possibilities for the
cabaret owner, and prostitution, "numbers," and other gambling thrived during the 1920s. One illiterate woman, through
the sale of cooked pigs' feet from a cart and shrewd investment
in real estate, became rich. And as early as 1918, Madame C. J.
Walker had become a millionaire, and had bought a mansion
at Irvington-on-the-Hudson, as a result of her processing and
treatment of the hair of Negro women. Harlem meant opportunity and promise for all kinds.

Understandably, thinking Harlem was the nerve center of
Afro-American life and the capital of the international black
man, its intellectuals who wanted to affect political change
had to raise their voices and speak to broad, general, and prin-
cipled issues. These spokesmen would be different from the
ward heelers and "bosses" who were part and parcel of city
politics during that period. Like their white reformer
counterparts—mugwumps and progressives—black intellectuals tended to see significant politics as above the muscle of
mechanism. Thus, the ward, the constituency, the manipulation
of small increments of power, the compromise—the only reali-

ties for the political practitioner—were ignored by Harlem's political spokesmen.

Like other progressives, Harlem intellectuals saw political issues and reform in moral terms and assumed a high moral tone. Racial problems were social aberrations due to moral corruption, fear, or ignorance. They offered no radical solutions therefore; the system was basically sound. The techniques they chose were familiar enough. The evil of racial injustice in all its varieties was exposed through a muckraking journalism that matched the best of that time. The assumption was that the moral weight of good would win once evil was exposed. The unreason, the illogic, the craven corruption that barred blacks from a fair chance in society could not stand, for men of good will, under the harsh light of right reason. And if reason could lay bare the evils and anomalies of American race practice, the same discipline and logic of mind could plot out remedies by means of the social sciences. And this exposure and rationality were not simply negative. A doubting and skeptical world had to be shown evidence of Negro ability, especially achievements in the arts and literature which all progressives equated with civilization.

This program of propaganda and persuasion was propagated by three Harlem magazines that had considerable influence among black people. The NAACP's *Crisis* was founded in 1910 and edited by W. E. B. DuBois. Seven years after its founding, A. Philip Randolph and Chandler Owen began publishing the *Messenger,* which claimed to be "The Only Radical Negro Magazine in America." The editors of the *Messenger* wanted to vie with DuBois as the most forthright and uncompromising in the Afro-American cause. In time, however, the *Messenger* abandoned its militant tone and became the organ of Randolph's larger enterprise, the Brotherhood of Sleeping Car Porters. In 1923, the Urban League's magazine, *Opportunity,* came into being. It reflected that organization's debt to the charity organization movement's doctrines of self-help and uplift. Each of these magazines manifested the Harlem intellectuals' commitment to progressive reform.

Show the problem to the readers, that was thought to be the first task. In regard to violence and injustice against the Negro, no one was a more ruthless muckraker than DuBois. *Crisis* focused on lynching, a public and national scandal. Every issue carried a statistical breakdown of violence against blacks. When the magazine would report an NAACP investigation of a lynching, its pages almost smelled of burned flesh. DuBois sketched in unrelieved sharpness how sub-human the white American was, once he was in a mob. And DuBois was quick to expose official duplicity, as when Woodrow Wilson refused to reverse the policy of government segregation that his administration had introduced to Washington.

The *Messenger* prided itself on being unrelenting. It criticized DuBois for urging Negro military service in the war, claiming that he had sold out the black man's cause. Rather, Randolph and Owen wanted to persuade Negroes not to enlist in the army; they were arrested for their pains, and the *Messenger* joined the elite of American periodicals, those confiscated by the Post Office under suspicion of sedition.

Opportunity exposed the race problem, but in a more studied and academic style than the others. The executive secretary of the Urban League, Eugene Kinckle Jones, wanted the magazine to "set down interestingly but without sugarcoating or generalization the findings of careful scientific surveys and facts gathered from research, undertaken not to prove preconceived notions but to lay bare Negro life as it is." Its pages were filled with scholarly studies by young social scientists such as Ira De A. Reid, E. Franklin Frazier, and Ralph Bunche. Articles by Melville Herskovits and Franz Boas also appeared. Charles S. Johnson, the editor, who was himself a sociologist, had contributed to that early massive study on civil disorders, *The Negro in Chicago* (1919).

It was much easier to expose corruption and evil than to find effective remedies. This was especially true for DuBois, whose mind seemed always to grasp the ultimate impossibility and to see the essential paradox of the Negro's position. His readers had to follow him from his demand for Negro political independence of the major parties to his anguished search for some meaningful political power for the race. They read of race as an international issue and experienced DuBois's frustrations with Pan-Africanism. But while DuBois shifted his ground under the torture of paradox, his argument, wherever he stood, was always literate and forceful.

Readers of the *Messenger* found solutions and programs much easier to come by. The editors were socialists and found their answers in the support of that party and the labor movement, never recognizing the bigotry in both groups. Randolph and Owen put their faith in reason and planning. Their guide was Lester Ward, whose *Dynamic Sociology* had tried to harness Darwinism to the purposive ends of social reconstruction. And for the editors of *Messenger* the answers would be clear enough once skilled social analysts defined the dimensions of the problem.

Each of these magazines saw as part of its role the encouragement of Negroes' work in the arts and the publishing of their achievement for blacks and whites to see. Langston Hughes's first published poem "The Negro Speaks of Rivers," appeared in *Crisis*. Claude McKay's "If We Must Die" was published in the *Messenger* after first appearing in the *Liberator*. And, even more than the others, *Opportunity* believed its motto—"Not Alms but Opportunity"—to apply to the arts. It sponsored a literary contest in the 1920s that became a major generating force for the renaissance.

Perhaps it was all shadow boxing. Did anyone out in that vague American white world read it? Did the blows tell? Were the points really made? What good would it do to expose President Wilson's racism? Even if he read it, he had a self-righteousness that was a match for any other progressive. All of that did not matter. The tone and the self-assurance of these magazines were the important thing. They gave a sense of importance to blacks who read them. They gave answers that had always failed the porter, the barber, the maid, the teacher, the handyman. They were the Negro's voice against the insult that America gave him.

In the October 1925 issue of the *Messenger*, George S. Schuyler wrote, "Today I believe it fair to say, Negro America looks to New York for advanced leadership and opinion." It was fair to say that, and that is what gave Harlem and its intellectuals a sense of importance. But were they deceived? It seemed clear enough that the past was dead, but had a new Negro day been born in Harlem? Did the circumstances promise more than they would deliver? That was the deception of Harlem. The leadership to whom Negro America looked turned out to be fairly impotent. Its failure exposed the irrelevancy of progressive reform to the Afro-American predicament.

The problem is best illustrated in the several issues to which DuBois attempted to give forceful leadership. From the beginnings of his editorship of *Crisis* DuBois had tried to give focus to Negro political energies, to make the Negro vote count. With America's entry into World War I, DuBois tried to use the Negro's participation in it as a lever to win democracy at home. And after the war he provided America's race problem with an international stage, placing the Afro-American behind the Pan-African movement. In all of these efforts he had to contend with the strong opposition of other Negro pundits. All of his efforts failed—as did those of others—because of the peculiar character of black leadership.

How could the Negro make his vote count in a political arena in which no major contender seemed to care much whether he won the black vote or not? The presidential election of 1912 illustrates this point. With four candidates in the field, the Negro vote should have meant a great deal. But President Taft showed little interest; having promised to appoint no federal officials whom white southerners found obnoxious, he effectively removed Negro Republicans from patronage lists. Both Taft and Roosevelt had shown indifference to Negroes and justice in the so-called Brownsville Affray. When the townspeople of Brownsville, Texas directed violence against Negro troops stationed there in August 1906, although there was little evidence that the soldiers responded violently, both Presidents Taft and Roosevelt colluded in their unjust prosecutions and dismissals from the army. Theodore Roosevelt's "Bull Moose" Progressives proved to be no better than the Republicans. DuBois proposed a platform plank that would have the Progressive party recognize "that distinctions of race or class in political life have no place in democracy." It asked for the "repeal of unfair discriminatory laws and the right to vote [for Negroes] on the same terms . . . other citizens vote." Joel Spingarn and Jane Addams struggled to get the plank accepted by the party, but Theodore Roosevelt would have none of it. Roosevelt saw some promise in wooing southern votes, and as a man much influenced by Booker T. Washington's Tuskegee Machine, he found DuBois dangerous.

DuBois was not so much an idealist that he could support Eugene V. Debs merely because that candidate and the Socialist party were closer to being right in principle and program. He had resigned from the Socialist party in order to avoid support of the ticket. It was a practical matter. "I could not let Negroes throw away votes." [11] DuBois refused to believe that the Negro vote counted for nothing. Of course, it had been the captive of the Republican party since the Civil War. That was understandable enough since the Republicans were the party of emancipation and Abraham Lincoln. But DuBois recalled that it was also the party that ultimately surrendered Black Reconstruction, leaving the southern Negro to southern white power. Anyway, no party deserved a people's unswerving support. The Negro could gain more if the major parties had to woo him than if his vote were sure. And the Democratic party was showing some evidence of liberalization through the influence of its growing urban support.

So DuBois's mind was open to the idea of Negro support for the Democratic party when Bishop Alexander Walters of the African Zion Church claimed to have influenced Woodrow Wilson in the Negro's behalf. In October 1912 Bishop Walters presented a letter from Wilson expressing his "earnest wish to see justice done the colored people in every matter; and not mere grudging justice, but justice executed with liberality and cordial good feeling. . . . I want to assure them that should I become President of the United States they may count upon me for absolute fair dealing, for everything by which I could assist in advancing the interests of their race in the United States." This was enough for DuBois to fly in the face of traditional Negro politics and to use his influence and *Crisis* to persuade Negroes to vote for the party of slavery and black oppression. Running counter to most Negro spokesmen and conflicting with almost the entire Negro press, DuBois supported Woodrow Wilson in 1912. He estimated that Wilson received one hundred thousand northern black votes, contributing significantly to his election.[12]

Yet it was hard to sense in the years that followed that Wilson recognized any debt to Negro voters, and he did not seem to want to keep their support. As many of DuBois's critics had predicted, the Negro suffered politically from Wilson's administration. Even if the President's intentions were most benevolent, his party had its greatest and most consistent support in the white South, and the party had been out of power since the Cleveland administration in 1896. There were many job-hungry party faithfuls to be rewarded. Petty southern Democratic bureaucrats were surely not going to appoint Negroes to federal jobs which were now open to their own constituents. Even James Weldon Johnson, who was consul to Corinto, Nicaragua, and protected by the civil service system, found himself up against what he termed "politics plus race prejudice" when he consulted Secretary of State William Jennings Bryan about a much earned promotion and transfer. His job could not be taken from him, but he could not advance. So he was eased out of the foreign service.[13]

Negroes who remained in Washington in the federal service were humiliated by Wilson's executive order establishing segregated dining and toilet facilities. Monroe Trotter, whose Boston *Guardian* had supported Wilson in the election, pleaded in an audience with the President that the administration's segregationist policies would make it impossible for Negro leaders to continue to urge support for the Democrats. Wilson claimed that segregation was for the Negro's own good, despite the fact that blacks and whites had shared facilities in Washington offices since the Civil War. Wilson was offended by Trotter's presumption of being able to barter votes; Trotter was humiliated as were most Negro spokesmen who had supported Wilson's election.[14]

The Negro press that had endorsed the Republican ticket made capital of the Democrats' embarrassment, and DuBois had to suffer along with the rest. The *New York Age*, for instance, wanted to make sure that the "Wilsonian Democrats" squirmed for their naïveté. But it was not only the black Republicans. A. Philip Randolph's *Messenger*, true to its radical image, far after the event took DuBois to task for his failure to support the Socialist candidate. If the incident proved nothing else, the *Messenger* editors were convinced that Negroes could

see the foolishness of support for either major party, since both
were hopelessly wedded to a corrupt and exploitative system.
DuBois, who had objected to the Negro's throwing away his
vote on Debs who could not win, had indeed encouraged his
readers to vote for a man and party that had contempt for
their votes. Was it not better to vote for a loser whom you
agreed with, than a victor, a lesser of evils, who would pay for
your support with insult?

DuBois was chastened by the experience, but he did not
give up the hope of making the Negro an effective political
weight. He continued to believe that Afro-Americans could act
as a "swing" in American politics, if they could support first
one major party and then another as it suited their interests.
This way, he believed, the Negro would have to be courted
and served. He persisted in this view throughout the 1920s,
urging Negroes to aid individual candidates who proved to be
friends of the race and to punish those who were enemies.

DuBois had taken an American way out. But political pragmatism to one man is opportunism to another; the *Messenger*
insisted that DuBois's approach was the latter. After all, there
was no principle or ideal involved, only convenience. And
what was worse, there was very little evidence that the policy
paid off—the true test of pragmatism. Of course, DuBois's position made sense. The Negro could not expect the social re-
wards of politics as long as his vote was unquestioned; he had
to be politically free to bargain. And the Socialist party—itself
not free of racism—was no viable alternative. DuBois's political ineffectiveness was not simply an error in his thought. He
shared with other progressives a faith in the efficacy of good
government to bring about fundamental social change. Like
the progressives, he could not take the machine alternative to
democratic politics. Unlike Marcus Garvey, for instance, Du-
Bois was unable, as well as unwilling, to mold the black masses into the kind of political constituency that might give him

the true power of leadership. Black progressives, doubtless more than whites, were plagued by the fact that effective politics in America often demanded the very kind of corruption that they abhorred.

The ultimate goal of DuBois's reform was a condition of social justice in which every man would be accepted on his merits as a man. A man with ability and talent would rise, and those without would not. Society would be color-blind; race would be of no account in the equation of human worth. Yet the realities of American life and politics demanded that the tactics to realize that goal exploit the race consciousness it hoped to deny. For the Negro to use politics to his ends, he had to do so as part of a Negro pressure group, not as a high-minded independent. But how could one attain a society of race denial with methods which were racially assertive? To organize effectively to use black power in politics seemed, even then, self-defeating. The dilemma was tortuous for DuBois. It explains much of the contradiction in his writings: sometimes supporting self-segregation for Negroes, sometimes asserting Negro superiority, sometimes demanding the extinction of racial distinctions. This quandary confounded any effort at an effective political program. Actually, "black power politics" had to be illusory because no Negro leader could have "delivered" the Negro vote to any candidate. Again, Marcus Garvey was a special case because he avoided the political paradox by advocating escape.[15]

The question of Negro participation in World War I illustrates further the perplexing character of Negro leadership. At a time when great violence was being done to Negroes through white mob action, when the Negro's life was being cramped and confined by laws and the custom of Jim Crow, when the American society seemed to choose every occasion to humiliate blacks, at the nadir of American race relations, the nation chose to lead the Western world's peoples toward social justice, democracy, and self-determination. The irony escaped no one. Most Negroes saw the wartime emergency as an opportunity to bargain for improvement in official policies toward black citizens. They were a bit encouraged as war industries opened to Negroes jobs that had been closed to them. Yet the War Department showed no eagerness to make full use of black citizens. Segregation in the armed services, of course, was taken for granted. But officials balked at granting new commissions to Negroes, promoting black commissioned officers, and assigning black units to combat status. There could have been no question of the Negro's ability to fight; recent army history in the Civil War, the Indian wars, and the Spanish-American War could hardly encourage such doubt. But martial virtues were not consistent with the Negro stereotype that white Americans cherished. There was also fear that the Negro could not remain docile once he had been battle-tested against the Germans. The Negro leader was left with hard alternatives. He could advise against Afro-American participation in a racist war effort which even questioned their right to fight—risking charges of sedition—or he could plead for the Negro to be allowed to serve as other Americans, as combatants as well as service soldiers. The latter choice was, in effect, to plead for the right of black men to die for their country.

Joel Spingarn, chairman of the board of the NAACP, believed that the war offered Negroes the chance to prove their capacity for leadership and courage. Spingarn succeeded in persuading DuBois to take this position too. Along with others, these men and the Association put great pressure on the War Department and succeeded in winning what they thought to be a significant concession—a segregated officers training camp at Des Moines, Iowa. Spingarn and the Association were troubled about the segregation—their proclaimed policy was to fight against all kinds of official discrimination—yet the Des Moines camp did assure that Negro officers would be commissioned; this was the best they could get. No less compromised, DuBois accepted even this arrangement as a regrettable but practical bargain.

DuBois wavered of course. He was angered that Negroes were forced to beg to give their lives to their country. We should worry, he charged, the Negro stood to win by the war, whatever the white man did. If he was not allowed to fight, the Negro would work in those jobs left by the white fighting man. "Will we be ousted when the white soldiers come back? THEY WON'T COME BACK!" If blacks were allowed in combat, on the other hand, DuBois knew that they would return different men. They would not be so easily lynched. DuBois was heartened when, despite its reluctance, the army awarded commissions to hundreds of Negroes who had trained at the Des Moines camp. But, then, in 1918 the execution of Negro soldiers of the 24th Infantry Regiment who were involved in the Houston race riot caused him to remind his readers of the oppressive conditions of society that produced such violence. And he took the occasion to attack the white political leadership, from President Wilson down, who assumed that black humiliation was normal and to be expected. He began to doubt whether the Negro's sacrifice in the war would be worth it.[16]

The Justice Department began to threaten; DuBois's critical tone might be considered seditious. The NAACP was anxious lest the Association be dragged by the *Crisis* into charges of radicalism and disloyalty. Doubtless, the combined pressure from these two sources helped tone down DuBois's editorials, but his ultimate position is reflective of his own ambivalence: he really *wanted* to be loyal to the United States. In the July 1918 issue of *Crisis*, he published "Close Ranks," which remained his position until the armistice. He voiced the same idealism that had won most intellectuals to Wilson's position on the war. The ultimate aims of civilization and democracy should command everyone's loyalty; its cause was the Negro's as much as anyone's. Then he urged, "Let us . . . forget our special grievances and close ranks . . . with our fellow citizens and the allied nations that are fighting for democracy." It was an unfortunate choice of language, for it embroiled him with other Negro spokesmen for years into the future.[17]

DuBois's critics were quick to note the similarity between this argument and the old Booker T. Washington kind of conciliation. Rather than forget, they insisted, the Negro should remember grievances now more than ever and make the adjudication of them the price of his full participation in the war effort. The War Department and the Committee on Public Information, anxious about hints of black sedition, had called a conference of Negro editors in June 1918 to urge unified Negro support of the war effort. The statement which these editors unanimously adopted insisted on minimal compliance with Negro demands as a price for their support. Conditions of public travel, lynchings, and Red Cross discrimination headed their list of complaints. Rhetorically, at least, they were not prepared to forget their grievances even for a little while. It was more a gesture and pose than a real complaint, however, for the vast majority of these editors supported the war without the slightest suggestion of possible defection. Their wrath was generally directed against DuBois and his "close ranks" position. Some even accused him of selling out for an army commission.

The *Messenger*'s editors, true to their radicalism, urged Negroes against the war. The nation had not earned the race's loyalty, and a war among capitalist, exploitative, and colonizing nations was surely not in the Negro's interest. Owen and Randolph were consistent and unmitigating in their criticism of the war. For their efforts they were jailed in Cleveland, and the magazine's second class mailing privilege suspended. According to Randolph, it was only the judge's doubt that black men were able to write such militant prose that saved them from long jail sentences.[18]

But how viable was this alternative to DuBois's "close ranks"? As attractive as bargaining might have seemed, the government was not so much in need of (or worried about) Negro participation that it was willing to make bargains. Despite many requests and pleas, the government made no effort to eliminate Jim Crow in its own facilities or in interstate commerce. Secretary of War Newton Baker told DuBois that we "are not trying by this War to settle the Negro problem." The government might have accomplished a great deal; the railroads, for instance, were nationalized during the war. Nor did it work in any way to protect the Negro from lynch mobs. Indeed, in the Houston riot cases, the Army allowed its own courts-martial to placate southern white opinion as it had earlier in the Brownsville Affray. Apparently, the Negro leaders had nothing to sell. On the other hand, as high-minded and consistent as the boycott of the war might have appeared, it was no better a choice. For that, too, depended on the willingness of ordinary Negro men to refuse to go into the service and to accept punishment as draft-dodgers. No Negro spokesman, at that time, had the influence to make such civil disobedience work. This alternative was especially harsh for a leader like DuBois. For had he urged Negro resistance to the war, he would have exposed the essentially unreal character of his leadership. With no real following, he had to urge compliance in order to maintain the illusion of leadership.[19]

DuBois's predicament was not a new thing, nor was it personal. He might well have remembered the tortured conscience of Frederick Douglass during the Civil War when he urged black men to enlist in the Massachusetts 54th and 55th Regiments with the assurance that the Union government would treat them fairly, only to be disappointed in that faith. Even Douglass' amiable audience with President Lincoln failed to secure redress of grievances: unequal pay to black soldiers, Union indifference to the mutilation and enslavement of those Negro Union soldiers captured by the Confederacy, the military's failure to honor black soldiers' valor and deeds. Even then it was clear that logic, dignified argument, and the urgent need of the Union for soldiers could not convince the govenment to risk racist criticism. Lincoln had merely insisted that the opportunity for Negroes to fight, support their cause, and prove their valor and manhood was enough to compensate them for inequities. Douglass, despite his misgivings and disillusionment, could do little else but continue to encourage Negroes to enlist as his three sons had. At least he could argue that they would be fighting, whatever the humiliating circumstances, to free their enslaved brothers. DuBois did not even have that comfort.[20]

Many years later, writing in Rayford Logan's *What the Negro Wants*, DuBois remembered the paradox before him. "I was . . . in a mad fight to make Negroes Americans." It was not easy. "I was fighting to let the Negroes fight; I, who for a generation had been a professional pacifist; I was fighting for a separate training camp for Negro officers; I, who was devoting a career to opposing race segregation; I was seeing the Germany which taught me the human brotherhood of white and black, pitted against America which was for me the essence of Jim Crow; and yet I was 'rooting' for America; and I had to, even before my own conscience, so utterly crazy had the whole world become and I with it." The problem was made no easier for him by the postwar reality which made it apparent that American racism had not even been touched by the war. If anything, the racists were more virulent. Even Negro combat troops, returning in triumph, had to swallow humiliation and violence against their persons from American military police in France.[21]

But the war had made evident to all Americans the realities of the world outside. And W. E. B. DuBois was one of the first American Negroes to take a new world-view. He helped to organize Pan-African Congresses in 1919, 1921, and 1923. The

Pan-African leaders wanted to influence the peace conference, and later the League of Nations, toward the international protection of African blacks. It was an opening wedge to place race issues, including ultimately those in the United States, before a world forum and to pressure Negroes themselves to ameliorate their condition. Although DuBois never lost his interest in Africa, he was to be disappointed in the congresses. He discovered that some important Africans, such as Blaise Diagne, Senegalese representative to the French Chamber of Deputies, could be as conservative a defender of colonialism as any white man. American Negroes, too, had their own ambivalences about blackness and Africa, nor was it easy for some to understand how identification with Africa would win them acceptance as full American citizens; regardless of appeals of race, American citizenship had been the consistent goal. Was not Pan-Africanism another kind of racism? DuBois found it impossible to keep free of the taint of Marcus Garvey. Even in his efforts to lead Afro-Americans toward a world-view of race —away from their provincialism—he was thwarted on the one hand by the complexities of international politics and on the other by the restraints imposed by his American progressivism.

The post-war effort to thrust Negro social thought into an international arena brings us to consider the Jamaican, Marcus Garvey, who taunted an exasperated W. E. B. DuBois perhaps more than anyone else in these years. A spectacular man, Garvey can no longer be considered an anomaly of American politics. First attracted to the United States to learn from the Booker T. Washington self-help school, he never abandoned this traditional American virtue, transforming it instead into a program which doubtless would have left Washington breathless. His style contained the flamboyant, the grandiloquent, which had always captured the imaginations of white and black Americans, whose addiction to lodge organizations and colorful parades is well known. His flair and rhetoric, despite vestiges of the accent of the British-style schools in Jamaica, suggested the political demagogue, it is true; but it was the style and manner of the popular preacher too. Even his promise of a future return to a powerful African nation echoed a traditional theme in Afro-American ideas. And, indeed, it secularized the strong "next world" character of Afro-American thought. Marcus Garvey and his program fitted neatly into the American setting.[22]

From 1917, when he founded the Universal Negro Improvement Association in Harlem, until his forced exile ten years later, Garvey was able to capture the imaginations and loyalties of countless blacks in the United States, Latin America, the Caribbean, and Africa. It was as if black common men the world over had been waiting for a Messiah; they were to follow Garvey as if he were one, some long after his imprisonment for fraud in 1925. And it was to the common man he made his appeal through his newspaper, *Negro World*, established in 1918. His message was simple and unambiguous: black people were a good and noble race. They were beautiful people with a grand history which had been hidden from them by their white oppressors. They were an enslaved people, true enough, but theirs was a servility of the mind—the effects of the brain-washing of the colonial system—not of nature. Once black men and women learned their true value, rid themselves of self-hatred, and asserted their natural nobility, they would overwhelm white oppression and come into their just inheritance. Their destiny was grand: to return Africa to the Africans.

It was a dream, of course. But Garvey's genius (and failure) was that he always provided a tangible and visible reality. What standard American lodges—Elks, Masons, Odd Fellows, etc.—did with elaborate hierarchies and colorful pagentries to give substance to their "mysteries," the Universal Negro Improvement Association (UNIA) did to give the African dream its sense of reality. The members became a nation in exile. They carried titles such as the Duke of Nigeria and the Overlord of Uganda. And all of the offices had appropriate uniforms and paraphernalia. Subscribers were decorated with bronze, silver, or gold crosses—depending on the size of their contribution. There were uniforms for everyone, enough to satisfy any taste in a parade.

In a parade, Garvey—uniformed in purple, green, and black with a hat of white feathered plumes—like any other potentate, would wave from his car to the crowds. Behind his touring car would ride other nobility, each with colorful sashes denoting rank. The African Legion, uniformed in dark blue with red stripes down the trousers, came next, to be followed by the rank and file of the Association.

The international appeal of the Association could not be questioned. In the convention of 1920, delegates came from Africa, Brazil, Colombia, Central America, and the West Indies. The racial renaissance that Garvey promised seemed to materialize at these frequent conferences. Some filled Madison Square Garden with black delegates from around the world. When Garvey exhorted such a throng with a rush of emotion, "Up, you mighty race!" the truth of the race's awakening was there for everyone to feel.

It was the persistent need to materialize the dream which caused Garvey and his enterprises to founder. His financial disasters, which hinted of fraud, were more the result of poor business judgment and bad management than chicanery. It was not enough, however, to establish offices and titles (ironically so suggestive of European monarchy), an army, and service organizations such as the Black Cross Nurses. Garvey was compelled by his own rhetoric and pretensions to produce grand results before he had the experience or organization to manage them. For hatching such grand schemes as the Black Star Line—a shipping line wholly owned and run by blacks—

and promised negotiations with African states, Garvey could always anticipate ridicule from other Negro spokesmen. W. E. B. DuBois and A. Philip Randolph knew that there were no Negroes with the kind of shipping experience needed to make such a line work. They cautioned Negroes about throwing their money away on schemes which were flimsy at best and fraudulent at worst. And DuBois knew better than any other man how the speeches and promises of Garvey glossed over the many complexities of the Africa for Africans scheme. Garvey's fantasies lightly ignored the realities of colonial power, as well as tribal, language, and ethnic divisions among black Africans themselves. It was as if one could build an African state simply on the basis of a common blackness. Anyone who knew Africa at all understood even that commonness to be a myth. But such sophisticated criticism could only urge him on.

Garvey's pen was a worthy weapon against his critics. He answered them regularly in the *Negro World:* they were merely self-defeating. According to Garvey, the very claim that Negroes could not do great things—run a shipping line—was the real shackle of slavery. Self-doubt was the cause of the Negro's impotence. Through such denial, Garvey insisted, men like DuBois betrayed their people and proved the failure of a Negro leadership wedded to white power. Garvey was cruel in slicing into those leaders who were torn by the dilemmas of accommodation. DuBois, he claimed, was a man who was part white and part black in mind as well as blood; he did not know who he was or where he was. It was Garvey's ability to reduce complexities to their most simple formulation that made him a charismatic leader. He could induce people to share his dream because his fantasies were untroubled by the kind of paradoxes that perplexed men like DuBois, Johnson, and Randolph. But the mind can only play tricks of imagination; it cannot produce power, experience, and mastery where it does not exist. And Garvey, goaded by critics and his own megalomania, was compelled to try to do just that—to give his dream a tangible reality.

Despite the nay-sayers, Garvey did purchase ships for his Black Star Line. While they pleased the Association's members and helped to raise money, this fleet of ships served to transport Garvey's fantasy into fiasco. Neither he nor anyone in the Association knew anything about ships, so they bought bad ones at outlandish prices. The fact that in the negotiations over the sale of these ships Garvey's people were made fools of by unscrupulous white men was slight comfort. The Line did have to use white captains and black crews of limited skill, on ships that were barely seaworthy. After breakdowns and repairs and the final collapse of these ships, the Black Star Line went into bankruptcy, losing hundreds of thousands of dollars of its subscribers' money.

The Association's efforts to colonize Africa were no more successful. From 1920 to 1924 the UNIA had been negotiating with the Liberian government. Their idea was to establish a colony of Afro-American technicians and settlers in that African republic. The Liberian government entertained this enterprise, perhaps to encourage American finance, perhaps to use the threat of the proposed settlement as a lever to raise European and white American capital investment. Blaise Diagne had already warned Garvey that he could expect no sympathy from Africans in the French colonies. They, the Senegalese deputy believed, were too blessed by French association to be lured into an Africa run by Africans, especially with Garvey the self-appointed leader. In June 1924 the Liberian government, after considerable duplicity, made members of Garvey's Association *personae non grata* in that country. And this, after careful and costly plans had been made by the UNIA to found this new colony for Afro-Americans, with the apparent support of that African republic's government. This treachery was doubtless the most telling blow to the dreams of Garvey and his followers; more indeed than his arrest and conviction for using the mails to defraud; more than his imprisonment; more than his subsequent exile from the United States.

Garvey's failures were total, but always of a petty character. His spectacular dreams deserved grander fates. On the other hand, his momentary successes were startling. He managed to convince masses of ordinary black men and women of the notion of their own collective potential. For a time, many Negroes believed that they could weld themselves into a powerful race and nation through the agency of Garvey's Association. He captured their loyalty as no other black leader had done before, nor would do again until the 1950s.

But for all of that, Garvey was threatening to other Negro leaders. It was precisely his talent to mobilize the common black man which challenged men like DuBois. His pandering to the superstitions and fantasies of the mob was exactly the kind of tactic that black and white progressives abhorred. His willingness to develop programs based on the most simple conception of reality was the very thing that appealed to ordinary men, and by the same token exasperated those leaders whose very lives were so torn by dilemma that simple conceptions were impossible. It was easy enough to make men cheer the rhetoric, "Up, you mighty race!" and "Africa for Africans." Nor was it hard to devise schemes. But somewhere one had to collide with the realities of French Africa and Liberia and finances and naval architecture and navigation. W. E. B. Du-Bois, whose Pan-Africanism became a lifelong commitment, felt that the problems were much too complex and torturous to be given into the hands of one whose ego tended to make its own realities. It was, finally, DuBois's very deep interest in Africa that made him so hostile to Marcus Garvey. For while he was seriously and painfully working to make the Pan-African movement work, Garvey was spinning dreams that frightened Africans as well as Europeans. While DuBois continued to try to acheive a careful balance of Negro integration in the American society as against a natural and essential ethnic identification, Garvey simply announced a kind of black separatism even to the point of collusion with the Ku Klux Klan.[23] And while DuBois carefully nurtured the image of a Negro leadership of reason, intelligence, and balance, Garvey was to DuBois's mind cutting the fool before the world. Most of Harlem's Negro leaders were relieved to see Garvey removed from the scene; he was disruptive. But most, like DuBois, also sounded a note of regret at his exile, because Garvey personified a spirit and genius for touching and moving men's souls to dream, a quality of leadership that they, in their aloofness, lacked.

George Schuyler was right therefore: Negroes throughout the country were looking to New York City, and to Harlem for the most advanced thought and opinion. Yet one is overwhelmed by the futility and impotence of it all. It was impossible to make political bargains where political leaders could not be convinced of the need of mass Negro support. And no leader could win political concessions when he was able neither to deliver nor to withold significant support. His role was confounded by the paradox of the Negro's situation. DuBois summed it up very well:

> Where in heaven's name do we Negroes stand? If we organize separately for anything—"Jim Crow!" scream all the Disconsolate; if we organize with white people—"Traitors! Pressure! They're betraying us!" yell all the Suspicious. If, unable to get the whole loaf we seize half to ward off starvation—"Compromise!" yell all the Scared. If we let the half loaf go and starve—"Why don't you *do* something?" yell those same critics, dancing about on their toes.[24]

Consistent leadership was impossible. Social hostility made integration impossible. Yet economic and numerical weakness made militant nationalism unreal.

But this Harlem leadership was weakened too because of its peculiar relationship to its following. All of them except Garvey—DuBois, Owen, Randolph, and James Weldon Johnson—had been weaned on traditional middle-class reform. Like their white progressive brothers they were committed to reason and truth and enlightened democracy to bring about desired change. Their magazines were filled with the same exposé literature that the muckrakers had used to reform trusts and the meatpacking industry, abolish child labor, and so on. And like their white counterparts, they were an elite, removed from the masses. A. Philip Randolph, of course, turned to organizing the sleeping car porters. But neither DuBois nor Johnson could have affected the political machine that in these same years had been winning minor concessions for immigrant masses in the cities. They were not involved in the block and precinct work that might have given them the kind of political leverage that the American political system understood. They, like other middle-class reformers, rejected that alternative as corrupt. It meant that Harlem intellectual leadership was epiphenomenal. It had no grass-roots attachments. Its success depended on its strategic placement, not its power. These leaders made themselves into conduits of Negro thought to white men of influence, and they attempted to channel white good intentions into effective reform. Except as white power could be inflected through them, they had no reason to believe that they could command black people's actions. Without mass support they were mere emblems of leadership, impotent to force change. That is why they and Harlem failed in what they promised to become.

From the end of the Civil War, Negro leadership had been tainted by elitism. The assumption always was that the final objective was the acceptance of the Negro into American society as an equal partner with whites and a full citizen. And it was also expected that the Negro had to prove himself ready;

he had to lift himself up. It mattered little whether the spokesman followed the Booker T. Washington line or the Niagara movement and W. E. B. DuBois. Technical and industrial training and business achievement, some said, would transform the Negro into an essential economic force whose place could not be denied him. On the other hand, it was argued that a "talented tenth," an intellectual black elite, was necessary to lead the skilled black artisan into breaking down barriers of caste. In either case, it was accepted that generations of slavery, oppression, and humiliating discrimination had unfitted the bulk of American Negroes for immediate claim to full citizenship. The leaders' role was to win for the people their opportunity for achievement and manhood.

Surely, this was understandable enough. Booker T. Washington knew the common Negroes in the South; James Weldon Johnson had taught them in rural Georgia; W. E. B. DuBois had taught them in rural Tennessee; and all had seen the rural peasant Negroes streaming daily into Harlem from the South; they could hardly make great claims for their unimproved condition. Nor would it have been in keeping with their progressive mentality to demand that men should be given more than they actually earned or deserved. All they asked, all they could bring themselves to demand, was that the track be open for a fair race. The Negro should be given every advantage and opportunity that other men were. They had the faith that in an open, fair race, where the truly best man was allowed to win, the black man would gain a good share of the laurels.

Whatever the justice of these assumptions, they gave a peculiar shape and thrust to Negro leadership. It, like progressivism, was superior, didactic, and uplifting. It often saw itself as an example for Negroes to follow and an example of Negro potential for the white world. Buried deep in this awareness of racial inadequacy was race guilt. Sometimes the Negro masses were a source of real embarrassment, something to be explained, to be understood. So they were when they responded so openly to the fantasy of Marcus Garvey. Never were the black masses a source of power, a true following. The black common man might well thrill to the sharp barbs and slashing wit of DuBois's attacks on white illogic and injustice, but he could never assume an identity with that fiery editor. There was a distance.

The association of this leadership with the white philanthropists and reformers also compromised them as far as the common man was concerned. Booker T. Washington's dependence on northern white benevolence and southern white tolerance has long been understood. Although more militant than the Tuskegee group, the NAACP was still a white organization. And that Association took considerable care that control remained in the hands of its white New York City board of directors. Even A. Philip Randolph and Chandler Owen were committed to the doctrine and politics of the Socialist party, whose attitude toward race relations was hazy, and to the trade union movement, dominated in the 1920s by the racially restrictive American Federation of Labor. If there was to be a voice of common black people, it would have to come from some other direction. Even when that voice did come—polemical and provocative—to lift black spirits with the dreams of a great race potential, it too was a deception which left them to founder in the realities of their limited power.

Harlem progressives cannot be wholly blamed for their failures as political leaders. Like many white reformers, they gave more weight to the power of morality and the essential rightness of the American system than either deserved. Their fault, if it can be called a fault, was in their innocent faith in the American liberal tradition. The problem was that racism, unlike child labor and unrestrained exploitation of natural resources, could not be touched by simple reforms and efforts at right thinking. Rather, it was so deep in the American psyche (black and white) as not to be consciously understood. Reform would not do; eventually it would require deep social convulsions to make black and white Americans conscious of its enormity. But the bedazzlement of new Harlem and the vision of a threshold of a new age of black achievement and mastery invited black intellectuals to fancy themselves a vanguard—new men.

2   The New Negro

The decade of the 1920s, with the Great War over, was one of general liberation; everything seemed in flux. America was self-conscious about a newness and change which had actually begun in the years before America's entry into the European war. This had been the theme of Van Wyck Brooks's *America's Coming of Age* (1915). Brooks announced that American arts and letters were at last free from the fetters of provincialism and Puritanism. The bracing winds from Europe had propelled the becalmed American culture and set it loose to find its own course. Van Wyck Brooks and the young intellectuals who had engaged in the prewar rebellion went into the war convinced that the day of American art and letters was at hand.[1] Despite the disillusionment that followed wartime idealism, the 1920s continued some of this spirit of emancipation, innovation, and newness. The aura of the postwar decade, epitomized in F. Scott Fitzgerald's "younger generation" and the Jazz Age, was reflected among Negro intellectuals too. They created the "New Negro."

By the end of the war, in 1919, Afro-Americans who called themselves radicals were already serving notice that the Negro of postwar America was going to be much more militant than his prewar brother. The *Messenger* had insisted that the "new style" Negro would not accept accommodation or ignore grievances even in the interest of the war. The Negro would no longer "turn the other cheek," be modest and unassuming. He would answer violence with violence rather than with meek though moral protests and requests for justice. That magazine had applauded the display of violence by Negroes in the recent racial disturbances in Longview, Texas, Washington, D.C., and Chicago. His willingness to fight showed that the New Negro was as anxious to make "America safe for himself" as he had been to make the world safe for democracy. W. A. Domingo, Jamaican and sometime contributor to Garvey's *Negro World,* tried to define the New Negro, this new man, in the *Messenger* August 1920 issue. In politics, Domingo claimed, the New Negro "cannot be lulled into a false sense of security with political spoils and patronage. The job is not the price of his vote." His labor was not to be exploited as the Old Negro's had been in the past. But, above all, he would insist on "absolute and unequivocal *social equality,*" which would be achieved by identifying his interests with those of the working classes. The Negro was mainly a worker, so his new leaders would reject association with capitalism and the bourgeoisie and support a labor party. He would focus on objectives that were to his immediate economic interest, working-men's goals: shorter working hours, higher wages, more jobs. He would join white labor unions where he could; he would form his own when white unions discriminated. He would educate himself and others in order to facilitate just race relations, but he would use "physical action in self-defense." To Domingo, the New Negro's methods were summed up in the rejection of the "old Crowd Negroes'" counsel of the "doctrine of non-resistance." [2]

Domingo, of course, viewed this new man through the eyes of a socialist, and so he added an economic class-consciousness. Few other Negro spokesmen talked in terms of a labor party as a viable political vehicle. But all would agree with Domingo on the broad strokes of the portrait. The New Negro was militant and self-assertive. He would not be content with second-class citizenship and only vague promises for a better future. And all agreed that the war had much to do with the changes. All Americans had just participated in a moral crusade to make political justice and democracy a reality to men throughout the world. American Negroes had joined in that struggle with the conscious intent of making this their fight too. They had made their contribution as military men, they had served their nation, and now they would insist on being treated like full citizens. Whatever they had thought of the war, Negro political leaders believed that it had bought the Negro some credit in American society; it had broadened him, and had given him a feeling of his power.

This new militancy was trumpeted to New York City and to America at large by the triumphal return of New York's 15th Infantry Regiment from Europe. An organization of Negro volunteers, it had been mustered into United States service in July 1917, only to suffer a series of official rejections and indignities lasting until the end of its service. The army's reluctance to permit black combat troops under its command resulted in this unit's being attached to the French Army as the 369th Regiment. Even so, white American anxiety about Negroes in the war was so acute that the United States Army had circulated among the French the famous document of August 1918: *Secret Information Concerning Black Troops.* This circular warned against black and white fraternization, lest Negroes rape French women. It also cautioned French officers and men

against treating American Negroes in other than the most official and perfunctory way. Yet, despite much provocation and
the persistent German propaganda which harped on American
racism, the 369th Regiment achieved an outstanding record of
valor and distinction in combat. It was the first Allied unit to
reach the Rhine. It was the first American regiment in the
French Army during the war (it had the longest service, therefore). It was in the trenches for 191 days. The entire unit was
awarded the *Croix de Guerre* for its action at Maison-en-
Champagne, and 171 officers and enlisted men were cited for
the *Croix de Guerre* and the Legion of Honor for exceptional
bravery in action. Nevertheless, this regiment of New York Negroes was brutally harassed by American military police while
they awaited ships to return to the United States. Their victory
parade in New York City, February 17, 1919, signaled something more, therefore, than the return of soldiers from the war.
These men had done more than most to prove themselves men
and Americans, and they accomplished their feats under the
most trying circumstances. They had come close, but they had
never succumbed to their rage. They had avoided, sometimes
quite narrowly, the violent reaction to bigotry and the subsequent punishment that had befallen the 24th Infantry Regiment at Houston, Texas. They had gone through it all and
brought back victory without blemish. It must have been a
proud day for them and for the black New Yorkers who
watched them.[3]

They marched down Fifth Avenue in massive company pha-
lanxes. Black Americans, fighting men. Lt. James Europe's
band, which had made itself and the new American jazz famous throughout France, led them down the broad avenue
under flags and banners reading: OUR HEROES—
WELCOME HOME. Through throngs of cheering New Yorkers they marched, through the newly erected victory arch at
25th Street, past the Public Library, continuing up Fifth Ave-

nue to 110th Street and the end of Central Park. Then it was
over to Lenox Avenue and up that street, through Harlem
(through home) to 145th Street. On these uptown streets, they
changed their tight phalanx to an open formation. The cheering crowds were darker with familiar accents; they called out
names and ran within the ranks to touch the men. Jim Europe's band of sixty brass and reed, thirty trumpet and drum,
swung into "Here Comes My Daddy Now"; all Harlem went
wild. For a moment—a day or two, or a week—Harlem, and
all of New York, thought these black men were heroes. Negroes cannot be blamed for thinking that the glory would last,
that this martial and manly spirit, these honors deserved and
won, would forever deny to white Americans the chance to
treat Negroes as less than men and citizens. Such expectations
were part of the stuff that fed the conception of the New
Negro.

The irony was considerable. Among other things, the postwar years saw a spectacular revival of racism; the new Ku
Klux Klan found white support throughout the country, and
violence against Negroes increased. Apparently, white Americans believed in the New Negro as much as black Americans
did; he was a threat to one as much as a hope to the other.

The black man's metamorphosis was assumed by everyone,
and thoughtful people knew that the change would have a profound effect not only on the American Negro but on American
culture and, indeed, the multi-colored world itself. Alain
Locke, a dapper, gentle, nut-brown man, a Rhodes Scholar,
and professor of philosophy at Howard University saw no limit
to the transformation. He brought together a varied group of essays, stories, poems, and pictures in *The New Negro* (1925), all
searching to define what was assumed to be a grand cultural
flux. Locke's editing of and contribution to this volume and his
energetic championing of the intellectual achievement of Ne-

groes in the 1920s made him the father of the New Negro and the so-called Harlem Renaissance.[4]

Locke insisted that a change in the Negro had occurred far beyond the measurement of the sociologist. The appearance of the New Negro seemed sudden and shocking only because the Old Negro had long since been a shadow and fiction, preserved in white minds through sentimentalism and reaction. The Negro, because he had found it paid, helped perpetuate this fiction through protective social mimicry. "So for generations in the mind of America, the Negro has been more of a formula than a human being—a something to be argued about, condemned or defended, to be 'kept down,' or 'in his place,' or 'helped up,' to be worried with or worried over, harassed or patronized, a social bogey or a social burden." Even the Negro intellectual tended to see himself as a social problem, Locke argued. He had to make his appeal in the face of the unjust stereotype of his enemies and the equally questionable stereotypes of his friends. In neither case could he see himself as he really was. "His shadow, so to speak, was more real to him than his personality." But a renewed sense of self-respect was forcing the Negro to look at himself afresh, to reject the stereotypes and clichés, and to insist on integrity of race and personality.

As Locke saw it, the traditional and fictional view of the Negro had been made embarrassingly obsolete by the changes in the realities of Negro life. The migration that had pulled the Negro out of the South, putting him in the Midwest and East, had made him an urban and industrial man. Only the most obtuse and sentimental could continue to find "aunties," "uncles," "mammies," Uncle Toms, and Samboes, in modern city life.

The city made a difference, in Locke's mind, because it forced the Negro from the simple to the complex life, from rural homogeneity to urban pluralism; he was forced to see himself in broad and sophisticated terms. Harlem was a perfect example. Not only was it the "largest Negro community in the world," but it brought together black men of the most diverse backgrounds and interests. There were Africans and West Indians as well as Negroes from the south and north of the United States. There were city men, town men, and village men; "the peasant, the student, the business man, the professional man, artist, poet, musician, adventurer and worker, preacher and criminal, exploiter and social outcast. Each group has come with its own separate motives and for its own special ends, but their greatest experience has been the finding of one another." This shared experience, Locke held, was race-building. Until that moment, he insisted, the Negro had been a race more in name than in fact, "more in sentiment than in experience." What had defined them as a race was a common condition and a common problem. What was needed to make a race, however, was a common consciousness and a life in common. Life in the city, life in Harlem, would satisfy that need. "In Harlem," he wrote, "Negro life is seizing upon its first chances for group expression and self-determination. It is —or promises at least to be—a race capital." Harlem was for the New Negro what Dublin was to the New Ireland, Prague to the New Czechoslovakia, and Belgrade to the New Yugoslavia.

Race-building, according to Locke, was forcing the Negro to reject old assumptions and old images. If the white man had erred in his defining the Negro in order to justify his treatment of him, the Negro too often had found his treatment an excuse for his condition. The new social sciences were taking a hard look at the realities, and the intelligent Negro would welcome the hard-eyed scientific evaluation in place of the soft and crippling judgment of the philanthropist. All racial groups had to be weaned from some dependency, and the Negro was no exception. Locke argued that the Negro's time had come to free himself from the patronizing and distant philanthropy of sentimental white society. The New Negro's race consciousness and racial cooperation were clear indications that his time had come to be a race, to be free and self-assertive. While expressed in racial and collective terms, Locke's view of the New Negro was strikingly familiar, an iteration of very traditional values of self-sufficiency and self-help, as American as the Puritans and the "self-reliance" of Ralph Waldo Emerson. Whatever else he was then, as Locke explained him, the New Negro was an assertion of America.

So, Alain Locke believed that the profound changes in the American Negro had to do with the freeing of himself from the fictions of his past and the rediscovery of himself. He had to put away the protective coloring of the mimicking minstrel and find himself as he really was. And thus the new militancy was a self-assertion as well as an assertion of the validity of the race. The Negro was in the process of telling himself and the world that he was worthy, had a rich culture, and could make contributions of value. And as Locke saw it, this new consciousness would be auspicious in two special ways. It made the New Negro the "advance-guard of the African peoples in their contact with the Twentieth Century civilization," and it also provided "the sense of a mission of rehabilitating the race in world esteem. . . ." He thus incorporated in his thinking the American sense of mission, a strange variation on the "white man's burden."

The New Negro's task was to discover and define his culture and his contribution to what had been thought a white civilization. In Locke's words, the Negro "now becomes a conscious contributor and lays aside the status of a beneficiary and ward for that of a collaborator and participant in American civilization." Thus, the considerable talents of the Negro could be released from the "arid fields of controversy and debate to the

productive fields of creative expression." So it was to be
through a cultural awakening that the Negro was to express
himself. Locke could not promise that the race would win the
long-desired end of material progress, but the enrichment of
life through art and letters would be an ample achievement.
What is more, the Negro would be a people rather than a
problem. Echoing the words of Van Wyck Brooks, who ten
years earlier had searched to find value in white American culture, Alain Locke announced the New Negro as the race's
"spiritual Coming of Age."

It was no mere coincidence that both Alain Locke and Van
Wyck Brooks saw crisis in terms of cultural maturity. Americans have been consistently perplexed as to what culture is,
what is distinctively American culture, and what of value
America has contributed to Western civilization. Concern over
the thinness of American culture forced many intellectuals to
give continued backward glances to Europe. Sometimes the
American's consciousness of Europe was ridiculed, as in the
probing satire of Mark Twain, sometimes it was marked by a
fascination with its richness, sophistication, and corruption, as
with Henry James. Always, it seemed culture was something
alien to the fresh and rough American; always something
learned, attained, achieved, never the natural gift of one's soil,
one's land, one's blood.

Malcolm Cowley has made this point very well in *Exile's
Return.*[5] In its early pages Cowley explains why a group of
young intellectuals around World War I felt no sense of value
in their own experience and past. All of their education, as
Cowley remembers, pointed them toward some other place
than home. They were trained out of their regional dialects
and into a colorless, school-learned Ameri-English which all of
their teachers had dutifully acquired. The stuff of imagination,
art, and literature was never pulled from the mysteries of their
own country and the experiences of their own people. Rather,

they were asked to dream of medieval European castles and English country life. It was as if the things that they could touch and see were unworthy of art and culture. Then, they were drawn to eastern colleges; fitting-rooms of culture, as Cowley remembers. Culture to the educated American had nothing to do with folk roots—one's past or one's life—rather, it was clothes that one could wear after a long process of divestment of the familial, the regional, the natural. Thus Cowley makes most understandable the feeling of uprootedness and alienation of the generation of young men who were in college, or had just finished college, around World War I. Set adrift from a past without meaning or value, or so their education had trained them to believe, they went searching for some roots in European civilization grafting themselves on to the only culture America had taught them to respect.

If anything, this alienation was more accentuated among Negro intellectuals. There had been little in the public schools or the colleges to give them a sense of their cultural past or the distinctiveness of their people. The black boy or girl who went to mixed northern schools and to white colleges could have expected little. But even the segregated southern schools provided little of their own past besides the names of heroines and heroes: Harriet Tubman, Sojourner Truth, Frederick Douglass, and of course Booker T. Washington. The fact that the line back to the past was snarled where enslavement and migration from Africa had begun made the racial past hazy, distant, and impossible to know. But even the more recent history of the Afro-American, that which could be touched and measured, seemed to provide little of the stuff for race-building. A society weaned on self-reliance and individual freedom could find little to honor in servitude, no matter how enforced. The shame that black men felt about their past was a measure of how much they had drunk up the values of the white American world around them. So they were left with the few names that had survived of the men and women who had defied oppression, achieved success in white men's terms, and who stood thus as proof that the past would not enslave blacks forever.

Shame of the past made the Negro reject much of the reality of his people's condition. In the mad rush from slavery, inferiority, and oppression into citizenship and manhood, much was garbled and confused. Those things reminiscent of the former condition—unskilled and field labor, enthusiastic religion—were to be denied. The professions (medicine, dentistry, law, the ministry, teaching, and undertaking) and business were to be embraced. One was to join the more sober Protestant denominations. It was not simply a matter of achievement or social mobility, these attainments were bench-marks measuring the distance a black man or woman had traveled from his past of chains. They were symbols which connoted to the Negro freedom and manhood. And they were not just in a few men's minds; they were built into those institutions, most of all the schools, charged with the impress of social values.

Of course, white schools transmitted "American culture," an ethnic cultural blandness—America was made up of many different peoples, but they were all the same. When the black child was well treated in such schools—not made to feel shame for his blackness—he was taught that he was like everyone else; a truth that his experience surely belied. And while Negro schools had many virtues in teaching the child that he had worth, they taught him also that he should be like white men, not like himself, and surely not like his father. It did not matter whether the teacher followed W. E. B. DuBois's philosophy of the "talented tenth" or Booker T. Washington's even more condescending notion that the Negro should prove himself acceptable as a citizen in white men's terms.

The point is not that teachers and schools were misguided or pernicious. White and black teachers gave many a young Negro his first feeling of genuine, personal worth. Rather, despite their best intended efforts they could not give to the black child a rich, dense, and mysterious sense of a past like that of traditional cultures. It was not merely that the ingredients were difficult to pull out of the American Negro's history, and that the sophistication and beauty of African cultures were not yet understood, but that the experience of American institutions worked against it. The object of American public schools was to make their charges American; which meant a rounding off of points of difference. Oriental and Jewish children were able to retain the gift of their past through special schools. But Negro children were swept into the cultural blender with other Americans, pulled into the vortex of Anglo-Saxon norms. Having no known culture to deny, the Negro was doubly damned. For when he discovered the emptiness and soulessness of the bland amalgam, or when he saw that the ultimate truth of the lie was that you had to be white, he had no place to return to. Adrift, his "shadow, so to speak, was more real to him than his personality."

Like white children, black children were taught that the speech of their fathers was not proper English speech. They were encouraged to leave behind their dialects and regional and ethnic idioms. The tales that they had heard the old folks tell were not the stuff of culture; they would read Jane Austen and Thackeray and dream of English romance. Nor were the special rhythms of their speech suitable for poetry when Keats and Shelley were the models. In time, they could learn to accept the spirituals, with their decorum and simple majesty, but never the more spirited gospel songs and surely not the profane blues. Culture was something distant and alien—generally English—to be studied, and, as Cowley remembers, fitted on like a suit of clothes. Negroes in provincial communities were introduced into Western culture by their churches. Vocal ensembles toured these towns, as well as soloists like Roland Hayes and Marian Anderson. Church members would

sell tickets to a performance which would include the standard
tour repertory with some spirituals. Local talent would be
given a chance to perform, and there was always an elocution-
ist who would read from classical English literature. One
would not have been surprised to find Browning Societies here
and there in black communities. Of course, the experience of
the people had been there all along. The folk wisdom that had
sustained Afro-Americans through their most devastating trials
persisted. The music in the language, the distinctive folk imagery, the drama of religion, the essential delight in music remained. In a very vital and real way, that folk culture and tradition was undergoing the genuine alchemy of art. Work
songs, gospels, and hollers were being transformed into blues,
ragtime, and jazz. But, strangely, although black intellectuals
were quick to acknowledge the contribution of black music to
America culture—the only distinctive American contribution
as it was often put—they were rarely willing to claim it was
serious music of high culture. And while many Harlem intellectuals enjoyed the music of the cabarets, none were prepared
to give someone like Jelly Roll Morton the serious attention he
deserved. Jazz was infectious entertainment and not an ingredient of high civilization. So, provincialism pulled the black
intellectual—like his white American brother—away from the
culture of his experience into the culture of his learning.

Since culture was not something that could be taken for
granted, the announcement of its attainment by both white
and black Americans seemed natural enough. The vogue of the
New Negro, then, had all of the character of a public relations
promotion. The Negro had to be "sold" to the public in terms
they could understand. Not the least important target in the
campaign was the Negro himself; he had to be convinced of
his worth. It is important to understand this, because much of
the art and letters that was the substance on which the New
Negro was built and which made up the so-called Harlem

Renaissance was serving this promotional end. Understanding this gives added meaning to the prose and poetry that were produced, and helps us appreciate their problems as art. Alain Locke and the others were correct in saying that there was a New Negro: an artistic self-consciousness of the Negro's human and cultural worth, the sense of an urgent need for self-assertion and militancy, and the belief in a culturally enriched past in America and Africa; these themes were real enough in the works of Negroes of talent. It was not merely Locke's imagination, although like an anxious parent he nurtured every suspicion of talent as if it were the bloom of genius. If the American context forced it to be artificial and contrived, it should not be thought Alain Locke's fault.

There is, however, a problem which promotions such as Van Wyck Brooks's New American and Alain Locke's New Negro share. It is in the metaphor itself. For whatever promise the new man has for the future, his name and the necessity for his creation imply some inadequacy in the past. Like the New Year's resolution or the "turning over a new leaf," the debut of the New Negro announced a dissatisfaction with the Old Negro. And since the New/Old dichotomy is a mere convenience of mind—Afro-Americans were really the same people all along—the so-called Old Negro was merely carried within the bosom of the New as a kind of self-doubt, perhaps self-hate. How can one take up the promotion of race (or nationality) through art without exposing this doubt? How can one say that Negroes are worthy and civilized and new men without at the same time acknowledging doubt and denial? Even the best of the poems of the Harlem Renaissance carried the burden of self-consciousness of oppression and black limitation.

Langston Hughes had just been graduated from high school in Cleveland and was on a strange journey to his father in Toluca, Mexico. His mother had made him feel guilty for wanting to go to college rather than to work, where he would be "of some use to her." While Hughes saw in his father a means of doing what he wanted—to go to college—he was perplexed because his father's bitterness had made him contemptuous of Negroes and a terrible man to live with. Hughes was on the train, crossing the Mississippi River at sunset, when he wrote a poem on an envelope that has since been most often printed as characteristic of his work.[6]

The Negro Speaks of Rivers

I've known rivers:
I've known rivers ancient as the world and older than the flow of
    human blood in human veins.

My soul has grown deep like the rivers

I bathed in the Euphrates when dawns were young.
I built my hut near the Congo and it lulled me to sleep
I looked upon the Nile and raised the pyramids above it.
I heard the singing of the Mississippi when Abe Lincoln went
    down to New Orleans, and I've seen its muddy bosom
    turn all golden in the sunset.

I've known rivers:
Ancient, dusky rivers.

My soul has grown deep like the rivers.

Hughes's use of the Mississippi here is traditional and symbolic. The river is an important symbol not only because it connotes the religious division between the temporal and eternal life, but because it is relentless, persistent, and timeless. It is eternity itself, with no beginning and no end. It pulls into itself the soil around it, and it sustains the life at its reaches. It is profound and enigmatic; its depths are somber and mysterious. And the rivers that Hughes mentions add to this point. The Euphrates, then thought the cradle of men, and the other three rivers are not only mother waters, sustaining life around them,

but they have known the black man and the black slave. And
Hughes says the black man has watched and known these rivers through the centuries, learned their inevitability, and,
through them, sensed eternity. The black man, therefore, will
persist because his soul has become one with the streams of
life.

Hughes has managed in this poem to capture some of the
force of the spiritual. Like many spirituals, it is so simple and
clear a statement that it is difficult to argue the truth of the
assertion. As in many spirituals, the Negro is the speaker and
identifies himself with eternal forces, transcending the facts of
life and the very conditions which make the statement necessary. And like many spirituals, there is great pathos in its promise of ultimate justice (the Negro's value is ultimate, indeed,
eternal), because no other justice is possible (or likely).

Another poem of Langston Hughes's shows something more
of his pathos.

Dream Variation [7]

To fling my arms wide
In some place of the sun,
To whirl and to dance
Till the white day is done.
Then rest at cool evening
Beneath a tall tree
While night comes on gently,
      Dark like me——
That is my dream!

To fling my arms wide
In the face of the sun,
Dance! whirl! whirl!
Till the quick day is done
Rest at pale evening. . . .
A tall, slim tree. . . .
Night coming tenderly
      Black like me.

Each stanza, here, is a variation on the same dream; but what is most striking in this poem is Hughes's contrast of day and night—black and white. The poet, again the Negro, identifies himself with the night; doubtless white men and the white world are the day and the sun. The white day is frenetic, harsh, and hot, while the night is cool, gentle, and tender. But what is this dance that the poet wants to do? Is it one of joy, defiance, or abandon? One senses a kind of suicidal defiance, because the "place of the sun" (suggesting simple freedom) becomes "in the face of the sun" (suggesting defiance). Arms wide, body whirling and spinning, is this not in spite of the white-hot materialistic civilization? But the statement seems a death wish. The Negro is like the night, and the night is death. For the speaker, from the "quick" day, comes to rest here, with a coolness about him and a monumental "tall, slim tree" over him. The night that he welcomes is gentle, pale, and tender like the sleep of death.

Here, too, Hughes's poem touches one of the major themes of the spiritual. Whatever the anxiety and torment of life, death is always a guaranteed release. As in so many of the spirituals, death in Hughes's poem is a welcome friend. And here, too, Hughes has joined the Negro to eternity and eternal forces through the simple association of the Negro with night and death, the untroubled, the tender and peaceful sleep. The white day passes, the sun sets, but the soft night, like the river, is eternal.

Like the spirituals, both of these poems gain power from the promise of a transcendent peace. Beyond the hardship and oppression of this life, there is an eternity and meaning which the poet claims to be his. The spirituals, unlike the poems, rest upon a metaphysic which insists that the "least of these" will be redeemed. It was not a racial matter; it was for all men. Negroes in religious expression found this message especially suited to their condition. When devout black men and women sang these songs, there was more than the self-pity of a lowly people claiming eternity for themselves. There was the sound of the triumph that Christianity promised, the glimpse of the eternity itself. So, while the spirituals were a racial expression, they were a universal message for all the dispossessed. Hughes's poems, on the other hand, are clearly racial. His poem is not merely speaking to the condition of everyman— that humbleness which Christianity promises to reward—but the condition of the Negro as a Negro. The pathos of his assertion is clear enough. But without the metaphysical or Christian justification, the claim to eternity and to ultimate worth lacks triumph and power. It is not that one denies the Negro's soul is deep or that justice to him is deserved and ultimate, but the secular expression lacks an important dimension. One need not ask a religious man why he feels it necessary to seek transcendent and eternal meaning for himself. But when a poet justifies his people in these terms, one suspects in him the initial doubt. There is doubt in the poet's mind, or he assumes doubt in his audience. Otherwise, he would not have to write about the matter in this way.

Ironically, the literature that was to be advanced as evidence of the Negro as a new man contained a strong odor of this pathos and self-doubt. It tainted all the pronouncements and exposed the vulnerability of the New Negro concept. Nowhere is this theme more clear than in one of Countee Cullen's poems:

Yet Do I Marvel [8]

I doubt not God is good, well-meaning, kind,
And did He stoop to quibble could tell why
The little buried mole continues blind,
Why flesh that mirrors Him must some day die,
Make plain the reason tortured Tantalus
Is baited by the fickle fruit, declare

> If merely brute caprice dooms Sisyphus
> To struggle up a never-ending stair.
> Inscrutable His ways are, and immune
> To catechism by a mind too strewn
> With petty cares to slightly understand
> What awful brain compels His awful hand.
> Yet do I marvel at this curious thing:
> To make a poet black, and bid him sing!

It may be argued that Cullen, influenced as he was by the English Romantics, was indulging in the self-pity that often captured those poets in their lesser expressions of inner anguish. There is something to this; Cullen turned to Tantalus and Sisyphus—mythological figures who fed the Romantic imagination—to give measure and equivalence to his torment. Yet, his torture is not personal, nor is it generic. It is racial, somehow the peculiar torment of black men who are sensitive and wish to sing. And Countee Cullen assumes that his audience, white and black, will know and immediately understand that there is a special godly and tragic condition here. But how can one know that? And why should everyone know that the black poet's trial is especially futile? Is it because he is wounded and limited? It could not be that he alone has more soul than voice to sing; that was the predicament of all poets, the Romantic would say. One cannot be sure what Cullen had in mind when he thought his reader would know the special curse of the black bard, but close to the surface is doubt which is not merely self-doubt but race doubt. Because it is a racial doubt and limitation rather than personal, the reader senses the pity of the futile effort, without the heroism of the tragic condition.[9]

Such doubt and presumption of limitation were inextricably a part of the New Negro vogue. Just as Van Wyck Brooks's *America's Coming of Age* was condescending about American art and culture, assuming it limited and wanting, those promoting the New Negro, even as they proclaimed the Negro's worth, provided evidence that they had to assert and prove it.

Part of the assertion of the Negro's value was the assumption of militancy. The assertion that justice ultimately would be his was not enough for the New Negro. Indeed, that had been the problem with the Old Negro, the docile and patient retainer who knew that his reward would be in heaven. Hughes and the young Negro writers of the 1920s were not saying that. The Negro had ultimate, eternal human worth. It should not only be asserted, but the Negro should assume in the present the posture promised him in eternity. He should be a man like other men.

Thus, the other face of the New Negro's *persona* was militant and self-assured. Indeed, the only way he was to claim his true manhood was to demand redress of grievances, to fight back. Some of the poetry and prose of the 1920s by Negroes iterated this theme. The most notable was a poem by Claude McKay.

If We Must Die [10]

If we must die, let it not be like hogs
Hunted and penned in an inglorious spot,
While round us bark the mad and hungry dogs,
Making their mock at our accursed lot.
If we must die, O let us nobly die,
So that our precious blood may not be shed
In vain; then even the monsters we defy
Shall be constrained to honor us though dead!

O kinsmen! we must meet the common foe!
Though far outnumbered let us show us brave,
And for their thousand blows deal one deathblow!
What though before us lies the open grave?
Like men we'll face the murderous, cowardly pack,
Pressed to the wall, dying, but fighting back!

Here was none of the non-resistance that the Old Negro had preached, nor the tone of superiority and righteousness of paci-

fism. Black men must fight back. This was the message of East
St. Louis, Illinois, and Houston, Texas. It was the same call to
self-defense that the *Messenger* and W. A. Domingo had applauded. The poem, itself, as an expression of the new black
spirit, alarmed conservative whites. Senator Henry Cabot
Lodge had it read into the *Congressional Record* as evidence
of the unsettling currents among black Americans. In later
years, when Arna Bontemps collected on a phonograph record
an anthology of Negro poets, McKay claimed that it was not
just a Negro poem. He said, following World War II, that he
had never considered himself a Negro poet. He claimed that
he had considered "If We Must Die" a universal poem, for all
men who were "abused, outraged and murdered, whether they
are minorities or nations, black or brown or yellow or white,
Catholic or Protestant or Pagan, fighting against terror." Yet,
in the *Messenger* in 1919 and in *Harlem Shadows* in 1922 no
one could doubt that the author was a black man and the "we"
of the poem black people too.[11]

The search for a personality for the New Negro necessitated
the rediscovery of a heritage. As much as the young Negro intellectuals wanted to proclaim a new day and to inter all vestiges of the old image, they felt a need to find justification in
the past. The heritage was to serve the new image. So, much
effort went into the explication of the Negro's folk traditions in
America and into the interpretation of whatever was known of
the civilizations of Africa.

The Negroes' importance to American culture, it was argued,
was that he provided its only genuine folk tradition. From the
Afro-Americans had come a rich and complex folklore and
music which was the most distinctively American contribution
to world culture. While the Negro had been denied by both
whites and sophisticated blacks, he was unconsciously pouring
out, in his own entertainment and for his own soul's needs, the

raw folk materials upon which any American music or literature would have to rest. With this argument in mind, Negroes
began to recover their folk traditions. Sophisticated Negroes began to find value in the peasant character of the mass of American Negroes. After all, it was from the common man and the
peasant stock that these ingenuous and fresh folk materials were
being produced.[12]

Arthur Huff Fauset was a teacher in the Philadelphia public
schools, but he turned his attention to the collection and study
of folklore. In 1925 he took a trip gathering materials in the
lower South. He had earlier done research in Nova Scotia
under the auspices of the American Folklore Society. He
turned his attention to Negro materials not only because of his
racial attachments but because of his fear that the rapidly
changing and urbanizing South would soon obliterate this very
rich source of the Negro's past. Fauset was convinced that
much that was distinctively Negro character was to be found
in his folk materials. At the same time, he recognized that the
main themes of folktales were intercultural. American Negro
folk-themes could be recognized in European and Oriental, as
well as African legend. So the compiling of the materials of the
southern Negro would both give America some cultural richness and texture and relate it to the vast and complex world
literature.

Arthur Fauset thought of folklore as documentary. Folktales
should not be tainted with the personality of the recorder.
Fauset had found this the signal fault of Joel Chandler Harris'
Uncle Remus tales. Harris had created in Uncle Remus a character who was artificial to the folk materials that were reported
through his words. Through his created character, Harris had
intruded and corrupted the folktales. Harris presented his view
of the ante-bellum southern Negro. The reader had to take Harris' sentiment in order to get to the starkly unsentimental folktales themselves. Fauset, on the other hand, conceived his role as

the gatherer and recorder of folktales just as they were spoken by the narrator, without any intrusion whatsoever. The value was in the tale itself, not in sophisticated or sentimental interpretation.

Zora Neale Hurston had more formal training than Arthur Fauset but was far less pure in her handling of folk materials. Orphaned at an early age, Zora Hurston had a very difficult time lifting herself from her poor Jacksonville, Florida, environment and getting a formal education. But she was strong-willed, aggressive, and tenacious; she managed through hard work, and the benevolence of white friends, to get into Howard University, finish at Barnard College, and take an advanced degree in anthropology under Franz Boas at Columbia University. Poverty and limitation had merely given her a keen instinct for opportunity and a single-minded will to grasp it when it came. In New York, she seemed constantly under the tutelage and patronage of white women; she was more comfortable under these arrangements than many of her Negro contemporaries.[13]

Negro folk materials were merely another opportunity for Zora Hurston, and she made the best of it. Gifted with a clear, uncluttered style and a keen ear for voice sounds and rhythms, she capitalized on her academic training, research, and the new public interest in Negro folk materials. She went beyond simple collection and used the common, rural Negro—his speech, manner, and superstitions—as the stuff for numerous short stories and plays. She was prolific, and her stories appeared in *Opportunity* and other magazines. Her talent for transcribing common speech brought her version of the rural Negro to the eyes of those who were trying to define the New Negro by contrasting him with his common folk.

Zora Hurston's imagination was the stuff of her stories. She provided the plot and voiced it with the speech of the lowly, rural Negro as her ear had captured it. She colored it with his superstitions and habits of mind. She did not give the reader full, well-developed characters. Rather they were types, folk types. So, these tales became Zora Hurston's general assessment of common Negro character and life. He was robust and passionate. He lived for the instant but was keenly aware of a world beyond. His life and his mind were uncomplicated; good and evil, strength and weakness, were not fuzzed by ambiguity. Yet, he lived in the constant presence of ghosts and supernatural powers—both good and evil. But this was Zora Hurston's interpretation, and Arthur Fauset could complain as much about the sentimentality and artificiality here as in Joel Harris' work. Harris, at least, had told authentic folktales, while the line between Zora Hurston's mind and her material was never clear.

Authentic or not, the popularity of folk materials among the promoters of the New Negro marks a significant step in the Negro intellectual's gaining self-consciousness and self-confidence. Remarkably, this Afro-American concern with the preservation of folk materials was paralleled by a similar white effort which began to discover value in mountain and rural folk-idiom. The American's willingness, white and black, to parade before the world his peasant origins was tantamount to stating his own sophistication and urbanity. One seems to have come of age when one can discuss with detachment and pride one's true origins.

In much the same way, the concurrent promotion of spirituals by black intellectuals was a sign of confidence in their urbanity. Of course, the Negro spirituals had long since been "discovered." It was 1871 when the Fisk Jubilee Singers brought these songs to the attention of American white audiences. In the years that followed, several Negro colleges sent ensembles on tour throughout the United States and to the

major cities of Europe. By the beginning of the twentieth century, whatever the white world knew of Afro-American expression came through these songs.

But it was not the white world alone that had to make this
"discovery." Like much that had been associated with slavery,
the spirituals were lost in the sophisticated Negro's rush to cast
off the garb of servility and simplicity. The spirituals, like a
rustic relative, were an embarrassment to some. But no Negro
could claim dignity for himself and his race while denigrating
so essential and distinctive a part of his people. W. E. B. Du-
Bois saw this. In *Souls of Black Folk,* he wrote a chapter about
these "sorrow songs," in which he ascribed to them a mystical
force which bound the race emotionally. They were the voice
of the common experience, essential to the soul of black people. After all, he, a black Yankee whose entire life had been
devoid of the experience from which these songs were produced, could instinctively sense, and be one with, the emotions
—the torment and labor—that had given them birth. DuBois
told his black readers that the spirituals were so essentially
them that their search for identity was futile until they found
themselves in this emotional seedbed that was the race's common spirit.

The early years of the new century saw a growing literature
on the Negro spiritual. By the end of World War I, a remarkable number of Negroes had turned their attention to these
songs. They included, of course, performers like Roland Hayes
and Paul Robeson, whose popularity was as much a measure
of white as Negro interest. More notable were men like Harry
T. Burleigh, James Weldon and J. Rosamond Johnson, Nathaniel Dett, and Hall Johnson who began collecting and scoring
these songs. A part of their motivation was similar to that
which compelled Arthur Fauset to collect and record folktales:
this rich and fundamental part of the Negro's life and history
would be lost as the Old Negro was transformed into the New.

And the promoters of the New Negro found more meaning in the spirituals than just the emotional and imaginative record of the Negro's past. Alain Locke saw those songs as a direct route to a rich and virtually untapped vein of folk art, the Negro's entire musical expression. Indeed, taking American culture as a whole, nothing so distinctive and so usable was available to the white American artist. Locke saw the spirituals, blues, and jazz as the stuff from which the American musicians would have to build their classical music. They would be the germ of modern music. He knew this would be, because he already had heard the soul sounds of Negroes in the music of new European composers: Milhaud, Dvořák, Stravinsky. It was only for Americans, white and black, to discover their souls in this true American folk music; then the American could truly come of cultural age.[14]

The discovery that Negro folk materials were usable in art was applicable beyond the realm of music. James Weldon Johnson had contributed to the gathering of the spirituals in the collection that he and his brother edited and arranged in 1925–26, and in 1927 he experimented with Negro folk idiom in poetry. His poems collected in *God's Trombones* were a fresh, distinctive effort. They took the rhetoric, idiom, and images of the Negro preacher and used them as poetic materials. Johnson had written dialect verse in earlier years, but these were different in two important ways. The subjects were serious, and the reader never forgets their serious intent; simple statement, and simple and direct figure, only add to their emotive force. And while the poet added syllables so as to "set that sun a-blazing . . ." and used ungrammatical expressions: "An he didn't hear no sound," these effects are euphonic and rhythmical and not the character of the poems as in dialect verse. "Creation" is Johnson's version of a Negro preacher's conceptualization of Genesis. "Go down Death" reduces orthodox Christian eschatology to human experience and imagination: death is the welcome friend and deliverer. Through these poems, Johnson tried to capture, for art, a basic Negro folk expression, the sermon.

Other Negro poets used everyday speech and the imagination of the black common man as suitable materials for poetry. Langston Hughes conceived of poetry as the music of the common people's language, captured and tied to the images of their minds. He saw himself and his poems as the means through which ordinary Negro men and women could become poets. And, perhaps, he could be the means for others to see their own beauty, see themselves as artists.

Many of his early poems were efforts to touch the dignity of the common man's life. "Mother to Son" in *Weary Blues,* and "Song for a Dark Girl" in *Fine Clothes to the Jew,* are clearly such efforts. But during this period, Hughes also made an attempt to transpose the blues into poetic form. Sometimes as in "Weary Blues," the poems borrow blues rhythms and incorporate entire blues phrases for emphasis and definition. In other poems, such as "Homesick Blues," Hughes seems merely to have transposed a blues lyric into a poem. It all added to Langston Hughes's insistent theme that Negro art would be achieved through capturing the common black man's experience in art forms.

Sterling Brown also chose the common man as the subject and source of his poetry. Brown's poems, however, were fed by the strong stream of American common-man mythology. His is backcountry tradition—the self-styled hero, with the bragging tone of the river boatman. He is Whitmanesque. "Odyssey of Big Boy" claims manly experience across the broad land and makes his *persona* one with Casey Jones, Stagolee, and John Henry himself.

The Negro intellectuals were attempting to build a race and define a culture. If there was validity in the notion of distinctive racial cultural contribution, it must be in the special experience of the race itself. So the whole people and the whole Afro-American experience had to be searched and exploited for clues to heritage. Folk materials and the expression of the common man had to be the essence of such a tradition. But heritage also demanded a continuity in the past, the transit of culture. When the promoters of the New Negro looked back to find his origins, or when they tried to discuss racial culture, they were always thrown back upon Africa.

Africa was an essential enigma in this culture-building enterprise. It was not only impossible for twentieth-century Afro-Americans to pick up any unsevered threads back to Africa, but it was difficult to find correspondence between the cultures of Africa and that of the American Negro. Alain Locke, who was quite knowledgeable about African art, was quick to admit this. The African had a strong tradition of graphic and sculptural expression, but the American Negro, true to an ascetic Puritan tradition, had little visual art to show. The untutored Afro-American could sense no more in a piece of African sculpture than could a European. There was an ocean and an age of experience between the black men of the two continents. Yet, Alain Locke was convinced that African art held a key to Afro-American artistic expression.[15]

African art was a legacy; its existence made evident the fact that black men were the craftsmen of a disciplined and classical art. So, the American Negro need not think himself "a cultural foundling without his own inheritance." He could be freed from imitativeness and indebtedness to the white Western culture. Thus, the knowledge of African arts should encourage American Negroes to pursue long-neglected lines: painting, sculpture, and decorative arts. Using his inheritance as a base, the American Negro, Locke dreamed, might then create new idioms from that tradition. With the African tradition to inspire him, the Afro-American could become the subject of art as well as the artist. He would be freed from the white dogma of beauty.

Locke observed that European artists had already been rejuvenated at the African fountain. Pablo Picasso and Georges Braque found in African sculpture the insight which led them into cubism. And sculptors like Constantin Brancusi and Wilhelm Lembruck were liberated through African sculpture to powerful restatements of human form. If they can, why can't we? Locke asked. Once known "and appreciated, this art can scarcely have less influence upon the blood descendants, bound to it by a sense of direct kinship, than upon those who inherit by tradition only, and through channels of an exotic curiosity and interest."

Alain Locke did not need to wonder long. Negro painters and sculptors began experimenting with the African motifs. Richmond Barthé sculpted several figures which exhibited strong African influence. Aaron Douglas was more consistently devoted to the African legacy than Barthé. Douglas developed a style of drawing which employed stark black silhouette. The figures were always angular and stylized. Like African graphics, Douglas' drawings were more decorative than representational; they were stark blocks of design. In the 1930s Douglas developed this technique into a series of large murals, using flat colors. They were elaborations on his early work; Africa and the exotic dominated.

It was easier to use the African artistic tradition as a means of giving racial quality to art than it was to discuss the significance of Africa to the Negro. Alain Locke had found it difficult and was reduced to a simple assertion of faith in a valuable African legacy. Other Negro intellectuals were equally perplexed by the African heritage. All seemed to know, or sense, that Africa should mean something to the race; there should be some

race memory that tied black men together; ambiguity and
doubt always left the question unresolved, however.

Countee Cullen's poem "Heritage" did little more than show
that poet's quandary. For he raised the question throughout
the poem, what is Africa to me? It is a long poem, with unrelenting tetrameter and a regular aa, bb, cc, rhyme setting up a
rythmic beat that echoes Vachel Lindsay's "Congo." And although the question recurs, and the poet tells of Africa's en-
chantment, he never convinces the reader that the question is
an honest one. Africa comes through as romantic and exotic,
no more or no less real for him as a black poet than it would
have been for a white one.[16]

. . .

> All day long and all night through
> One thing only I must do
> Quench my pride and cool my blood,
> Lest I perish in their flood,
> Lest a hidden ember set
> Timber that I thought was wet
> Burning like the dryest flax,
> Melting like the merest wax,
> Lest the grave restore its dead.
> *Stubborn heart and rebel head.*
> *Have you not yet realized*
> *You and I are civilized?*
>
> So I lie and all day long
> Want no sound except the song
> Sung by wild barbaric birds
> Goading massive jungle herds,
> Juggernauts of flesh that pass
> Trampling tall defiant grass
> Where young forest lovers lie
> Plighting troth beneath the sky.

. . .

Doubtless, Africa was a large question for the black intellectual searching for identity and heritage. It was compelling because of the rootlessness and placelessness of the Afro-American and his search for the springs of a race's origins. It was not
answered by the romantic ejaculations that Cullen used for
passion. Langston Hughes came to the question more honestly
in

Afro-American Fragment [17]

So long,
So far away
Is Africa
Not even memories alive
Save those that history books create,
Save those that songs
Beat back into the blood—
Beat out of blood with words sad-sung
In strange un-Negro tongue—
So long,
So far away
Is Africa.

Subdued and time-lost
Are the drums—and yet
Through some vast mist of race
There comes this song
I do not understand,
This song of atavistic land,
Of bitter yearnings lost
Without a place—
So long,
So far away
Is Africa's
Dark face.

America and Americans were provincials. That was the
problem. Black men as well as white men were forced through
condition and education to look elsewhere for the springs of

civilization and culture. Afro-Americans could not submit to the judgment that Europe was their cultural parent. Such an idea jarred reason, and relegated non-whites to aboriginal and primitive origins which denied them civilization. Whatever self-denial white Americans indulged in to tie themselves to Europe was intensified among blacks, whose road back to Africa was unclear; and when they looked they saw only a dark continent. It was dark because little was known about it; its civilizations and its people had not been high in the order of importance for European scholars. So, black men yearned, as American provincials, to find meaning and identity in Africa; their frustration was a measure of their Americanization.

World War I had been a kind of puberty rite for peoples the world over. Self-determination, an aim of the Allies in the war, became a slogan in the 1920s. Black intellectuals saw in the Yugoslavs, Czechs, and Irish a clue for their own emancipation and uplift. They, too, were a people to be defined. The New Negro was a product of this era of race-building. Afro-Americans were to reforge the long-severed links between the world's black peoples. From this effort would come a revitalized black culture and self-esteem. Whatever else, the era produced a phenomenal race consciousness and race assertion, as well as unprecedented numbers of poems, stories, and works of art by black people. Harlem was making it all happen, because black men were coming together there, some intending to build a cultural capital of the black world. So, Harlem intellectuals looking at themselves, thought of the renaissance.

3 🝑 Heart of Darkness

The Negro, for sufficient reason, has felt himself outside American society. And white Americans, on the other hand, while intent on excluding Negroes from the mainstream of American life, were nevertheless dimly conscious of the black man within it. "Negroes," as Henry May has said, "like white Southerners, had to break into the dominant respectable culture of the day before they could break out of it." [1] Yet the black-white relationship has been symbiotic; blacks have been essential to white identity (and whites to blacks). This interdependence has been too profound to be measured by the simple meting out of respective contributions to American culture. Whites have needed blacks as they have needed the blackface minstrel mask—a guise of alter ego. And blacks—sensing this psychic dependency—have been all too willing to join in the charade, hiding behind that minstrel mask, appearing to be what white men wanted them to be, and finding pleasure in the deception which too often was a trick on themselves. The way that the Negro has been used by whites, and the way he has permitted himself to be used, exposes the deep moral tensions that have characterized American race relations. Harlem in the 1920s gave to this interdependency a sophistication and charm, but at its very core the game of masks remained the same.

If black Harlem had been left alone, not been discovered by whites, the whole story might have been different. Chances are not so much prose and poetry (good as well as bad) would have been published. The sense of urgency to promote culture might have been less. And whatever the artistic output (bad and good), it might have been more honest. But black Harlem could not be left alone, for in a sense it was as much a white creation as it was black. "Harlem on My Mind," in the 1920s or in the 1960s, brings into focus the necessary black-white association in American culture.

At first, Harlem seems contradictory to the main thrusts of the American tradition. There was none of the austerity and anguished conscience of the Puritan fathers, none of the flighty idealism of the transcendentalists, nowhere Benjamin Franklin's dicta—temperance, industry, frugality, chastity—nor Ralph Waldo Emerson's "self-reliance." Indeed, one might look in vain for that secularized Protestant Ethic, Social Darwinism. These compulsive (some would say, anal) traits of American character seem absent from the black metropolis. For the popular mind, Harlem was associated with spiritual and emotional enthusiasm (some would say, soul), indulgence, play, passion, and lust. Where could these fit into the American past?

On second thought, Harlem fits very well into that American tradition. There had of course always been antipodes to those pillars of American tradition. Puritanism contained arminian and pantheistic tendencies. And the same romanticism which generated transcendentalism could be subversive to decorum, emotional austerity, and rational intellect. The same sense of human volition that could sustain self-reliance opened itself to the tumultuous religious revival. The latter believed in the intuition. It was the stuff of the democratic faith because it was

hospitable to the unschooled intellect. Innocence without artifice was an ultimate value. With such faith, the child could be
father to the man. Black men, indeed, could be tutor to white.

Furthermore, Harlem and black men had exotic potential in
America, and the literature and personal accounts of Americans evidence a deep and abiding fascination with exotica.
Charles Brockden Brown's *Wieland*, the fantasies of Edgar
Allan Poe, the writings of Herman Melville, Ambrose Bierce,
Lafcadio Hearn, James Branch Cabell, Joseph Hergesheimer.
In certain views of the West, there was always something of
the "heart of darkness." Meriwether Lewis' fascination with
the West was highly seasoned with a mystical darkness; and
his compulsion was not abated by his successful expedition
into the Louisiana Territory. Or consider the way that China
and the Orient have affected American imagination from before the clipper ships into our own time. Economic and political realities have often been distorted through our fantasy. Indeed, some aspects of America's sense of mission can be
explained by this continuous pull of the exotic.

Americans have lived with their contradictions or, better,
poles of tension. Should we be surprised that Melville and
Emerson, both under pronounced Puritan influence, were
drawn to exotica, the one to the South Seas, the other to the
mysticism of Eastern religion? Will we pause at the notion
that a people wedded to a work-save-build ethic would fantasy
a black stereotype of indolence and appetite, and would find
deep in their souls a thirst for the hot-blooded and impulsive
life?

The years following World War I seemed to encourage the
obverse side of things. Or, as some saw it, to loose subterra-
nean forces that had been held long in check. Nowhere was
this more apparent than in sexual attitudes. The sexual life of
the middle-class American of the late nineteenth century had
been marked by denial and restraint. Practical as well as mor-

alistic, the young go-getter could not get very far burdened with a large family. Idealized notions of the sexual union, however, made non-procreative sex lustful and demeaning. The answer, the proper answer that is, had been delayed marriages and continence. The tension was great. Monument to the failure in practice was the unbroken success of brothels and "red-light" districts in every community of size in the country. But the failure produced revulsion. Thus, the revivalistic crusades against vice which closed those houses and dislodged the whores until backsliders started them up again.[2]

Changes which undermined the moral code came, however, in the early years of the twentieth century. Americans were moving away from rural areas; they were living in large cities, not small towns. Urban anonymity diffused community censure; family control was less immediate and important where children had greater mobility and earlier economic independence. But more jarring still to the traditional moral code was the popularization of Freudian psychology among young intellectuals and sophisticates.

By the United States's entry into World War I, Freudianism had become faddish in sophisticated circles. The Freud (or the psychology), however, that appeared in the popular press would not be recognized as that of the master. Much popularized psychology was heavily charged with naïve optimism which presumed the liberation of the soul from the strait-jacket of moralizing conventions.[3] Freudianism had made popular the conceptions of the id and the super-ego. It could be understood too simply: the human-animal hungers which are forever seeking fulfillment are controlled by social forces made necessary by civilization, order, and decorum. Overburdened with conscience and guilt, civilized man indulged his passions always at the risk of neurosis or greater psychic disorders. By the same token, the man who was least touched by civilizing influences could be more immediate, more passionate, more healthy. Civilizing artifice stripped away, men could dance, sing, and love with freedom and abandon. Seen through such lenses, looking at Harlem, it was easy to believe that Negroes had more fun.

Another kind of primitivism played its part. Early in the century, European intellectuals, particularly the French, had discovered the sophistication of African culture. They saw forceful aesthetic statements in African art and music. The post-impressionists allowed the Africans to influence their sculpture and painting; this was particularly true of "cubism," which like African art "analysed" form rather than reproduced it, emphasized design over representation. What the African craftsmen had accomplished was pure and essential. Could it not be their innocence of civilizing conventions and artifice, their simplicity—which made them primitive—that allowed them to be so pure?

The war, too, had served to produce a disenchantment with civilization. The word "civilization," itself, and other abstractions—loyalty, honor, truth, democracy, liberty—were war casualties because the war, especially for Americans, had been fought in terms of them. These values had lost currency in the postwar moral depression. It had been understood that the difference between the civilized man and the savage was less a matter of technology and materialism than it was of manners and style. It had been thought that the civilized man lived with inner checks which allowed him to create an environment of decorum and gentility. For the savage, on the other hand, natural forces were the only restraint to his inner freedom, so that his environment was chaotic, disorderly, and inhumane. Yet, mass warfare, the trenches, the gas, the weapons of the Great War exposed the ugly brutality that lurked beneath the surface of genteel manners. The most sensitive observers could see it all as a grand illusion. Was the sacrifice worth it—the surrender of the essential self to manners, decorum, and artifice—if the ultimate end of that civilization was a savagery beyond the ken of the most backward and primitive man?

Postwar America was prepared to view the Negro from a different angle. Afro-Americans and Harlem could serve a new kind of white psychological need. Even if Harlem blacks had wanted it, there was little chance that they would have been left alone to shape and define their own identity. White Americans had identities of their own to find, and black men were too essential to them to be ignored. Men who sensed that they were slaves to moral codes, that they were cramped, and confined by guilt-producing norms which threatened to make them emotional cripples, found Harlem a tonic and a release. Harlem Negroes' lives appeared immediate and honest. Everything they did—their music, their art, their dance—uncoiled deep inner tensions. Harlem seemed a cultural enclave that had magically survived the psychic fetters of Puritanism.

How convenient! It was merely a taxi trip to the exotic for most white New Yorkers. In cabarets decorated with tropical and jungle motifs—some of them replicas of southern plantations—they heard jazz, that almost forbidden music. It was not merely that jazz was exotic, but that it was instinctive and abandoned, yet laughingly light and immediate—melody skipping atop inexorable driving rhythm. The downtown spectator tried to encompass the looseness and freedom of dance. Coffee, chocolate, and caramel-brown girls whose lithe long legs kicked high, bodies and hips rolling and tossing with insinuation; feline black men—dandies—whose intuitive grace, teased and flirted at the very edge of chaos, yet never lost aplomb. In the darkness and closeness, the music, infectious and unrelenting, drove on. Into its vortex white ladies and gentlemen were pulled, to dance the jungle dance. Heads swaying, rolling, jerking; hair flying free and wild; arms and legs pumping, kicking, thrusting—going wherever they, them-

selves, would go—chasing the bass or drum or coronet;
clenched eyes and teeth, staccato breath, sweat, sweat—bodies
writhing and rolling with a drum and a beat as they might
never with a woman or a man.

It was a cheap trip. No safari! Daylight and a taxi ride re-
discovered New York City, no tropic jungle. There had been
thrill without danger. For these black savages were civilized
—not head-hunters or cannibals—they would not run amok.
At worst, if a man strayed from the known paths in search of
the more forbidden exotic, he might get fleeced, but in a most
"civilized" way. So, as if by magic, convention returned with
little evidence that it had gone, except, perhaps, for the deeply
insinuated music, the body-remembered rhythm, and the subliminal tease; the self had been transported to a region of its
own honesty which it could know again.

How much was illusion? The white hunter in New York's
heart of darkness would not see (doubtless, would not recognize) his "savage-primitive" drummer and dancer, on sore,
bunioned feet, picking their way on morning's concrete to
cold-water flats, to lose their rhythm-weary bodies in sexless
sleep. Nor could he know the deep desolation of "savage" life
that found only slight escape in alcohol, exotic fantasies in cocaine. Primitive, romantic Harlem was too simple a conception
to survive the cold light of day. So, too, was the romantic
view of Africa. Illusion though it was, it served the deep needs
of those who nurtured it, provided some black men a positive
image of themselves, and, most important, it brought downtown money uptown. What was looked for was found.

Paul Morand, the French journalist, found Harlem the only
relief from the relentless engine of America. Morand saw Negroes to be primitive men, but they had been ripped from their
jungles and forever lost in the machine of the West. But Harlem allowed "these blacks [to] recover their identity and the
quarter again becomes a place of exotic gaiety." Blacks were a

great relief to the traveler, because "they shatter the mechanical rhythm of America . . . people had forgotten that men can live without bank balances, without bath tubs." Civilization, however, was always too close at hand. "Standing erect at the street-crossing, symbolic of white civilization, the policeman keeps his eye on this miniature Africa." Perhaps unwittingly, Morand conjured up the image of the super-ego and the id when he wrote of the policemen on a Harlem corner. If "that policeman happened to disappear, Harlem would quickly revert to a Haiti, given over to voodoo and the rhetorical despotism of a plumed Soulouque." [4] Nor was Morand alone. Carl G. Jung, whose psychology often implied racism, thought it inevitable that European Americans would be affected by the primitives in their midst. Indeed, that behavior which was peculiarly American, he thought, could be traced to African and American Indian influence.[5]

So viewed, Harlem was a means of soft rebellion for those who rejected the Babbittry and sterility of their lives, yet could not find within their familiar culture the genius to redefine themselves in more human and vital terms. The Negro was their subversive agent—his music, manners, and speech. Sheet music and phonograph records could be taken into the home (though the Negro could not) to undermine the sentimentality of conventional American popular music as well as the un-American formality of the standard classics. And the Negro's speech, jazz speech—secretive, "in," casual, and fluid—could be carried abroad to shatter the philistine with its impudence.

Harlem was also therapy for deeper white needs. The most forbidden was most available: whiskey of course, but also cocaine and sex. The fantasy of Negro sexuality is fed by deep springs in the white psyche. Brown and black bodies—the color seemed lustier than white—full lips that quickened flesh to move, whole selves enlivened to blood-heat, seemed closer to the jungle source. Negroes were that essential self one somehow lost on the way to civility, ghosts of one's primal nature whose very nearness could spark electric race-memory of pure sensation untouched by self-consciousness and doubt. Fumbling self-doubt, groping for some hand known to the mysteries, seeking to untie the knots and let the welled-up passions flow; passion without ambivalence, love without guilt. Sensitive and tortured white men and women, whose psyches had somehow been wounded so that they cringed before their own white world, could find a strange comfort and peace among Negroes. It was not that Negro life was less brutal than their own; if anything it was more cruel. But whatever the wounds they brought with them, they were still more whole than the blacks from whom they sought succor. For white men were superior men. No matter how benevolent or genuine their love, they could not help but know that they were better than the Harlem Negroes they saw around them. Although they might damn and curse and spit epithets at a system that brutalized the beautiful blacks, they did so knowing that they were white. Their sense of wholeness could become more full as they watched the anguish of those more deeply hurt than they.

White Americans got much out of blacks in Harlem, but there was a price. The money that fed the joints and cabarets, that kept Harlem flowing with bootleg liquor, that kept the successful pimps dressed and fed, that made Harlem jump, came from whites following a sex lust, or escape, or bindings for their inner wounds. Their money let Harlem Negroes, square and hip, live. Yet some whites paid more than money. Few were injured or lost their lives, but many discovered the narcotic that Harlem could be to the wounded soul. For while guilt might fly in the arms of a black whore, necessarily callous and indifferent, she could hardly have the gentle hands to make a man really whole. Sex, furtive and fugitive, could nurture another kind of guilt. Some whites, pulled into the black vortex, paid the ultimate price of their identity. They defected, became apostates; they became Negroes.[6]

Of all the whites to become associated with black Harlem in the 1920s, Carl Van Vechten was the undisputed prince. He had the reputation of knowing Harlem intimately, not only the places of entertainment but also the important people. He not only enjoyed Harlem, but he also catered to Harlemites by maintaining a kind of downtown salon to which Negroes were welcome as important guests. Indeed, he almost made a career of promoting, socially and professionally, Negro artists and performers. He counted James Weldon Johnson as one of his closest friends; Countee Cullen, Langston Hughes, Richmond Barthé, the sculptor, Ethel Waters, and Paul Robeson were befriended by him. He listened, without weariness or apparent condescension, to Negro writers and artists. He read and viewed their work, urged their interests before publishers and producers, made the important introductions, and, in that way, acted as a kind of midwife to the Harlem Renaissance. Even Langston Hughes, who had slight patience with patrons, welcomed Van Vechten's friendship and supported and defended him against his Negro critics.[7] Beyond this, Van Vechten was responsible for the gathering of Negro manuscript materials at Yale University, encouraging James Weldon Johnson to contribute the nucleus of the collection. Still, it is open to question how well, or in what way, Van Vechten served Harlem and the Negro.[8] It is at least as important, however, to ask how Harlem and the Negro served him.

Born in Cedar Rapids, Iowa, in 1880, Carl Van Vechten, whose productive life extended into the late 1950s, had a career that was not only long but varied. While his interests were always cultural, he exploited them in many different ways. Critic of music, art, drama, and literature, journal-

ist, novelist, and photographer, he followed his mind and talent through successive changes of interest and fascination. And
while at each point he demonstrated exquisite taste and potential, he never found anything wholly absorbing. Van Vechten
was a dilettante in the best sense of the term, excelling where
he had the talent, and pulling it off where he did not. Through
all of the change, however, there was consistency. He was a
collector of rare *objets d'art* and of rare people; rare, in both
instances, because no one had stopped to see or think about
them properly until Van Vechten showed them how. He enjoyed the discovery, and he enjoyed the display, as any collector would. He thrived in that thin, dangerous, and exhilarating
atmosphere where one makes *approving* critical judgments
about the very new and the very off-beat.[9]

It is remarkable how often his judgments—usually daring,
seldom cautious—were right. As early as 1915 he recognized
the revolution—predicted the influence—of Igor Stravinsky
and Arnold Schoenberg. His championing of the modern in
music extended to an early devotion to the blues, Clara and
Bessie Smith. He wrote with discernment and appreciation
about the modern dance of Isadora Duncan. He was responsible for getting Gertrude Stein's *Tender Buttons* published
(theirs was a lifelong friendship, and he became her literary
executor). Wallace Stevens' early poetry was published by Van
Vechten. Elinor Wylie felt indebted to him. And in 1921 he
took the occasion of reviewing a biography of Herman Melville to make the startling, for that time, statement that *Moby
Dick* far surpassed all other American work and stood "with
the great classics of all times, with the tragedies of the Greeks,
with *Don Quixote,* with Dante's *Inferno,* and with Shakespeare's *Hamlet.*"[10] And, subsequently, Van Vechten went on
to properly adjudge Melville's minor novels, *Mardi* and *Pierre,*
as being serious, powerful, and successful works of art. To this
list should be added the Negro writers whom he helped. His

publisher, Alfred Knopf, was persuaded to publish James Weldon Johnson, Nella Larsen, Rudolph Fisher, and Chester Himes. Van Vechten, more than Vachel Lindsay, was responsible for Langston Hughes's first book of poems, *Weary Blues*. And, through Van Vechten, Hughes found his way to the pages of *Vanity Fair*.

Of course, Van Vechten did support and promote writers who would not be recognized today, novels that enjoy the same oblivion as his own. It was more than a simple matter of literary judgment that caused his appreciation of writers like Edgar Saltus and Ronald Firbank, the British author; Firbank, at least, was a writer of consummate imagination and skill. Rather, here was further evidence of Van Vechten's penchant for collecting the exotic and his fascination with decadence. For both Firbank's and Saltus' novels were fantasy creations. Firbank's artificial worlds, which could seem more real than reality, contained the strong flavor of evil and decay that had thrilled the late Victorian readers. It is not surprising that, when Van Vechten concocted his own novels, they too would have the heavy odor of *fin de siècle* decadence.

Reviewing Carl Van Vechten's *Blind Bow-Boy* (1923), Edmund Wilson called it a "burlesque fiction of which we have all too little in America." [11] Wilson noted how this novel and Ronald Firbank's *The Flower Beneath the Foot* harked back to the European literary decadence of the 1890s, specifically Oscar Wilde and Aubrey Beardsley. Conscious artificiality, aestheticism, cultivation of the perverse, and experiment (adopting evil as in the Black Mass) characterized this early movement. The American counterparts were mild; Henry F. May has called them "amoralists." What was at work in the *Blind Bow-Boy*, as in the other Van Vechten novels, was a deliberate dislocation of conventional moral sensibilities, such that each novel, in some way, demanded of the reader some inversion of accepted values. Although Van Vechten's novels, and his moral commentary in them, are serious, the tone is always light and comic. In *Spider Boy* (1928), and especially his last novel *Parties* (1930), a tragic element is heightened; *Parties*, especially, foreshadows some of the recent tragicomic art of the absurd. Indeed, throughout Van Vechten's novels the absurd is given the face of reality, reality become absurd. There is a standard for human behavior, however. The ultimate and only truth is the self, properly expressed. The highest good is the indulgence of one's mind and one's sensations; the greatest fear is boredom.

Carl Van Vechten's fiction echoes late Victorian attitudes which have been brilliantly discussed by David Daiches in his Ewing Lectures in 1967.[12] With much of the traditional basis of faith shattered by science and higher biblical criticism, many intellectuals embraced skepticism. Faith in purposeful order seemed no longer possible—ego without immortality meaningless—so they assumed attitudes which would justify action without purpose on the one hand or would allow them to retreat to aestheticism on the other. Daiches identifies W. E. Henley, A. E. Housman, and Rudyard Kipling as characterizing the late Victorian "mood of stoicism of heroic endurance for its own sake."

> The game is more than the player of the game,
> And the ship is more than the crew!

The aesthetes, like Oscar Wilde, lacking a world of external values, sought the intensification of experience for its own sake. "The aesthetic view of value," says Daiches, "is entirely solipsistic: all the aesthete seeks is to multiply and diversify inward personal experience." Both the stoic activists and the aesthetes converted life into a game, the one sought meaning in the tests of sport and war that tried man and his endurance (the struggle had no meaning or purpose beyond itself) and the other re-

duced society and life to artifice and a game of wit. Carl Van
Vechten was clearly an heir to the Wildean aesthetes. For him,
too, purpose and meaning were to be found only in the personal experience, and the game itself was the ultimate value.

Peter Whiffle, the subject of Van Vechten's first novel, has
spent a lifetime—a restless experiment in art, in sensation, and
in literature—searching for a form with which to build a body
of work.[13] He is finally told that his conscious self is what
holds him back. Rather than think and search, he should abandon thought so that his true self can come through. Ideally, he
should be like the jazz musician who knows his instrument,
knows his music, and knows himself on a level beneath
thought. He should imitate the cat—the feline—in its self-centeredness. Campaspe Lorillard—who appears in *The Blind
Bow-Boy, Firecrackers* (1925), and briefly in *Nigger Heaven*
(1926)—achieved what Peter Whiffle could not: satisfying inward personal experience. Whatever was within was part of
the self and needed celebration. "If it is there, *in us,* it can neither be virtue nor vice. It can only be ourselves. Whatever it
is, if we admit that it belongs to us, we need it to complete
ourselves." Campaspe wanted to live herself, to be, what E. E.
Cummings called, an IS; to make herself into a verb.

The idea was to take oneself and life as they came, enjoying
the entertainment they provided—develop one's taste to its
finest, and savor. Here too are the values of a dilettante and
collector. Van Vechten created the character, Gareth Johns,
who appears in several novels as a stand-in for himself. Johns,
a young novelist, describes what makes a novel work: ". . .
you must think of a group of people in terms of a packet of firecrackers. You ignite the first cracker and the flash fires the fuse
of the second, and so on, until, after a series of crackling deto-
nations, the whole bunch has exploded, and nothing survives
but a few torn and scattered bits of paper, blackened with
powder," which can be taken not only as a scheme for enter-

taining oneself in a varied world, but also as the formula for a
good party—a salon. The trick was to avoid boredom. Since
spontaneity and extroversion were key values, there was a necessary dependence on the existence of an environment and
people who could be catalyzed into enjoyment. Except for *The
Tattooed Countess* (1924) and *Spider Boy* (1928), the characters in all of Van Vechten's novels live in an exotic and artificial atmosphere. The artificiality defines the rules of the social
games that are to be played. Some characters, like Campaspe
Lorillard, master this life. *Peter Whiffle,* an "autobiography"
which is really fiction, since it claims to be the subject's life
and works (Peter Whiffle has actually written nothing), was a
game in itself. Van Vechten's last novel, *Parties* (1930), is a
crazy flight from boredom. Truly an example of the art of the
absurd, it shows everyone on an endless round of parties. One
drunk is succeeded by the next, so that the parties and the alcohol create the most artificial of worlds. The main characters
—David and Rilda Westlake—have one brief, sober moment
when they can talk to one another. This great chase and point-
less round continues because the characters fear the emptiness
that would remain if the parties were to stop. *Parties* is the
logical end of Van Vechten's fiction, the *cul de sac* where self-
indulgence ends.

Van Vechten's most controversial novel, *Nigger Heaven*
(1926), exemplified this inversion of values and fascination
with the exotic. That work was a high point in Van Vechten's
long interest in Negroes.

In his interview for the *Columbia Oral History,* Carl Van
Vechten remembered that his interest in Negroes began very
early. Even as a child, in Cedar Rapids, he remembered that
his parents had insisted on the Negro servants being called Mr.
and Mrs. In the first years of the new century, when Van Vechten was attending the University of Chicago, his broad cultural
interests outside the University had brought him in touch with

popular Negro performers. He had met Bert Williams, for instance. And his penchant for promoting Negro artists was foreshadowed. He recalled bringing Carita Day, who was "very beautiful and sang like an angel," to his fraternity house; she was then performing with Ernest Hogan's "Georgia Minstrels." In 1902, black theatrical entertainment was considered a bit bawdy, so Van Vechten's introduction of Carita Day to his fraternity brothers showed not only his characteristic desire to display and share his own taste, but also his lifelong posture of being *intime* with the underside of life.

In 1912, even New York sophisticates and intellectuals were not accustomed to Negroes close up—except for servants perhaps—surely people did not invite them into their apartments. Carl Van Vechten persuaded Mable Dodge Luhan to allow two Negroes he had "discovered" to entertain at one of her parties. It was a thrill, of sorts. "While an appalling Negress danced before us in white stockings and black buttoned boots, the man strummed a banjo and sang an embarrassing song. They both leered and rolled their suggestive eyes and made me feel first hot and then cold, for I had never been so near this kind of thing before; but Carl rocked with laughter and little shrieks escaped him as he clapped his pretty hands." [14]

It was in 1922, after the publication of *Peter Whiffle*, that Van Vechten, to use his words, became "violently interested in Negroes." "I would say violently," he emphasized, "because it was almost an addiction." Walter White had just published *Fire in the Flint*, and Van Vechten got to know him through Alfred Knopf. Walter White took him everywhere—parties, lunches, dinners—introducing him to everyone who mattered in Harlem.

It was during this intensive induction into Harlem that he met James Weldon Johnson, who was to become his closest and most lasting Negro friend. In about two weeks, Van Vech-

ten recalled, "I knew every educated person in Harlem. I knew
them by the hundreds." Paul Robeson, Rose McClendon, so
many names and faces and talents; it was exhilarating. Nowhere but in Harlem could it have happened at the time. For
nowhere were there so many Negroes, widely varying in talent
and degrees of sophistication. Not in Chicago, and surely not
in Cedar Rapids. Carl Van Vechten was drunk with the experience. "I remember once coming home almost jubilantly after a
night in Harlem, and telling my wife in great glee that I hated
a Negro, I'd found one I hated. And I felt that was my complete emancipation, because now I could select my friends and
not have to know them all." It was as if he had discovered an
unknown country.

It was not only the people but the life of Harlem that Van
Vechten tasted—especially the night life. "I frequented night
clubs a great deal. They were very popular at the time in New
York—at least they were popular after I started going because
I used to get other people to go and it became quite a rage for
a year or two, to go to night clubs in Harlem." He became, indeed, for those years and some years to come, the undisputed
downtown authority on uptown night life. If you were white,
even if you knew some Negroes, he was the man to see to put
you in touch with the right person. It was a considerable privilege to be given a Van Vechten tour of the Harlem night; he
knew the "authentic" places. He was always being asked to
serve as a guide; it was expected. Doubtless, he delighted in
the curator's role. He recalled a considerable reluctance to
guide William Faulkner, at Bennett Cerf's request. He was
mildly embarrassed by Faulkner's persistent request of the musicians to play the "St. Louis Blues" when that song was out of
fashion. It is hard to imagine, however, anyone knowing Carl
Van Vechten and refusing or forgetting to ask him for a tour of
Harlem. It would have been rude, like asking a performer *not*
to do his act. Even foreigners knew where to turn to see the

real Harlem. "Paul Morand," Van Vechten remembers, "wrote me immediately when he got to New York . . . and the first thing he said to me—he wanted me to take him to Harlem. That was almost my fate, for ten years at least: taking people to Harlem." Morand told his readers a different story. He had been guided away from such glitter as the Cotton Club, Sugar Cane, and the Second Part of the Night, and to the "African Room" of the Harlem Club, which featured murals by Aaron Douglas, and female impersonators. But Morand said that his guide was from Martinique. It may have seemed more authentic that way.[15]

The cultural interchange was two-way as far as Van Vechten was concerned. From 1923, he began to invite Negroes to his home and to the parties for which he became quite famous. "I don't think I've given any parties since 1923, until the present, without asking several Negroes," he said. Other white New York intellectuals copied Van Vechten's parties, at least for those years that the "Negro was in vogue." The idea was to compose parties of human ingredients that were electric and exciting, like setting off a string of firecrackers. Characteristically, Van Vechten prided himself on his singular taste in bringing just the right combination of people together. Late in his life, the charm still worked. When Isak Dinesen came to New York in 1958, she asked for, and got, a Van Vechten party. He remembered that the Danish noblewoman was particular: no " 'magazine or book editors, and not many authors —no ambassadors—and absolutely no merely social people. What I would prefer is to have you give me a Negro Party.' " He was, needless to say, happy to arrange it. He pleased himself, especially, with the fine touch of choosing as the countess' escort that irascible, Menckenesque journalist—become editor of the *Pittsburgh Courier*—George Schuyler.

It was at one of the annual benefits for the NAACP that Van Vechten met Langston Hughes and Countee Cullen. Neither

poet had published a book. Van Vechten was able to get
Knopf to take Hughes's *Weary Blues* (1925), which began a
long publishing association of Hughes with Knopf's firm. Countee Cullen, on the other hand, declined Van Vechten's help,
choosing his own way; in time, Harper published *Color* (1925).
Van Vechten's eagerness to help Negro writers and to broadcast Negro culture—as he understood it—knew no limit. He
used his association with Frank Crowninshield, editor of *Vanity
Fair*, to get Hughes's and other writers' works in that magazine. And he wrote many feature articles for that magazine
about Negroes: Paul Robeson, Ethel Waters, Bessie Smith, and
others. "I wrote about these people as I would write about
white people." And he spread the message wide. "Everything I
wrote about Negroes was published, and this did a lot towards
establishing them with other editors because at that time it
was very rare to have a story about a Negro even in the news-
papers. And the magazines! . . ."

He had almost been brought into a new life by the Negro and
Harlem. He was thrilled by it all and devoted much of his energy to being a midwife, a patron, an interpreter of Negro culture. It "soon became obvious to me that I would write about
these people, because my feelings about them were very
strong." The novel he wrote about them was *Nigger Heaven*.
Most of the Negro commentary on that novel must have made
them appear very insensitive, very ungrateful, to Van Vechten.

Nigger Heaven tried to make two points. In the first place, it
wanted the reader to know Harlem as a social microcosm of
New York City. The reader had to reject definitions of the
Negro as a type. There was a wide variety of characters, tastes,
and values. You could witness as many kinds of social
experiences—parties, intellectual salons, elegant dinners,
brawls, and bashes—in Harlem as you could in the rest of
New York. Harlem was no monolith, and the Negro fit no stereotype. Yet, at the same time, the reader was expected to ac-

cept the Negro as a natural primitive. Where he was true to himself, he was saved from civilized artificiality, and had preserved his mental health. Indeed, the novel seems to argue that the Negro "civilizes" himself at great cost. These rather contradictory assumptions are never reconciled. Present-day readers, however, should not underestimate the daring of the first point. Until the publication of *Nigger Heaven,* no generally read novel had chosen the Negro as its subject and abandoned the stereotype. It was not for many years after 1926 that the other popular medium, the movies, could dare to do the same. Whatever the novel's faults then, it was a historic event.

Nigger Heaven opens and closes with scenes of the "sporting" side of Harlem life, beginning with a street scene on Seventh Avenue and ending in a cabaret. Both focus on Anatole Longfellow, sometimes known as the Scarlet Creeper. He was sharp:

> He wore a tight-fitting suit of shepherd's plaid which thoroughly revealed his lithe, sinewy figure to all who gazed upon him, and all gazed. A great diamond, or some less valuable stone which aped a diamond, glistened in his fuchsia cravat. The uppers of his highly polished tan boots were dove-coloured suede and the buttons were pale blue. His black hair was sleek under his straw hat, set at a jaunty angle.

The reader is not informed how the Scarlet Creeper makes his way in life—pimp, male prostitute, narcotics pusher, numbers runner, bootlegger—but one or several of these occupations is implied. Whatever it is, he is good at it. His name, as well as his own words, tell us that he provides sexual interludes for women whose men are not watching. Almost as soon as he is introduced, he gets a prostitute to persuade him to let her pay for an evening's sport. "Oh, Ah been full o' prosperity dis evenin. Ah met an ofay wanted to change his luck. He gimme a tenner." The Creeper assents, but maintains indifference through it all. "Ah sho' will show you some lovin' daddy, she promised." The reader can only suppose that she did, because the Creeper does not appear again until the end of the book. But his very absence makes him hover over the central story.

The plot tells the story of Mary Love, a prim, proper, and pretty Harlem librarian who falls tragically in love with a would-be writer, Byron Kasson. Byron has just graduated from The University of Pennsylvania, and while he has only published short things in *Opportunity*, he was told at college that he has promise. "I know what they meant, he added, pretty good for a coloured man." Mary's prudishness, sexual self-consciousness, and self-restraint and Byron's petulance and self-doubt, in time destroy whatever promise their love had. For Mary, unlike most of the Negroes she sees around her, takes love and sex quite seriously, which is not to say passionately. She expects, consistent with conventional canons of the moral order, to give herself—beyond passion or lust—to a man whom she can honor and live for. Until Byron, no man in Harlem has made the grade, especially not Randolph Pettijohn, the Bolito (numbers) King, who is relentless in pursuit of Mary as a " 'spectable 'ooman" to wife. Pettijohn is definitely out of the question; it may be a class matter. He made it the wrong way: hot-dog stand to numbers to wealth. And he does not speak good English the way Mary and her friends do: "Ah ain' got no eddication lak you, but Ah got money, plenty of et, an' Ah got love." That is no way to capture a girl like Mary. Byron, on the other hand, has the deft touch of innocence:

> Somehow, Miss Love . . . it was his turn to be embarrassed . . . you, stand out in a crowd like this. I couldn't help liking you, even before I talked to you.
> I saw you first . . . diving.
> He smiled. That's the only thing I do well.
> You do *that* well. Is it your profession?
> I haven't any profession yet. I want to write, he went on.
> You're a writer! Mary exclaimed with enthusiasm.

As it turns out, Byron is not much of a writer. At least, he fails to get any commercial recognition. He fails despite Mary's love (surrender?), devotion, and encouragement. The reader never knows whether or not Byron has real talent. Neither does Byron, as a matter of fact. Sensitive to racial discrimination, he can never distinguish between his own limitations and social oppression. His despair (a present-day reader might say self-hate) compels him into an orgiastic interlude with Lasca Sartoris, a totally self-indulgent woman of pleasure. Lasca disposes of Byron in her own time. Mary's pride and Byron's compounded humiliation frustrate any possibility of turning events and redeeming their love. Byron, at last, goes to the Black Venus Club intending to kill Randolph Pettijohn, who has taken Lasca Sartoris from him. But, alas! the fine hand of the Scarlet Creeper robs Byron of even this desperate assertion of manhood; the Creeper kills Pettijohn first. Byron is reduced to the ultimate futility of emptying his pistol into the corpse. "Mary, he cried aloud, I didn't do it! I didn't do it!" as the white hand of the law takes him away.

Those reviewers who liked the book, and there were many, insisted that one of the novel's strengths was its restraint from propaganda, from making sociological points. Edward Lueders, Van Vechten's literary biographer, concurs in that judgment. In the sense that the novel does not probe very deeply into race relations (or racism) or engage the reader in any fundamental moral problem, this assessment is correct. But propaganda and sociological points the book makes, plenty of them. Carl Van Vechten goes to great lengths to show that besides the Scarlet Creepers and the Randolph Pettijohns, Harlem has some very cultured and intelligent people. Mary Love reads everything that is up-to-date and illuminates her bedroom with a single, framed reproduction of the "Mona Lisa." Stravinsky is a part of her life, as well as the blues and spirituals—it is all culture. Mary quotes, from memory, poems by Wallace Stevens and, if that were not enough, about a page of "Melanctha"

from Gertrude Stein's *Three Lives*. A dinner at the wealthy
Aaron Sumners' allows Van Vechten to employ his talent for
description of rich furnishings and appointments. It also permits the famous author, Gareth Johns, to be openly astonished
by the refinement of Negroes. They have read his books. They
know Paris. One of the guests, Leon Cazique of the Haitian
consulate, allows the conversation to drift into French, in
which language Mary talks about an authentic African sculpture exhibit that she has arranged and, at another point in the
novel, discusses Cocteau, Morand, and Proust with M. Cazique, who turns out to be something of an expert on modern
French literature. In short, culture abounds. On reading *Nigger Heaven*, it is impossible to escape the feeling of being for-
cibly drawn to acknowledge these facts of Negro life, which
have little, if anything, to do with the story. They are *obiter
dicta* and no less propaganda because they condescend to the
reader.

The reader is also instructed about the "Blue Vein Set" and
"passing." The problem of Negroes' being served in downtown
restaurants or seated in the theaters is explained, as well as the
advantages of light-skinned over dark-skinned Negroes in almost every walk of life, and other social differences among Negroes. Often, characters' conversations are mere lengthy disquisitions on these subjects. The points of view are authentic
enough, but they are designed to instruct the reader more than
to develop the novel. Lest the reader draw racist generalizations from Byron Kasson's failure, Van Vechten is careful to
contrast it with the success, after long struggle with frustration,
of Howard Allison, the fiancé of Mary's apartment mate. The
presentation of statistics on the number of Negroes who pass
every year is gratuitous. Often, speeches are no more than
whimsical fantasies about how the "problem" will disappear,
for instance through interbreeding. Van Vechten, throughout
the novel, amuses himself by commenting upon the joke on the

white world that "passing" is. All of this is propagandistic and sociological in petty ways. What is missing in the novel is a clear moral or intellectual perspective that might engage the reader in the dramatic issues of Negro life.

The essential limitations that frustrate Mary and Byron are personal rather than societal. Racial problems form a backdrop for, indeed, inform everything they think or do, but it is character that makes them fail to be their best selves. They suffer, in fact, two varieties of the same malady. They are alienated from their ethno-spiritual roots but are unable to be anything else. Mary is plagued with her inability to be passionate, essential, primitive. Although spirituals or Clara Smith's singing the blues can bring her to tears, she cannot abandon herself to men or to the Charleston until she meets Byron. She is said to be cold, and she has doubts about her priggishness and her persistent propriety. Her inhibitions keep her from what she really wants. When Lasca Sartoris charms Byron at a dance, Mary's inner rage and jealousy make her want to kill Lasca. But she is reduced to priggish impotence by Lasca's deft, feline verbal slashes. Mary is proper and polite; she has just witnessed two women fighting and screaming over a man and was revolted by the scene. Her impulse to act is throttled by her civility. Her inability to act on her feelings defeats her.

Byron, on the other hand, is a very spoiled young man who has no nerve for the struggle forced on Harlem Negroes. He was educated in a white college, and he has lost all contact and sensitivity with Negro people. He despises the rich Negroes because he thinks them snobs. He resents the young, successful professionals and writers because they make his failure evident. He abhors the poor blacks because they shame him. Except for small checks from his father, he refuses help from anyone, turning down a good job when he learns that Mary had arranged it. His writing will be worth something, he is told by a magazine editor—a thinly disguised H. L. Mencken

—if he observes what is around him, if he looks at Harlem life close up, and writes about it. Of course, Byron could not bear to look at Negroes, and he could not really see anything else. Rejected and defeated at every turn, he leaps into the arms of Lasca Sartoris. She uses him and rejects him after unmanning him.

Present-day readers would be likely to interpret Mary's and Byron's problem as race-hate and self-hate. Neither of them can accommodate to the blackness they see around them and the suggestion of the blackness within them. Rejecting the Negro that they see, they must also deny themselves, which makes them less than whole. But Carl Van Vechten, true to his nineteenth-century influences, treats the matter differently. Both Mary and Byron, in characteristic ways, drift away from the primitive, natural, and intuitive springs of the race. Mary can only be abandoned in her dance as a result of her rage over Byron's obvious receptivity to Lasca's charms. Byron's sexual passion turns to mere lust. And he lacks—as is made clear in a letter of advice from his father—that intuitive sense that has allowed the Negro to survive: the acceptance of the humble portion for the moment, the expectation of being helped and patronized, and the desire to be useful. In the end, neither Mary nor Byron can find the words, because of pride, to say what can reconcile them and avert tragedy. Pride is their fault. To Carl Van Vechten, their tragedy is that they have become civilized. Thus the epigraph of the novel is from Countee Cullen:

> All day long and all night through,
> One thing only must I do
> Quench my pride and cool my blood,
> Lest I perish in the flood.

The sad thing about *Nigger Heaven* is that Mary and Byron, although the core of the novel, are not the most interesting characters. Mary is a sad little thing; one might feel sorry for her ineptitude; her problem is not fully enough understood to feel more than that. As librarian, Mary's difficulties could as well be an occupational stereotype as anything, and Carl Van Vechten does not develop them enough for the reader to know. Byron, on the other hand, is too miserably weak; the reader is moved to disdain too quickly for any sense of tragedy to develop. Perhaps excepting Peter Whiffle, all of Van Vechten's strong characters have been women, and emasculating women at that. Here, again, in this novel, the truly strong character is Lasca Sartoris. She overwhelms everything. The Scarlet Creeper, also, whose role is limited in the novel, is deftly drawn. Briefly introduced in the Prologue, making only one appearance before the concluding pages, the Scarlet Creeper is like a cocked pistol throughout the story. The reader is not disappointed: the pistol goes off; the Scarlet Creeper shoots Randolph Pettijohn and then disappears as the novel ends.

Lasca Sartoris is a true Van Vechten female character. Like Campaspe Lorillard, she has all the right ingredients: self-centeredness, self-indulgence, moral inversion, indifference, and abhorrence of boredom. "She has found what she had wanted by wanting what she could get, and then always demanding more, more, until now the world poured its gifts into her bewitching lap." That is Byron's assessment. Her apartment, like herself, is richly and sumptuously decadent. Those chapters she shares with Byron are the most lively in the book. They go to the Winter Palace, get high on champagne and cocaine. They leave at six in the morning and go to a Black Mass:

> It's a garden where champagne flows from all the fountains and the paths are made of happy dust and the perfume of the poppies is opium. Kiss me!
>
> I'd like to be cruel to you! she cried after she had momentarily slaked her thirst. I'd like to cut your heart out!
>
> Cut it out, Lasca, my own! It belongs to you!

I'd like to bruise you!
Lasca, adorable!
I'd like to gash you with a knife!
Lasca! Lasca!
Beat you with a whip!
Lasca!
She drew her pointed nails across the back of his
hand. The flesh came off in ribbons.
My baby! My baby! she sobbed, binding his bleed-
ing hand with her handkerchief, kissing his lips.

The Black Mass—they descended to a ring of hell:

They stood in a circular hall entirely hung in vermilion velvet; even the ceiling was draped in this fiery colour. . . .
The floor was of translucent glass, and through this clouds of
light flowed, now orange, now deep purple, now flaming like
molten lava, now rolling sea-waves of green. An invisible
band . . . began to perform wild music, music that moaned
and lacerated one's breast with brazen claws of tone, shriek-
ing, tortured music from the depths of hell. And now the hall
became peopled . . . men and women with weary faces,
faces tired of passion and pleasure. Were these faces of dead
prostitutes and murderers? Pleasure seekers from the cold
slabs of the morgue?

Into the awful scene of evil and decay a girl suddenly stood,
bathed in purple and green light, mist and shadow. A pipe
sounded, as if far away, accompanied by a faint reverberation
of tom-tom. A bell in the distance tinkled, and the cloak fell to
the floor.

The girl—she could have been no more than sixteen—stood
entirely nude. She was pure black, with savage African features, thick lips, bushy hair which hovered about her face
like a lanate halo, while her eyes rolled back so far that only
the whites were visible. And she began to perform her evil
rites . . . Byron groaned and hid his face in his hands. He
could hear Lasca emitting little clucks of amazement. Standing before him, she protected him from the horror . . . while

> she watched. When he looked again, the light on the body
> was purple; the body was purple. The girl lifted a knife. . . .
> A woman shrieked. The knife . . .

Then follows a lacuna heavy with meaning. The story resumes
three days later as Byron awakens at four in the afternoon in
Lasca's bed. Avoiding objective description, Van Vechten employs
the period's style of heavily suggestive language to imply the sensuality, the depravity of their lust:

> There were rages, succeeded by tumultuous passions; there
> were peaceful interludes; there were hours devoted to satisfy-
> ing capricious desires, rhythmical amours to music, cruel and
> painful pastimes; there were the artificial paradises. Then,
> late one afternoon, Byron awakened to find himself alone.

After reading these passages, Mary Love and her "New Negro"
intellectuals pale for the reader as well as for Byron Kasson.
   The Scarlet Creeper, his masterful criminality (almost, but a
not fully developed "MacHeath"); Lasca, the description of her
environment, her "decor," the suggestions of her lust; the Black
Mass—it is in these particulars that the novel is most effective.
After all, it was there that Van Vechten's heart had always
been. No wonder, considering Van Vechten's life and style,
that no matter how hard he tried, Mary Love, Byron Kasson,
and all of the goody-good, respectable Negroes would seem
bloodless next to his imps of Satan. And the message is strong;
although perverted, the Creeper and Lasca are permanent, en-
durable, and perversely heroic because they have accepted
without qualification their primitive and predatory natures—
civilization, respectability, propriety, manners, and decorum
are for others, for "niggers." Try as he might to illustrate that
Negroes were much like other people, Van Vechten's belief in
their essential primitivism makes him prove something else. It
stands to reason, after all. Had he thought Negroes were like
white people, he would not have adopted Harlem the way he

did. His compulsion to be fair to the race while he exploited the exotic and decadent aspects of Harlem caused the novel to founder.

The title of this novel, coming from a known friend of the Negro, was startling—no doubt intentionally so. Most of the reviewers who objected to the book—white and black— objected in some way to the title. That was unfortunate because Van Vechten and his admirers defended the novel by defending the title, ignoring the serious defects of the novel itself. There had been a precedent. Edward Sheldon wrote a play—*The Niggers*—which appeared on Broadway in 1909, and took a sympathetic (to Negroes) view of the Reconstruction period in the South. A few years before he published his novel, Van Vechten succeeded in getting Ronald Firbank to change the title of his *Sorrow in Sunlight* to *Prancing Nigger* in the American edition. Van Vechten insisted that in his own novel the title was used ironically. It was a play on the geography of Manhattan Island, where Harlem sits like a segregated balcony over the white "orchestra" of downtown New York.

Within the novel, the term is used variously. The prostitute, who with the Scarlet Creeper begins the novel, apostrophes "Nigger Heaven!" as she sees the joy around her and contemplates the pleasure before her in the Creeper's arms. In the too-frequent "race" discussions, characters refer to Harlem as the "Mecca of the New Negro," and "Nigger Heaven" with a tone of sarcasm, but the irony is unclear. Byron Kasson, at a point of great despair, defeat, and self- (race-) hatred, begins a long apostrophe: "Nigger Heaven! Byron moaned. Nigger Heaven! That's what Harlem is." Byron plays out that figure of speech by imagining the whites in the "orchestra" below. "It doesn't seem to occur to them either, he went on fiercely, that we sit above them, that we can drop things down on them and crush them, that we can swoop down from this Nigger Heaven and take their seats. No, they have no fear of that! Harlem!

The Mecca of the New Negro! My God!" It is impossible to know from the novel what Van Vechten meant by all of this. Given Byron's character and the context of his speech, Edward Lueders is not justified in reading here an "authentic prophecy." [16]

Criticism of the book by blacks apparently stung Van Vechten, because much of his interview for the *Columbia Oral History* was taken up with a discussion of the novel; and most of that with the title. He meant the title ironically, he reiterated, and only "emancipated people" like George Schuyler, James Weldon Johnson, Mrs. Alice Dunbar, and Langston Hughes understood that. Other Negro journalists complained about the title and charged that the author had exploited his friends in Harlem to get material for this highly commercial and sensational book. The problem was irony, "and irony," he at last told his interviewer, "is not anything that most Negroes understand, especially the ones who write for the papers." And Langston Hughes joined him in that judgment. [17] Unfortunately, most of those who accepted Van Vechten's view were too close to him to make free judgments. Van Vechten had both Hughes and Johnson read the manuscript for authenticity, and he discussed with these men his intentions. The same, too, can be said for Edward Lueders, who had the privilege of interviews with the author as well as correspondence. Surely, Van Vechten could be convincing about his intentions. The problem is, however, that they are not clear in the novel, where it counts. It is not irony that the reader, then or now, comes away with. Sensation is a better word.

The title, the subject, and Van Vechten's handling of the material evoked the sensational. Nor should that be surprising. Carita Day, Arnold Schoenberg, Ronald Firbank, Herman Melville, Gertrude Stein, Campaspe Lorillard, Lasca Sartoris, Harlem itself, his Negroes, his parties—all had a sensational ingredient, and that is what had attracted Van Vechten to begin with. Nor should one ignore the sensual element in the sensational. And when the white man with the reputation for sensuality, and for knowing Harlem and Negroes best, wrote a book from the "inside," there should have been little doubt what was looked for and what was found. The book sold 100,-000 copies almost immediately. It was its pretense to be something else that made the book seem false. When all of the hysteria had filtered out, it was this central problem that caused intelligent critics to reject the book—men as disparate as D. H. Lawrence and W. E. B. DuBois.

D. H. Lawrence failed to see reality or honesty in the book, describing Harlem, he said, in "the daytime, at least, the place aches with dismalness and a loose-end sort of squalor, the stone of the streets seeming particularly dead and stony, obscenely stony." He saw here a "nigger book" which feebly copied the luridness of Cocteau or Morand. The respectable characters were indistinguishable from whites, and the love affair a "rather palish brown." "And the whole coloured thing is peculiarly colourless, a second-hand dish barely warmed up." And Lawrence saw nothing fresh in the luridness of "the usual old bones of hot stuff, warmed up with all the fervour the author can command—which isn't much." At bottom, however, the real problem was that for all its pretense there was no blackness in the novel's black people. Lawrence doubted that there was much in reality. "Reading Negro books, or books about Negroes written from the Negro standpoint, it is absolutely impossible to discover that the nigger is any blacker inside than we are. He's an absolute white man, save for the colour of his skin." He touched a crucial feature of white-black relations.

> It is rather disappointing [the sameness of Negroes and whites]. One likes to cherish illusions about the race soul, the eternal Negroid soul, black and glistening and touched wth awfulness and with mystery. One is not allowed. The nigger

"Home to Harlem." The 369th Infantry (New York's 15th)
in victory parade up Fifth Avenue, World War I.

Elegant Edgecomb Avenue, "Sugar Hill," overlooks Harlem.

Harlem street scene, ca. 1920. A black policeman gives directions.

"Gay Northeasters."

W. E. B. DuBois at work in the *Crisis* Office.

Marcus Garvey
on parade.

Langston Hughes,
a young poet.

Countee Cullen.

Carl Van Vechten, "Self-portrait."

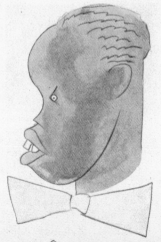

Carl Van Vechten,
"A Prediction,"
caricature by Miguel Covarrubias.

a prediction to Carl from COVARRUBIAS.

Claude McKay.
Photograph by Carl Van Vechten.

Aaron Douglas.
Photograph by Carl Van Vechten.

Nella Larsen.
Photograph by Carl Van Vechten.

Zora Neale Hurston.
Photograph by Carl Van Vechten.

is a white man through and through. He even sees himself as white men see him, blacker than he ought to be. And his soul is an Edison gramophone grinding over the old records.[18]

DuBois insisted that he had no objection to the use of "nigger" *per se*. "As employed by Conrad, Sheldon, Allen and even Firbank, its use was justifiable." But he was offended that Harlem should be so called. For in common parlance "it means . . . a nasty, sordid corner into which black folk are herded, and yet a place which they in crass ignorance are fools enough to enjoy. Harlem is no such place as that, and no one knows this better than Carl Van Vechten." But, beyond the title, DuBois disliked the book's pretension of verisimilitude. It was dishonest. The distinctive in Negro character was subtle and could not be defined in "wildly, barbaric drunken orgy in whose details Van Vechten revels." Nor, in DuBois's view, did the novel stand up as art. Conservative and echoing the standards of the Genteel Tradition, DuBois asked:

> Does it please? Does it entertain? Is it a good and human story? In my opinion it is not; and I am one who likes stories and I do not insist that they be written solely for my point of view. . . . Real human feelings are laughed at. Love is degraded. The love of Byron and Mary is stark cruelty and that of Lasca and Byron is simply nasty.

DuBois objected to every part: to the casual and superficial discussion of serious issues, to the flimsy treatment of character. "I cannot for the life of me see in this work either sincerity or art, deep thought, or truthful industry. It seems to me that Mr. Van Vechten tried to do something bizarre and he certainly succeeded." [19] Perhaps, if the book had been promoted as unquestionably bizarre, or had it engaged itself more deeply in the psychological, emotional, or moral reality of Harlem, neither DuBois nor Lawrence would have been so offended by it.

Van Vechten reported to his interviewer for the *Columbia Oral History* that a hostess once put DuBois and him in a room, because " 'I thought you two ought to know each other better.' " Nothing much came of it. But Van Vechten remembered the occasion with more perception than he might have realized. In recalling DuBois, he concluded, "I guess he thought maybe white people shouldn't say anything at all about Negroes."

Whatever DuBois's wish, the 1920s witnessed a wave of white literary efforts to take up the Negro as artistic subject. By 1926, the field was well worked. Eugene O'Neill had already startled New York with *Emperor Jones* (1920) and *All God's Chillun Got Wings* (1924). E. E. Cummings had already developed the child-primitive black, Jean Le Nègre in *The Enormous Room* (1922), to be followed a year later by Waldo Frank's in *Holiday*. In 1925 Sherwood Anderson published *Dark Laughter* and DuBose Heyward *Porgy*. And just two years later, Heyward completed *Mamba's Daughters*. Van Vechten's novel was no isolated phenomenon in white American writing. Van Vechten's Mencken-like editor apparently was echoing professional opinion when he told Byron Kasson that he was interested in Harlem and Negro subjects. Harlem, he advised, "is overrun with fresh, unused material. Nobody has yet written a good gambling story; nobody has touched the outskirts of cabaret life; nobody has gone into the curious subject of the divers tribes of the region. Why, there are West Indians and Abyssinian Jews, religious Negroes, pagan Negroes, and Negro intellectuals, all living together. . . ." White America had become interested in the Negro. There was a market, success, and acclaim for the author—white or black—who could treat the subject properly. If Carl Van Vechten had any genuine news to tell in his novel, that was it. The author lectured the reader about it, and, if that was not enough, the remarkable commercial success of the book made the message all too clear.

For some, the Negro had always represented the true American tragedy. In a time of moral disorder and despair the pathos of Negro life, as illuminated by DuBose Heyward, could be beautiful. To one unsettled by the growing societal destruction of the individual, the primitive purity of Jean Le Nègre could seem a "Delectable Mountain" in that pilgrim's progress to his own true self. To a generation frightened by the Babbitt which the logic of their lives and values guaranteed, *Nigger Heaven* was a haven from the philistine. Tantalized and horrified by the machine, the Negro was essential to white Americans because of his humanity.

So when Russett Durwood tells Byron Kasson to write about what he knows—Harlem, the Negro—there is no sentiment, it is purely commercial. The strange thing is that Byron does not know much about Negroes and does not want to know much about Harlem. Durwood even admits that Byron's best writing is about whites: "You must have spent a lot of time with white people to understand them so well." He does not tell the young man to forget about Negroes and write about whites, whom he understands. Harlem and Negroes are the only subject for him. But whites are different. "Well, if you young Negro Intellectuals don't get busy, a new crop of Nordics is going to spring up who will take the trouble to become better informed and will exploit this material before the Negro gets around to it." Indeed, the editor suggests Cocteau and Huysmans as models, and he points out that a white author whom Byron had met in a cabaret had just submitted a story, "a capital yarn about a Negro pimp. I don't suppose he even saw the fellow. Probably just made him up, imagined him, but his imagination was based on a background of observation. The milieu is correct. The story is credible. It jumps ahead; it lives. I'm featuring it in the June number." Van Vechten's message is more insidious than it first appears: the Negro was to write about what he knew best, himself; but the trick was to do it so that white men would recognize it as authentic.

By 1926, then, white Americans were prepared to patronize the Negro, not only his prostitutes and cabarets but his art and literature as well. It was intoxicating. After a history of struggle, of being an outcast, of being viewed with contempt or pity, the Negro was now courted and cultivated by cultured whites. How grand it was to be valued not for what one might become—the benevolent view of uplift—but for what was thought to be one's essential self, one's Negro-ness. Whites and Negroes shared James Weldon Johnson's expectation that the America of the machine and philistine could be transcended by men of talent, sensitivity, and art. Racial accommodation would begin, indeed it had already begun, among artists and creative people. The possibility was there, the Negro need only exploit it. It was so easy, all the Negro artist had to do was to be true to himself, and he would be honored and sustained, ironically, by the very commercial apparatus that the *avant garde* traditionally distrusted. Few Negroes permitted themselves the thought that patrons—commercial or not—often exact a price in integrity.

Two novels by Negro writers appeared in 1928 having those qualities which would appeal to the audience that *Nigger Heaven* discovered. Rudolph Fisher's *Walls of Jericho* and Claude McKay's *Home to Harlem* were something more than merely cynical efforts to exploit white fancy, yet they developed themes suggested by Van Vechten. Both authors had published before. Fisher had done several short pieces for *Atlantic Monthly*, and Claude McKay was on the editorial staff of the old *Liberator* and had achieved notice as a poet and essayist. True to Van Vechten's predictions about the genre, both of these novels met with commercial success; *Home to Harlem* was the first fictional work by an Afro-American to reach the best-seller lists.

Joshua "Shine" Jones, Rudolph Fisher's proletarian hero, has several walls to bring down. There is the barrier of race, of course, which remarkably is the least of his concerns. His resentment is directed primarily against class distinctions and the pretensions of high-toned Negroes. Thus, Fisher wrote the only novel in the decade that exposed class antagonism among Harlem blacks. "Dickties is evil—don' never trust no dickty" is Shine's pronouncement. But his main energies go toward overcoming the resistance of Linda Young, a sweet and innocent housemaid who knows enough to distrust the intentions of Harlem men. Shine's problem was to become respectable enough to deserve and convince Linda, yet not lose his essential honesty. Linda, who worked first for a white do-gooder, Agatha Cramp, and then for a near-white attorney, Fred Merrit, wants to improve the quality of her life. So she prods Shine to move beyond his almost irresponsible life as a piano mover. His deep distrust of respectable Negroes, however, makes him resist until he is drawn into an alliance with Fred Merrit against Henry Patmore, a Harlem underworld character. This breaching of the class barrier permits Shine to accept Merrit's financing of his piano-moving company, solving his problem with Linda.

Fisher's novel is a kind of happy union of "field hand" with "house servant." Shine is saved from irresponsibility and Linda is rescued from the sterility of middle-class artifice. Shine's character permits the author to examine the underworld of cabarets, gambling, and prostitution—which Shine is familiar with but not a part of. Linda, on the other hand, allows the exposé of both white and black society—where they interact— from the perspective of the pantry. Neither character, therefore, is tainted by the sordidness or the phoniness of the extremes of Harlem life. With characters who are essentially

innocents—a device as old as Henry Fielding's novels surely
—the reader enjoys the titillation of corruption without the undermining of the romantic resolution. Thus, the ambiguity that
plagued Van Vechten's novel is avoided; the lovers in *Walls of
Jericho* never fade from focus.

Fisher's novel also differs from *Nigger Heaven,* as well as all
the period's other novels about Harlem, in that it deals with
race hatred as something other than a topic of casual conversation. Fred Merrit's feeling about whites is almost pathological.
He talks about it as naked hatred. Although he can "pass" for
white, Merrit conspicuously asserts his blackness in the white
neighborhood he moves into. He cares less about living in the
house than he does about indulging his "chief joy in life . . .
making them uncomfortable." Perhaps Van Vechten's whiteness shielded him from this variety of black passion, for neither
his novel nor any other comment by him hints at it. But Fisher
even goes so far as to explain Merrit's anger in terms of white
sexual exploitation of black women—specifically his mother,
resulting in his own bastardy. Through Fisher, the reader can
see a hint—slight though true—of the worm in the apple, of
the snake in the white man's black paradise.

Rudolph Fisher had genuine talent as a light satirist; black-
white relations, Negro society, and Harlem were targets to his
wit. He managed in Miss Agatha Cramp a deft caricature of a
do-gooder white matron, reminiscent of Dickens' Mrs. Jellyby.
Miss Cramp was a benefactor for almost any cause, but never
with true sympathy. She came to be interested in Negroes because of what began as a casual conversation between herself
and Linda. One might say, that before this talk with her maid,
Miss Cramp was unaware of Negroes. But once she became
aware, she would support the General Improvement Association (the National Association for the Advancement of Colored
People?) with the same eager enthusiasm as she had supported
Russians and Poles. And with the same disinterest; for she,

mistaking Fred Merrit as white, confesses her belief in the Negro's inferiority, all to Merrit's amusement. Black pretense is as
much ridiculed as white. Linda innocently describes the General Improvement Association to Miss Cramp: "Well, they collect a dollar a year from everybody that joins, and whenever
there's a lynching down South they take the dollar and send
somebody to go look at it."

So while Fisher's novel pretends to introduce the reader to
Harlem as it was, it shies away from the sensationalism of *Nigger Heaven.* In some ways Fisher achieved greater distance
from his subject than did Van Vechten, who could not (dared
not?) use satire as a device for critical judgment of Harlem
blacks. An outsider, Van Vechten seems to have been "taken
in" by blacks on all levels of society; Fisher was too much an
insider for that. Nor did Fisher's novel exploit exotic taste
through decadence. There is no inversion of values. Whatever
went on in Harlem joints, evil and good, is clearly defined, and
there is no doubt that the author stands for good. The reader
cannot doubt that Linda is right to remain aloof from Shine's
wooing until she is certain of his intentions. And such conventional behavior does not give rise to doubts about her sexuality
and passionateness as with Mary Love. Linda is sure of herself,
she merely wants to be sure of Shine before she jumps into his
bed. There is nothing very primitive about that. The love story
—apart from the Harlem setting and the race issue—was like
many others of the time. So, while *The Walls of Jericho* exploited the commercial interest in Harlem exotica, it reserved
a kind of gentility and propriety that was absent from *Nigger
Heaven.*

The more popular *Home to Harlem* made no such reserva-
tion. Claude McKay was not very much troubled by
conventional moral issues, and unlike Dr. Fisher he did not let
class and professional distinctions intrude into his story. Jake,
Home to Harlem's hero, has values that are based on a free,

open confrontation with life. He is driven by love and enjoyment. Living is drink, food, dance, and sex. Evil for Jake is
what threatens his pleasures or his loyalty to friends. Men like
him, because he is a man's man, and he is irresistible to
women because of his uncluttered sexual instincts.

Jake deserts from the army when he discovers it has no intention of letting him fight Germans. In time, hungry for Harlem and black women, Jake works his way back home on a
freighter. Without hesitation, he gives his last fifty dollars to
the first Negro woman who catches his eye in a Harlem cabaret. The morning after, walking down the street, " 'I ain't got a
cent to my name,' mused Jake, 'but ahm as happy as a prince,
all the same. Yes I is.' " But as he puts his hand in his pocket,
he discovers that Felice has returned his money with a note:
" 'Just a little gift from a baby girl to a honey boy!' " Being
loved by women is Jake's fate. Yet, he cannot find Felice when
he looks for her, and the novel becomes a series of episodes
(almost picaresque), held together by his vague longing and
search for her. Like *Nigger Heaven,* McKay's Harlem novel
uses the device of a frame—the Scarlet Creeper and Felice
open and close the novels with no other appearance—so that
the rest of the novel can be almost random episodes, descriptions of Harlem life, and discussions from Harlemites' points of
view. Thus, in *Home to Harlem,* the reader is carried into
house parties, cabarets, and dives. Jake takes a job with the
railroad, so one sees the dining-car life, the dormitories of the
black railroad crews, as well as the brothels that serve these
men. Authentic views of Negro life abound, even to the description of a fight in a Harlem backyard between two nude
West Indian women over a man; the Jamaican won because of
her adeptness in butting with her forehead.

Ray, a West Indian intellectual and would-be writer, becomes a close friend of Jake's and serves as a foil to his primitive simplicity. Ray is fascinated by Jake's power and inno-

cence. He is envious, for his own education cripples him. " 'The fact is Jake . . . I don't know what I'll do with my little education. I wonder sometimes if I could get rid of it and go and lose myself in some savage culture in the jungles of Africa. I am a misfit. . . .' " It is Jake who sustains Ray and defends him against antagonists among the dining-car crew. In fact, Jake patronizes him. He continues working as a dining-car cook long after wanting to quit because Ray needs him around. "The other cooks and waiters called Ray 'Professor.' Jake had never called him that. Nor did he call him 'buddy,' as he did Zeddy and his longshoremen friends. He called him 'chappie' in a genial, semi-paternal way." Jake is lucky with women because he is irresistible. Wherever he goes prostitutes, dancing girls, fun-girls want to give him their bodies: commercial women do not accept money from him. Ray, on the other hand, has been made impotent by thought. He is unable to enjoy himself in the brothels with Jake because he wants to remain true to a nice girl in Harlem. But he cannot find satisfaction with Agatha either, for that would mean marriage: "he would become one of the contented hogs in the pigpen of Harlem, getting ready to litter little black piggies." Neither able to fornicate freely and play with the whores nor domesticate himself, Ray, confused and still searching, finally ships out as a messman.

Jake is highly respectful of Ray's education and even claims that he would like a little: " 'Ef I was edjucated, I could understand things better and be proper-speaking like you is. . . . And I mighta helped mah li'l sister to get edjucated . . . and she would be nice-speaking like you' sweet brown, good enough foh you to hitch up with. Then we could all settle down and make money like edjucated people do, instead of a you gwine off to throw you'self away on some lousy dinghy and me chasing around all the time lik a hungry dawg.' " Ray also recognizes that his education makes him more alive than

Jake in certain ways—he can be sensitive to a wider range of things. His education has allowed him to experience vicariously and has opened him to varied and complex sensations. "Life burned in Ray perhaps more intensely than in Jake. Ray felt more and his range was wider and he could not be satisfied with the easy, simple things that sufficed for Jake. Sometimes he felt like a tree with roots in the soil and sap flowing out and whispering leaves drinking in the air. But he drank in more of life than he could distill into active animal living. Maybe that was why he felt he had to write." Mind and training make Jake's primitivism impossible for Ray.

McKay's novel is far more evocative than Van Vechten's. The fact that *Home to Harlem* was written from the "inside" is apparent from its confusion. Van Vechten's novel described life that the author had observed as a chosen part of his experience. McKay, on the other hand, wrote about his own context and his own frustration; he could not detach himself through an act of mind or will. He tried to be light and amoral with Jake, yet he was burdened by the heavy seriousness of Ray, whose mind would not let him escape the large issues of race and civilization. He wanted to emphasize that the simple primitive values were life-sustaining and humane, yet he was compelled to describe the violent, self-destructive, and life-destroying acts that gambling, prostitution, and narcotics occasion. He could choose to be ecstatic about the sensualness of Harlem—"'Harlem! . . . Where else could I have all this life but Harlem? Good old Harlem! Chocolate Harlem! Sweet Harlem! Harlem, I've got you' number down.'"—but "How terribly Ray could hate it sometimes. Its brutality, gang rowdyism, promiscuous thickness. Its hot desires." These ambiguities are not merely described, they are deep within McKay—his own ambivalence.

Jake is not the "noble savage" traditional in American literature. Most notably, he is completely and enthusiastically urban; there is not the slightest whimsy about his living by rural or country values. While his morality is simple and direct, his values are strictly personal and have no universal application. Jake does not despise and cannot hate; he is ashamed and sick on the two occasions when he is moved to violence. Like Natty Bumpo in James Fenimore Cooper's novels, Jake's life is a criticism of conventional morality and order. But unlike Cooper's "noble savage," Jake is unconscious of the disparity; he is indifferent to the larger society. Nor is he bigger than life, as is characteristic of the folk hero: McKay would have liked to have drawn Jake equal to life. Jake is a child-man, having the simplicity and innocence of Mark Twain's Nigger Jim, and the childlike openness and spontaneity of E. E. Cummings' Jean Le Nègre.

Jake's personal code permits him a rather wide moral swath. Cocaine, alcohol, and sex are all part of living. He does not care about the other men who have been in his women's lives. He refuses the many offers to be a "sweet man" or a pimp, but he sympathizes with a pimp and defends him as one who "also loved." His venereal disease discomfits him, but only because of the pain and the proscription of food, drink, and sex that it demands. He just does not want to hurt anybody, that is his singular moral judgment.

In many ways *Home to Harlem* amplifies themes that are in *Nigger Heaven,* treating them more authentically and forcefully. The lurid and sensational character of the book doubtless contributed to its commercial success. The reader could find here the apotheosis of the savage. Yet, beneath the surface lurked notions that were more ominous and critical. Ray, as McKay's voice, attacks with genuine bitterness the United States, white men's civilization, and European domination of dark people. The focus of the novel is elsewhere—on Jake's search for Felice—but there is a foreshadowing of a radical, racial primitivism (that rejects white men) which would domi-

nate McKay's next novel, *Banjo* (1929). But that novel will be
discussed in a later chapter. Notably, too, *Home to Harlem* totally lacks any accepted basis of order. Van Vechten, whatever
his fascination with the exotic, had no doubt that commercial
success was worthwhile—to "make it" was the idea. Byron
Kasson and nearly all the other characters are prepared to accept the notion that a published story in a major magazine is a
signal of one's worth. Overtly as well as covertly, McKay,
through Ray, attacks progress, achievement, and success as
measured by the alien white world—the human-consuming
machine of the European-American culture. Van Vechten, like
Cooper, is moved to find a respectable, proper, and moral lady
to be the official heroine of his novel—it is a fault in *Nigger
Heaven*. Agatha, Ray's nice girl friend, however, promises him
only the life of the "hog." She is not intended to be a paragon.
Actually, none of McKay's women are fully drawn. They are
mere instruments for male behavior. Thus, he skirts the problem of an amoral heroine. Without a stable sense of moral
order, *Home to Harlem* has none of the appeal to decadence
that is apparent in *Nigger Heaven*.[20] Van Vechten had to assume a morality in order to invert it. McKay's novel accepts no
moral order; thus it does not experiment with it. Ironically, despite its disparagement of white values and commerce, the
novel became a best seller precisely because it pandered to
commerical tastes by conforming to the sensationalism demanded by the white vogue in black primitivism.

McKay's life was marked by a deep skepticism, and he at
one time or another assumed many of the attitudes of the late
Victorians: sometimes an aesthete, as in his insistence on personal values and an intense life; sometimes a decadent, as was
his close friend Frank Harris; sometimes a stoic activist, as in
many of his sonnets. But, altogether, it made a difference that
he was black and hardly a real part of that tradition that the

late Victorians found in disarray. McKay seemed to believe that the man nearest to nature and his instincts did not have to worry about purpose or games. But the paradox was, as Ray made clear, when one knew enough to understand that, it was already too late.

The vogue in black primitivism had encouraged the commercial press to patronize black writers, and Rudolph Fisher's and Claude McKay's novels were products of that arrangement. Necessarily, the significant barometer was the white reading-public's taste. Where, as we will see, McKay's interest in primitivism and its relationship to Afro-American culture went beyond the strange and sensational, the market became much less sure. If he had a genuine interest, a preoccupation with the market would prevent his exploring it too far. He could not deal with the subject more seriously or much longer than the amused tolerance of his white audience would permit. That, of course, is the predicament of all patronized intellectuals—white and black. When one ceases to amuse, one is out of luck. Sadly, all of Harlem—especially the entertainer, the artist, and the writer—was in some way, at one time or another, obliged to the white patron. The racial character of the relationship made it more damaging to the art and more galling to the artists.

Throughout his life, McKay was strangely tied to some white patron. A white Jamaican discovered his talent and encouraged him in his first dialect verse. In his early years in the United States he was supported by Frank Harris of *Pearson's Magazine*. Then he joined the *Liberator* under Max Eastman, who helped him publish his most widely known poems, *Harlem Shadows* (1922). At the end of his life, McKay found himself in the Catholic Church. None of these associations was casual. A poem which he dedicated to Max Eastman was "A Prayer" which asked for guidance:

>The wild and fiery passion of my youth consumes my soul;
>In agony I turn to thee for truth and self-control.

And Eastman, for his part, although he would not see it so, disclosed the patronizing character of their relationship: "His [McKay's] laughter at the frailties of his friends and enemies, no matter which—that high, half-wailing falsetto laugh of the recklessly delighted Darky—was the center of my joy in him throughout our friendship of more than thirty years." [21] And years later, in interview, Eastman recalled that he "loved Claude," but he had never invited the poet to his summer home on Martha's Vineyard. His memory failed to capture a reason or motive, but the very blackness of McKay and the fact that "we always swam in the nude here" came together in the old man's mind.[22] Then, in the last days of his life, McKay surrendered totally to the authority of the Catholic Church from which citadel he rejected everyone—Negroes, communists, liberals, and radicals. At no point was he free from some dependency.

It was a difficult thing for the Negro artist to maintain his racial and artistic integrity under the aegis of the white patron. Yet, the Negro artist was necessarily dependent. He had no force or leverage within the publishing or critical establishments. Opinion was against black artists. In the 1920s, except for some earlier individual writers, Negroes were new—self-consciously new—to the commercialized arts. They needed supporters and advocates, defense and encouragement from those who were supposed to know. The fact that whites became interested in the Negro would seem fortunate from this point of view. Yet, the question had to be asked in time: whose sensibilities, tastes, and interests were being served by such art, the patron or the patronized? Of course, this is no problem peculiar to blacks. Any artist must ask how much the market, the critics, the profit-oriented apparatus distorts his statement.

But it is different when it is racial. There is, at first, the suspicion that the patron values Negro-ness, not talent. Nor was the Negro artist assumed to be the final judge of truth and the relevant statement. The patron—as best illustrated by Van Vechten—was a teacher, guide, and judge; his search for authentic Negro voices was dictated by his own needs. Without the help and friendship of white men and publishers, there probably would have been little production of commercial black art in the 1920s. But white guidance and encouragement probably prevented those few men and women of real talent from wrestling with their senses and plodding through to those statements which the thrust of their lives and experience would force them to make. Whatever other burdens Negro artists carried, this arrangement stigmatized Negro poetry and prose of the 1920s as being an artistic effort that was trying to be like something other than itself.

For a time, Zora Neale Hurston, Louise Thompson, and Langston Hughes were supported by the same elderly Park Avenue matron and shared a cottage in Westfield, New Jersey. She was a very generous old woman, who kept herself spiritually alive by supporting the arts and artists—entertaining them in her apartment high above the streets of New York. Hughes was still at Lincoln University when he was first her guest. As he left that first evening, she pressed something into his hand: " 'A gift for a young poet,' she said. It was a fifty-dollar bill." When she discovered that Langston Hughes wanted to write a novel, she supported him by covering all of his expenses so that he would not have to work during the summer. That summer he finished a draft of *Not Without Laughter*. After his senior year, having revised his novel with his patron's help and advice, Hughes was given a monthly allowance that permitted him a rare year of economic freedom. The same woman gave Zora Neale Hurston two hundred dollars a month for two years, and for a short time similarly supported Louise

Thompson. All three recalled her the same way—beautiful, generous, with strong primitive tastes—but their personal reactions to her were sharply different.

Louise Thompson was very restive and did not continue the relationship long. She did not like the dependency, but more particularly, she felt that the good woman was indulging her fantasies of Negroes. Her black guests were primitives, savages, or they were not being themselves. The slightest thing could be distorted for the patroness' self-gratification. "I might comment on the beauty of a flower arrangement in her apartment, and she would be greatly pleased. 'I knew you would like them, you *would* like red.' " Whoever Louise Thompson was— she, herself, was not sure—she was not the pagan savage that it pleased the good woman to imagine. She had to get out, not for artistic integrity—she never was much of an artist—but for her womanness. She was especially sensitive to the crippling dependency of paternalism; her keen nose made even less obvious and direct support noisome. She found it difficult, for instance, to work on the staff of *Opportunity* because she detected the white hand of philanthropy working through the Urban League in that magazine.

Zora Neale Hurston seemed to thrive on this kind of dependency. Her character—or perhaps her style—made her into the exuberant pagan that pleased her white friends. Her Negro contemporaries saw her as "playing a game," using white folks to get what she wanted. Langston Hughes said as much in *The Big Sea*. Louise Thompson remembered her talking on the phone: "Here's your little darky" and telling "darky" stories, only to wink when she was through so as to show that she had tricked them again.

That, too, was Wallace Thurman's impression. In *Infants of the Spring*, Zora Hurston is presented as Sweetie May Carr, a short-story writer noted more "for her ribald wit and personal effervescence than for any actual literary work. She was a great favorite among those whites who went in for Negro prodigies." She lived up to their expectations. "It seldom occurred to any of her patrons that she did this with tongue in cheek." As Thurman portrayed her, Zora (Sweetie May), given a white audience, "would launch forth into a saga of the little all-colored Mississippi [Florida] town where she claimed to have been born. Her repertoire of tales was earthy, vulgar, and funny. Her darkies always smiled through their tears, sang spirituals on the slightest provocation, and performed buck dances when they should have been working." She was a master of dialect (Zora Hurston collected Southern Negro folk materials for her graduate work at Columbia University), and a great storyteller. Her great weakness was carelessness or indifference to her art. "But Sweetie May knew her white folks."

" 'It's like this. . . . I have to eat. I also wish to finish my education. Being a Negro writer these days is a racket and I'm going to make the most of it while it lasts. Sure I cut the fool. But I enjoy it, too. My ultimate ambition . . . is to become a gynecologist [Anthropologist]. And the only way I can live easily until I have the requisite training is to pose as a writer of potential ability. *Voila!* I get my tuition paid at Columbia. I rent an apartment and have all the furniture contributed by kind hearted o'fays. I received bundles of groceries from various sources several times a week . . . all accomplished by dropping a discreet hint during an evening's festivities. I find queer places for whites to go in Harlem . . . out of the way primitive churches, sidestreet speakeasies. They fall for it. About twice a year I manage to sell a story. It is acclaimed. I am a genius in the making. Thank God for this Negro literary renaissance. Long may it flourish!' " [23]

Langston Hughes liked Zora Hurston, and his report of her in *The Big Sea* reflects his affection and amusement. Of course Hughes was never unkind or critical about anyone, except his father, perhaps. But he too remembered her success in getting

things from white people, "some of whom simply paid her just
to sit around and represent the Negro race for them, she did it
in such a racy fashion." "To many of her white friends, no
doubt, she was a perfect 'darkie,' in the nice meaning they give
the term—that is a naïve, childlike, sweet, humorous, and
highly colored Negro." When she graduated from Barnard, she
took an apartment on West 66th Street, near the park. "She
moved in with no furniture at all and no money, but in a few
days friends had given her everything, from decorative silver
birds, perched atop the linen cabinet, down to a footstool. And
on Saturday night, to christen the place, she had a *hand*-
chicken dinner, since she had forgotten to say she needed
forks." [24] Making it was simply cleverness and personality.

Zora Neale Hurston's recollections in her autobiography,
however, make it hard to imagine her relations with her white
patrons as an act, a "put-on." The patronness she shared with
Langston Hughes and Louise Thompson, she called "Godmother." They shared a mystical primitive bond: "She was just
as pagan as I." Under the guise of an extrasensory, spiritual
union, Miss Hurston would take chiding and criticism: "You
have broken the law. . . . You are dissipating your powers in
things that have no real meaning. . . . Keep silent. Does a
child in the womb speak?" Zora Hurston, Langston Hughes,
and others would read their work to their patron. She knew
what was good and right; she had a primitive instinct you
might say. "Godmother could be as tender as mother-love
when she felt that you had been right spiritually." But what
her instincts told her were false, were false: " 'That is nothing!
It has no soul in it. You have broken the law!' " "Godmother"
was a ruthless critic of what she thought to be pretense and artificial. Zora Hurston did not question those instincts, nor did
she really wonder about art and artifice.

"Godmother" wanted what was authentic, real folk, in her
Park Avenue apartment. The contrast might have given Miss

Hurston cause to wonder. "There she was sitting up there at the table over capon, caviar and gleaming silver, eager to hear every word on every phase of life on a saw-mill 'job.' I must tell the tales, sing the songs, do the dances, and repeat the raucous sayings and doings of the Negro farthest down. She is altogether in sympathy with them, because she says truthfully they are utterly sincere in living." [25] But she never did wonder, it appears, about what her "Godmother" was asking of her, or even what her earlier patron, Fannie Hurst, charged for her indulgences.

It is impossible to tell from reading Miss Hurston's autobiography who was being fooled. Her Negro associates were led to believe that she was putting on an act. If that is so, by the time she wrote the story of her life, she had become the act. She had learned, when in graduate school, from "Papa Franz" Boas not to use an educated diction in searching out folk materials. She had to become one of the folk to be a successful researcher, and the characterization served her well in the Park Avenue parlors. In the end, the folksiness, the idiom was so much her style that she had become the character Wallace Thurman thought she was acting.

There was something in the arrangement Langston Hughes could not stand. He returned his patron's generosity with his own in *The Big Sea*. His description of the episode is filled with compassion and the pain of unrequited love. "Her powers filled the rooms." She had been a friend of presidents, bankers, distinguished scientists, and famous artists. Famous people from all over the world came to see her. Hughes was honored: "I do not know why or how she still found time for me."

She had been "devoted in a mild way to the advancement of the Negro and had given money to Negro schools in the South." In this era of the "New Negro," she had found a cause that fitted her artistic impulses. "She was intensely excited about each new book, each new play, and each new artist that came out of the Negro world." But Hughes saw that Negroes occupied only a small corner of that good woman's interests. She had her hand in many things, but did not allow her name to be associated with her beneficences. It was in honor of that wish, as well as because of the hurt he bore, that Hughes never mentioned her name.

Langston Hughes was greatly pleased, and touched by this woman's interest. "I was fascinated by her, and I loved her. No one else had ever been so thoughtful of me, or so interested in the things I wanted to do, or so kind and generous toward me." Beyond that, her support gave him real security for the first time, "an assured income from someone who loved and believed in me." He had a suburban apartment, the leisure to work. He had "boxes of fine bond paper for writing, a filing case, a typist to copy my work, and wonderful new suits of dinner clothes from Fifth Avenue shops, and a chance to go to all the theaters and operas and lectures." Price did not matter, nothing mattered; "all I needed to say was when and where I wished to go and my patron's secretary would have tickets for me." But it could not work.

It was not all pleasant. Hughes felt pushed to produce, even when he did not feel like writing. "I didn't realize that she was old and wanted quickly to see my books come into being before she had to go away." The contrast of elegance and poverty that the association heightened troubled him also. She insisted that he be driven everywhere, even to his Harlem rooming house, in her limousine chauffered by a "rather grim and middle-aged white man." "I knew he *hated* to drive me, and I knew he had to do it if he wanted to keep his job. And I dislike being the cause of anyone's having to do anything he doesn't want to do just to keep a job—since I know how unpleasant that is."

The depression, the human misery in Harlem and New York, brought the social disparity sharply home to Hughes. It was

difficult to write about the mystery and mysticism and spontaneous harmony of Negroes' souls when what they really shared
was cold, and hunger, and despair. Hughes wrote a poem, re-
sponding to that real awareness. "Advertisement For the Wal-
dorf-Astoria" invited all the white and black poor to come and
take over the newly opened "palace." It was really a parody on
an advertisement in *Vanity Fair.*

> Take a room at the new Waldorf, you down-and-outers—
> sleepers in charity flophouses.
> They serve swell board at the Waldorf-Astoria. Look at this
> menu, will you:
>
> > GUMBO CREOLE
> >
> > CRABMEAT IN CASSOLETTE
> >
> > BROILED BRISKET OF BEEF
> >
> > SMALL ONIONS IN CREAM
> >
> > WATERCRESS SALAD
> >
> > PEACH MELBA

The poem had a very clear and radical message: "Dine with
some of the men and women who got rich off of your labor,
who clip coupons with clean white fingers because your hands
dug coal, drilled stone, sewed garments, poured steel to let
other people draw dividends and live easy."

When Hughes showed his patron this poem, he knew she
did not like it. " 'It's not you. . . . It's a powerful poem! But it's
not you.' " Who was he? Wasn't that the problem? Who was to
decide? Who was to know?

She had wanted him to be a primitive, but he knew that he
was not primitive. What she felt in him to be true, he knew to
be false. "I knew that my friend and benefactor was not
happy," Hughes wrote, "for months now, I had written nothing
beautiful." He felt that she was anxious to fulfill herself, her
life, in the works of her black protegés. He was not helping.

"So I asked kindly to be released from any further obligations to her, and that she give me no more money, but simply let me retain her friendship and good will that had been so dear to me."

But the relationship that permits a patron cannot produce a friend. There had been only one thread binding them together. "When that thread broke, it was the end." It was a deeply wrenching awareness for Hughes. He became physically ill as a result of their last meeting, and to the end of his life he could not bring himself to talk about it without strong emotion. "That beautiful room, that had been so full of light and help and understanding for me, suddenly became like a trap closing in, faster and faster, the room darker and darker, until the light went out with a sudden crash." She did not let him go without her words about his character, his talents, his limitations. She told him what she thought. She had every right to. "I fought against bewilderment and anger, fought hard, and didn't say anything. I just sat there in the high Park Avenue drawing-room and didn't say anything. I sat there and listened to all she told me,-closed my mouth hard and didn't say anything." [26]

If black New York had been left alone, it all would have been different—how, who knows? But that was impossible because Negro life and culture and art were important to white men. They had their lives and identities to work out too. The relationship between black and white had to be. "So, in the end it all came back very near to the old impasse of white and Negro again," Hughes claimed, "white and Negro—as do most relationships in America." But because of where they were, white and Negro, the Negro was naturally patronized in his art to serve a white dream and fancy. As Hughes learned, the fee that the patron claimed could be humiliation.

4 🖤 Art: The Black Identity

It has been the fate of all Americans to struggle to accommodate the individual and his particular ethos to the broad general American culture. Black men and white men, immigrant and native, have been subject to crises of identity because the American Dream promises to include them all in a common culture which has not been realized. The problem is paradoxical. For the tradition of America is change, and the singular characteristic of its culture is vague indefiniteness. For the individual to define himself in terms of American experience has been therefore problematic. Identity could no more be taken for granted than could culture itself. The immigrant and his children tried to belong to the adopted culture: learn the language, drop old ways, adopt new styles and mannerisms. But, in time, the adopted mannerisms, life styles, language, and materialism became feeble substitutes for genuine culture. And third and fourth generations of immigrant families attempt to rediscover an ethnic tradition. The native American and his children have been no more secure. Constantly dislocated in the flux of an ever-changing society, they have tried to translate the uncertainties of newness into what has been understood as traditional. Foreign or native, one sooner or later would find comfort in ethnic identification.

Negroes, too, were to discover, after the decades of struggle following emancipation, that the America they wanted to get into was a spiritual "nowhere." They began the search for their own selves. The quest was intensified because of the general postwar uncertainties, because American intellectuals generally were displeased with the manifestations of American culture, and were themselves in search—in Paris and elsewhere —for themselves. It was a hard, perplexing task for Negroes. Unlike the immigrant, the Negro as a native American did not have ready at hand the surface manifestations of a former culture which, no matter how diluted and distorted, could serve as a link with the past. Nor could the Negro easily imagine a place where his history began. The Italian or the Greek or Serb could know of a village or a place to which he could return (to visit) where his family would still be remembered, where, indeed, his family still lived. His imagination could work himself back into the community, the tough and austere life, and even the oppression of gentry, or Turks, or Cossacks. And while he reconstructed it, he could congratulate himself on the distance that he had placed between himself and that past. Steel, railroads, coal, business, cities, were the present stuff of his life, not the grudging and churlish hills of his homeland. Being American for many immigrants meant being a part of progress and the future, with a strong and real sense of a different past.

Negroes, on the other hand, had no such clear sense of the past; it was a general and abstract thing, slavery. Those whose past was northern were like the other undifferentiated city dwellers without the possibility of having "first family" identification—they were Yankees and native sons without the attendant self-satisfaction. And those from the South could seldom, even if they wanted to, find the plantation, the farm, the cabin of their origin; except for a rare few, family could seldom be traced beyond two generations. The Negro's search for self was closer to that of the deracinated young postwar intellectuals that Malcolm Cowley describes in *Exile's Return* than to that of the immigrants. Both the Negroes and the uprooted youth were cut off from a past to which they could not return, and with which they could not identify. At the same time, they were both unrelated to American progress in amassing wealth, building machines, and producing things—the one because he was repulsed by the Philistine, the other because racism denied to him the American Dream. Both were American— having no other past—and thus were subject to greater hopes, expectations, bitterness, and despair than were the immigrants. There is a very real and important difference between being alien and alienated: being a stranger to something which is your becoming, or being native to something of which you are not a part.

The task of Negro intellectuals, as they have addressed themselves to the issue of race in American life, has been to delineate Negro character and personality in the American context. Did the Negro belong? Was he distinctive? How? Was he merely a white man with black skin? The problem was to define the Negro as a part of the American future; few were willing to touch the American past.

The general picture that one gets of the Negro through the eyes of his intellectual interpreters is that of the man rejected, the citizen denied. The American Dream held out the promise to all men: through industry, self-reliance, and individual talent the limitless vista of progress were theirs. Most black men wanted to say that this promise of American life was theirs— logically, rightfully, morally—as much as it was other men's. The issue is not, as many interpreters insist, a matter of assimilation—segregation vs. integration.[1] These matters were incidental. Faced with the past of slavery and a present of racism, could the Negro become a part of an American future that honored its own precepts?

Justice John Harlan, dissenting from the "separate-but-equal" doctrine which was proclaimed in *Plessy vs. Ferguson* (1896), might well have said that the American Dream, rather than the Constitution, was color-blind—the future, progress, hope, color-blind. For that was the issue for black men. A great deal rested on whether one affirmed or denied that the American Dream included black men. A yes answer had to mean, at least ultimately, the end of formal segregation and legal discrimination. This was not merely because "separate but equal" is necessarily a fiction, nor simply because Negroes wanted to reject their blackness and become white. It was rather that segregation and discrimination ignored the individual, contradicted self-reliance, denied the promise. If, on the other hand, one answered no, that the Dream was for white men only, there was nothing to do but escape. But even when one looks at those who have said no and dropped out—the colonizers of Liberia, Garvey's supporters, the Black Muslims —the Dream persisted in their very efforts.[2] It does not matter that, in practice, the American Dream has been imperfect or even fanciful. It was a myth deeply believed by American people of all conditions, people who would call reality a lie before they would deny the future.

But due to the real social, economic, and political discrimination, those Negroes who were yea-sayers to the Dream had to explain continually the disparity between black Americans and others in their progress, their achievement. Implicit in discriminatory practice was the doubt that black men could really compete individually; hence the justification for bars to competition. Despite the circularity of the logic, barriers which limited Negroes' mobility were defended because of the observable inequality of Negroes and whites, which, of course, the barriers guaranteed. Indeed, the majority opinion in *Plessy vs. Ferguson* is a classical example of this circular argument. So, black believers in America's capacity to absorb Negroes, and in the black man's potential, bore the onus of race while they promoted individualism. They had to explain the whole race in order to gain advantage for anyone. The emphasis was on achievement. Every instance of advancement—a successful business, a new professional, a patriotic act or service— became ammunition in the barrage against arbitrary barriers. On the other hand, every failure, every crime, every black man's foolishness became a spot of shame that had to be rubbed away. Every act of a Negro that came to public attention had emotive connotations far beyond the significance of the act itself. The Negro intellectual, the leader, was image-conscious. It is within this context that the Harlem leadership's hysterical reaction to Marcus Garvey must be understood. He appeared a fool, impractical, a charlatan; and as his movement foundered in financial and legal straits, it became essential to black intellectuals that the public know the difference between a showman and the real thing. But it is also within this context of image-consciousness that one must understand the promotion of Negro artists, poets, and novelists during this decade. But what is really remarkable is that these black yea-sayers, in their struggle to uphold the American virtues of progressivism, individualism, and self-reliance, were obliged by circumstances to be group-conscious and collective. The American Dream of open-ended possibility for the individual was for them another paradox.

The Negroes' history, out of slavery and beyond emancipation, threw this paradox into sharp focus for those black spokesmen who straddled the decades of the nineteenth and twentieth centuries. Booker T. Washington and W. E. B. Du-Bois illustrate this point. Despite all of their apparent differences—in spirit, tone, and self-image—these two men

were in remarkable agreement on essentials. In *Up From Slavery* and *Souls of Black Folk* these authors agree that the race is
downtrodden, and both project the progressive bias of uplift in
their imagined solutions. Both men were one with the bed-rock
virtues of America—frugality, industry, temperance, competition. Washington's autobiography has a strange identity with
Andrew Carnegie's *Gospel of Wealth*, and DuBois's own
achievement, he stressed, was the result of intense individualistic competition. The differences, of course, are significant. Du-
Bois wrote his book to make "the ears of a guilty people tingle
with truth"; Washington dared not so to presume. Both, however, were men of their time and place, progressive Americans
—mired in the collectivity of race. They both believed in the
ultimate justice of an economic system in which the laws of efficiency and quality automatically discriminated among men.
Washington believed in it so uncritically that he was prepared
to sacrifice his contemporary Negroes' expectation of dignity
and citizenship to the inevitability of that justice. Present-day
efforts to find in Washington the roots of modern black nationalism should take into account that he never lost faith that the
Negroes' future was within the American context. Nor did he
assume a segregated future, for racial antipathy would decline
when economic necessity warranted it and when the economic
disparity between the races diminished. Washington, indeed,
was honored among whites (probably more than among
blacks) because he allowed himself to be seen as the black evidence that the Dream was real.

The challenge to find a black identity within the American
cultural context was made more difficult because the stereotype which defined Negroes for most Americans was the obverse of the Protestant Ethic, that convenient measure of de-
serving character. Laziness, slovenliness, and excessive sensual
appetite deserved no reward except poverty and dishonor. Furthermore, the range of black character that whites would ac-

cept was extremely circumscribed, if one judges by those who appear in print. The Negro was pathetic or humorous, loyal or treacherous, servile or savage. Thus, it was a delicate problem for the black writer who wanted to develop Negro character. For he had to delineate—to an audience with such bias and which judged character, growth, and change by progressive and materialistic measures—a man who was honorable and sympathetic but nevertheless constrained within the limits of actual Negro experience. And until World War I, any such literary effort would have to conform to the "trinity" of genteel dogma: a focus on morality and uplift, a faith in a progress conveniently linked to morality, and the aspiration of a learned (not native) culture.[3] Nor could the black hero be aggressively critical of the order of things, North or South. The critics and the publishing establishment were anxious to bind up the wounds from the Civil War and to eradicate lingering bitterness between northern and southern whites.[4] It was a tight and narrow place for a black hero to breath.

The model of such a hero can be found in Mrs. Stowe's Uncle Tom. He has become a much maligned old man, his name synonomous with fear, obsequiousness, and servility— surely not heroic characteristics. To an age that knows *Uncle Tom's Cabin* mainly through commentary, it is probably nearly impossible to think that Uncle Tom is in any way heroic. Yet that was Mrs. Stowe's intention, reasonable if one accepts that era's values and assumptions. Uncle Tom's guiding virtue is an unquestioned faith in God and loyalty, principally to his first owners. This obligation is based on an honestly reciprocal affection, which Tom feels bound to even to the point of obedience to a new master and overseer after circumstances force his sale. Tom has the sense of honor to serve his loved master even beyond the grave. But his character saves him from mere servility when he refuses, under the threat of death, to flog a slave for Simon Legree. Tom, indeed, has virtues which appealed to nineteenth-century Americans—industry, temperance (moderation), selfless loyalty to others (not servility), and a strong sense of duty to a moral order. While grievously cramped and confined within the oppressive institution, while tested by the inhumanity of a vicious overseer, Mrs. Stowe's Uncle Tom can remain patient and human despite all. He is noble and heroic precisely because he refuses to do mean and low things—in contrast to the whites who enslave him; he will not allow his essential self to be corrupted by passion and the conditions of life. He is a powerful indictment of the institution of slavery all the more, not because he rebels against it, but because he overcomes it through that essential inner humanity —through character. And what a moving example of life that was to people who nursed at the nipples of Puritan duty and transcendental immanence.[5]

The Negro writer was moved to project the image of the black man who, contrary to the stereotype, suffered under the unfair and arbitrary problems and restraints that beset him. The protagonist in James Weldon Johnson's *Autobiography of an Ex-Coloured Man* (1912) finds the difficulties of realizing his musical talent as a Negro insurmountable. Becoming ashamed of the impotence of the American blacks (after witnessing a lynching), he decides to become white. Johnson was careful to keep his apparently white protagonist's action from being dishonest, or deceitful. Everyone had always taken him for whatever he acted; he merely chooses to no longer act Negro. Honor is always central in his thinking:

> I argued that to forsake one's race to better one's condition was no less worthy an action than to forsake one's country for the same purpose. I finally made up my mind that I would neither disclaim the black race nor claim the white race; but that I would change my name, raise a moustache, and let the world take me for what it would; that it was not necessary for me to go about with a label of inferiority pasted across my forehead.[6]

Coming to this resolve, the young man drops his professional
interest in music and becomes devoted to the business world.
And he succeeds like any Horatio Alger hero, working hard
and watching for opportunities to make wise investments. His
most crucial trial of honor comes when he falls in love with a
white lady and must decide to tell her, risking her love and,
perhaps, all that he has achieved. Of course, he does the honorable thing, he reveals his secret, and true to genteel formula,
love ultimately triumphs. The wife dies, after bearing two children, and the protagonist is left with some ambivalence and
mild guilt. His children and their futures justify, for him, his
continued life as a white man, yet he has lingering doubts
about the greater self he might have been had he continued
with his music to define the genius of his black people. Johnson wanted his readers to understand that being white was not
a desideratum of Negroes; circumstances and bitter frustration
forced subterfuge. The tragedy, as he saw it, was not merely
the protagonist's abdication of his art (and his essential self)
but, more, that the society had lost the cultural synthesis that
might have been possible through the genius of this marginal
man. And, further, the message is clear that civilization, virtue,
honor, gentility, and success were qualities of individuals, not
races.[7]

A year earlier than the publication of *Autobiography*, that
other black man of letters, W. E. B. DuBois, published his first
effort in prose fiction, *The Quest for the Golden Fleece* (1911).
The central purpose of the novel was to show the influence of
impersonal and distant forces in controlling personal destiny.
DuBois used cotton and its far-flung, international power as
the force that frustrated the human aspirations of little people
—poor white farmers as well as his main black characters,
Zora and Bles. The novel thus parallels Frank Norris' *The Oc-
topus* and *The Pit*, not only in its use of a commodity as the
symbol of impersonal force (Norris used wheat) but in its na-
turalistic determinism as well. It should be recalled that Nor-

ris' and DuBois's novels came at either end of that agrarian
Populist upheaval which had stressed the individuals' impotence under the oppression of industry and finance. This helps
to explain their similar preoccupations. Zora and Bles begin
their story as innocents who are one with the life and the nature that blesses them. Their struggle with King Cotton's empire,
however, forces on them a sobriety and sophistication which is
at once tragic and hopeful. Zora is a clear link with slavery
and the past. She is very dark, exuberant, and "savage" as the
novel opens. As a child, she had been forced by her mother, a
slave, to gratify the lust of her former master. And, like a slave,
Zora felt little compunction about lying or stealing. But with
the help of Bles and a Yankee school-mistress, Zora becomes a
respectable heroine—respecting education and purposeful industry. Of course, DuBois was only a man of his times in
knowing that a true heroine could not be morally compromised.[8] Zora's and Bles's final resolve to fight the system with
black share-cropper cooperatives, as well as the book's suggestion that white-black, poor farmer alliance was the ultimate so-
lution, are suggestive of Populism. In any event, DuBois had
tried to thrust his black characters into the mainstream of
American moral and political values. Whatever their historical
limitations, the Negroes' character, virtue, and education were
the future's hope to destroy artificial barriers.

Jessie Fauset tried to project the Negro image in very conventional terms. Indeed, it was her intended purpose in writing novels to place the Negro in the context of standard American life. Her first novel, *There Is Confusion* (1924), will
sufficiently illustrate how she used the clichés of genteel realism to construct stories of the "respectable" Negro middle
class. Joanna Marshall comes from such a family; her father is
a typical American businessman, despite the fact that the
source of his middle-class comfort is a catering business. The
novel turns around a very erratic and temperamental romance

between Joanna and Peter Bye, a young man whose genealogy is entangled in main-line Philadelphia Quaker stock (thus the title). Joanna is much enamored of her father and his success, and she has a compulsive ambition to "amount to something," which almost destroys her romance with Peter. Peter is very bitter about his ancestry; the black Byes produced the wealth that the white Byes enjoy, yet they are not even acknowledged as part of the family. His bitterness would have destroyed him except that Joanna goads him on, using her love and promised marriage as inducement. But Joanna, too, is ambitious for herself and finds it hard to commit herself wholly to Peter. Hoping to make himself worthy of Joanna, Peter puts away personal indifference and takes up the study of medicine, but in time Joanna's games cause him to break off with her completely and to drop out of medical school too. All to Joanna's grief; she learns through his rejection how much she really loves him.

Jessie Fauset's strong class bias is evident in her treatment of Joanna's friend, Maggie Ellersley, who helps run her mother's boarding house. Maggie falls in love with Joanna's brother, Philip, and he loves her, although he is much too shy to let her know. Joanna becomes so enraged at Maggie's social presumption that she writes her an ugly and hurtful letter. Maggie impulsively runs off to marry an older man, whom she later discovers to be a gambler. Maggie remains thus degraded until Peter, on the bounce from Joanna, rescues her. But even that ends as Peter makes up with Joanna and goes off to join the war in Europe.

Miss Fauset resolved her conventional novel in a conventional way. Peter happens to meet Meriwether Bye (white) aboard the troop ship to France. He happens, also, to be present at Meriwether's death on the battlefield. The pathos and the genuine humanity of Meriwether soften Peter's heart, dissolving the last of his hatred and bitterness. Maggie and Philip are also reconciled in Europe—she, a social worker, he, a desperately ill soldier. They each learn for the first time that they had loved the other in their youth. And Maggie, true to the Victorian code for a woman with her past, devotes herself to his care and to a life of selfless service. Of course, Peter and Joanna are married on his return from the war; she is resigned to him. They soon have a child who promises to complete their lives. Ironically, the white Byes are without a male heir with the death of Meriwether, and the old family head comes to Dr. Peter Bye and offers to take his son to be reared into the legacy. Of course, Peter Bye says no, but Jessie Fauset sees the triumph in that he said it without bitterness. For, the truly genteel values of uplift, self-perfection, and honor burden all of Miss Fauset's novels and give all of her approved Negro characters the image of conventional respectability.

Of course, these works, as would be inevitable, had a purpose and function besides the purely artistic. They all tried to project the image of the Negro as exemplary within the context of conventional morality. Where those who peopled these stories achieved success, it was simple to understand as a matter of character overcoming the unusual obstacle of race. But the realities of life forced Negro writers to confront the frustration of black people. It was no easy task to handle that problem honestly within a conventional model which had strong stoical ingredients and which could not accommodate bitterness or anger at personal misfortune. Everyman was to bear his burden without self-pity and complaint. That was Uncle Tom's heroism, and it could be seen—if viewed through the lens of tradition—as the beauty and triumph of the Negro.

This image was utilized by Countee Cullen, among others, in poetry having a racial subject. Characteristically idealized, Cullen's "Simon the Cyrenian Speaks" transforms the black man's servility—through act of will and sensitivity to ultimate virtue—into a triumphant act.

Simon the Cyrenian Speaks [9]

He never spoke a word to me
And yet He called my name;
He never gave a sign to me,
And yet I knew and came.

At first I said, "I will not bear
His cross upon my back;
He only seeks to place it there
Because my skin is black."

But He was dying for a dream,
And He was very meek,
And in His eyes there shone a gleam
Men journey far to seek.

It was Himself my pity bought;
I did for Christ alone
What all of Rome could not have wrought
With bruise of lash or stone.

For Langston Hughes, on the other hand, this same theme,
which transforms humiliating and frustrating labor into virtue,
is more earthy and immediate.

Mother to Son [10]

Well, son, I'll tell you:
Life for me ain't been no crystal stair.
It's had tacks in it,
And splinters
And boards torn up,
And places with no carpet on the floor—
Bare.
But all the time
I'se been a' climbin' on,
And reachin' landin's
And turnin' corners,
And sometimes goin' in the dark

Where there ain't been no light.
So, boy, don't you turn back.
Don't you set down on the steps
'Cause you finds it's kinder hard.
Don't you fall now—
For I'se still goin', honey,
I'se still climbin',
And life for me ain't been no crystal stair.

It is a very delicate problem for, as one can see in these poems, pride inevitably wrestles with pathos. Power and clarity of image suffer in the uncertainty.

In his poetry, Claude McKay chose another way of conceptualizing the black man's existence within oppression and frustration. The unfair restraints were a challenge to test the mettle of the unconquerable self. McKay showed the undaunted will triumphant against impersonal corruption.

America [11]

Although she feeds me bread of bitterness,
And sinks into my throat her tiger's tooth,
Stealing my breath of life, I will confess
I love this cultured hell that tests my youth!
Her vigor flows like tides into my blood,
Giving me strength erect against her hate.
Her bigness sweeps my being like a flood.
Yet as a rebel fronts a king in state,
I stand within her walls with not a shred
Of terror, malice, not a word of jeer.
Darkly I gaze into the days ahead,
And see her might and granite wonders there,
Beneath the touch of Time's unerring hand,
Like priceless treasures sinking in the sand.

Here, too, one reads the late Victorian stoic mood; the bravado of tone is more than reminiscent of W. E. Henley: "I thank whatever gods may be/For my unconquerable soul." McKay, here and in his other poems, is careful to avoid pathos and self-pity. But he also consciously struggles against projecting bitterness. As he says in "White House," "Oh, I must keep my heart inviolate/Against the potent poison of your hate." As in most of his poetry, written after his migration to the United States, McKay assumes the *persona* of the Victorian stoic activist—Henley, Housman, Kipling—alone against the ravages of external, impersonal forces. Although a self-statement, McKay projected himself as exemplary, and therefore without violence to his intent one can understand this poetry as the idealization of the Negro against his oppression: a black Prometheus in the twentieth century.

Yet image-making and image-conceptualizing were no easy things. For if the Negro were really no different from other men, if he were a white man with black skin, so to speak, if the objective differences were solely environmental and not matters of character, then there would be nothing but the biology of color which set him off from whites. There would really be nothing that he could claim as distinctive, except for history and immediate condition. The future which unfolded itself in inevitable progress would ultimately obliterate distinctions, even these superficial differences would disappear and all would be as one. No matter how much one wanted to claim that discrimination against Negroes was arbitrary and that the society ought to be color-blind, since there were no differences among people, still one felt the need to hold onto some claim of distinctive Negro character. Abandoning all distinction was a total rejection of the past, a kind of self-obliteration. Those qualities of American life which had germinated in black soil had to be explained. The spiritual, the music, the dance, the language, were distinct because they were from a Negro source. Without distinct Negro character, there could be no Negro genius.

None of these writers would have denied the black man his special gift. W. E. B. DuBois was eloquent and moving in evoking the germ of that idea in *Souls of Black Folk* (1903), and James Weldon Johnson touched it too in "O Black and Unknown Bards." The novels of both of these authors reflect the ambivalence that grows out of the effort to balance the conventional Protestant Ethic with the recognition and approval of a distinctive Negro spirit.

DuBois, for instance, was unable to resolve the contradition of Zora's and Bles's initial innocence and the necessary sophistication of the cooperative economic venture which is their final strategy against the civilized cotton machine. While he is fascinated with Zora's primitivism—her wild, half-nude dances —he must bring her, through education and conventional virtue, to contend with her environment. Her primitivism and innocence had been corrupted by her institutionalized environment; the former master and the plantation—remnants of slavery—are translated into the cotton empire as the modern exploiter. Love, innocence, and purity of self will not sustain Zora; she must become educated and sophisticated—tough. While, doubtless, DuBois approves of this transformation— thinks it imperative—there is nonetheless a trace of regret over the lost black Eden.

Johnson's novel shares this regret. Descriptions of Negro life, whether in the New York cabaret or the southern rural revival meeting, are charged with the sense of distinctive spirit and color. Marshall's (an actual Negro social club in pre-Harlem New York) is described with genuine affection. White entertainers who made a profession of blackface use the club to pick up their "authentic" black material. The novel also assumes that the protagonist's quite remarkable musical talent is really ethnic. His special genius—being a marginal man between white and black—is that he is as fresh in his interpretation of ragtime as Chopin. His unrealized ambition—his calling, indeed—is to bring that distinctive black genius, which bursts naturally from the souls of ragtime musician or gospel singer, into a cultivated musical statement. When the protagonist decides to leave the world of race, he relegates his music to a hobby and concentrates his energies on real estate, investment, and money-making. Thus, Johnson draws a line between the humane, artistic spirit of black Americans as against the hard materialism of whites. The tone of regret that ends this narrative reiterates the lost hope—the Negro soul denied.

Langston Hughes's *Not Without Laughter* (1930) confronted this dilemma head-on—unfortunately, as Hughes himself confessed, without real success. Sandy, the little boy around whom the novel revolves, lives in the tension between the flight and abandon of music and laughter and the sober duty of achievement. Each member of his family presents a different face to the problem. Aunt Hager, his grandmother, is sober and religious. She has raised three daughters by taking in washing, and now helps with Sandy. Of the daughters, Tempy, with great self-discipline and energy, devotes herself to getting ahead and accumulating property. Harriet, the youngest, is hurt, and angered by racial injustice, and has become pleasure-seeking and blindly rebellious. Annjee, Sandy's mother, is married to Jimboy, an itinerant blues singer and guitarist, who comes and goes like a spirit. Jimboy is the ultimate artist, a troubador whose music generates his life, for whom life and joy are united even in life's sadness. It is his laughter and life-giving spirit that sustain Annjee despite his irresponsibility. Harriet's humanity, too, is sustained by Jimboy, for it is his music and her dance and song that free her from the corroding bitterness that she holds within. For Tempy, joy and laughter are time-wasting. Pleasure and play are the Negro's curse, according to Tempy, her husband, and their friends. Aunt Hager had great ambitions for her children, hoping that they would

achieve something for the race. Annjee and Harriet have disappointed her, dropping out of school, so she has placed all of
her hopes on Sandy:

> "I wants you to be a great man, son," she often told him, sit-
> ting on the porch in the darkness, singing, dreaming, calling
> up the deep past, creating dreams within the child. "I wants
> you to be a great man."

But Aunt Hager was not simply a religious woman who abandoned joy.[12] Her faith has been her joy. "Sandy remembered his grandmother whirling around in front of the altar at
revival meetings in the midst of the other sisters, her face shin-
ing with light, arms outstretched as though all the cares of the
world had been cast away." Only Tempy fully rejects this
Negro gift of joy and laughter, and she has become enslaved to
utter materialism. Hughes wanted the reader to understand
that Sandy had absorbed the uplift and the moral character of
Aunt Hager while still being possessed by the spirit and
beauty of the Negro genius. It was this combination that was
the Negro's hope, in so far as Sandy was the future.

The conventional American ethic proved inadequate in several significant ways when it was applied to the Negro. In the
first place it was racist. For the "Custodians of Culture," [13] the
Negro was not central. He was an aberration, a kind of Caliban in a demi-paradise. When the critics and commentators
considered culture, they used Anglo-Saxon models; American
literature and art in the prewar years were judged mainly in
terms of English models. If white Americans were merely cousins to that English tradition, black Americans could only be
curiosities. In the second place, conventional values were optimistic. While they might be heavily moralistic, and while one
might find beauty in the persistently moral life without reward,
the basic assumption was that progress was inevitable and,
being the signature of God, tied to the moral life. Whatever

Booker T. Washington's faith, the twentieth century found this convention invalid for the Negro experience. Individual achievement aside—it was painfully small and often bought at a dear price—the Negro was experiencing greater violence against him, greater restrictions, greater oppression than before. Indeed, in the postwar years it seemed that racism was being formalized—as a fact of American life—rather than erased by the transforming force of inevitable moral law and principle. Progress, in fact, was a lie. With such an awareness, the poor-but-honest and the moral-but-oppressed Negro image not only became a bore, it became irrelevant.

What the war and the postwar years seemed to prove, if nothing else, was that the American system had no place for blacks. What all of the restrictive legislation, the riots, the lynchings, the popularity of the Ku Klux Klan (North as well as South, urban as well as rural) proved was that for the black man the American Dream was fantasy. No matter how much the Negro might affirm it and aspire to it, the Dream itself seemed to say no. Indomitable and awful reality made it impossible for black men to project themselves into some American future that they would want. If the remarkable popularity of the Garvey movement tells us nothing else, it attests to the willingness of thousands of Negroes to put their dimes and dollars into another dream. Decades later, a white American character in drama echoes this same dream-quest and the same frustration: in Arthur Miller's *Death of a Salesman* Willy Loman badgers the spirit of Uncle Ben who had gone into the African jungle and come out a rich man.

But even before the war, forces were at work among white American intellectuals to transform traditional values, at least superficially. Henry F. May has described the prewar "innocent rebellion" which opened the door for the rather spectacular cultural eruption of the 1920s. Young people had gleefully and casually combined their distortions of Dostoevsky and

Freud with H. G. Wells's demand (prediction) of rational social reorganization and Henri Bergson's ejaculations about
élan vital. Convention, order, formalism were suspect. The
truth of life itself, as testified in experience, became the measure. As May explains it, the "Liberation was, in its own way,
pragmatic: it believed with [William] James that ideas should
be judged not by their conformity to any preconceived truth
but by the quality of life they contained." [14] This "rebellion"
and "liberation" emphasized spontaneity, suspected that which
was too rational and logical, criticized the harsh materialism of
American life, and challenged conventional moral (especially
sexual) standards. Henry May makes it clear that these "rebels" merely redefined traditional norms; they did not destroy
them. They could become moralistic in their advocacy of free
love or sexual experiment. They substituted an easy and naïve
optimism for a belief in progress. And while they were quick to
abandon the conventional apotheosis of Anglo-Saxon culture,
they were equally eager to accept authentic exotics: Italians in
Greenwich Village and Negroes in Harlem. James Weldon
Johnson shared their optimism about culture, believing that art
and poetry would be the bridge between races in America. [15]
The war did much to destroy the optimism of these people no
longer young. Yet those who had the greatest influence on Harlem intellectuals were precisely those who held fast to their
prewar innocence: Floyd Dell, Max Eastman, Carl Van Vechten, Carl Sandburg, and Vachel Lindsay. [16]

So the postwar years found traditional values in disarray. A
very articulate and sophisticated segment of the white society
appeared ready to stand everything on its head. Where industry, frugality, temperance (including moderation and decorum)
had been the touchstones, now exuberance, spontaneity, irresponsibility (to be crazy), and sexual freedom were the new
norms. The Negro, who had long fought a white imposed stereotype found that those very traits which he had denied were

now in vogue. One need merely rework the old minstrel model, and one had a new Negro image that both conformed to contemporary values and laid claim to a distinctive Negro self. It also provided, for those who read reality as a denial to the Negro of the American Dream, the illusion of a half-way house between resignation and rejection.

As the decade of the 1920s came to a close, the new wave of Negro literature chose to unearth the grotesque and exotic in black men, to abandon genteel standards and the embarrassment over what had been accepted as Negro traits (the stereotype). Indeed, the new effort was to accept those traits rather than to deny them, to convert them into positive and appealing characteristics. With this reversal of values, one could sometimes treat the Negro as superior to white men.

Nella Larsen, native to the Virgin Islands and of African-Danish ancestry, explored through her novels the uncompromising dilemma of the cultured-primitive Negro. Her characters seemed always to be pulled between the poles of refined civility and passion. In her best novel, *Quicksand* (1928), Helga Crane is overwhelmed by the ethnic war within her mulatto psyche. Helga moves from Naxos—a narrow, regimented, authoritarian southern Negro college—to Chicago, to bourgeois Harlem, and then to maternal relatives in Copenhagen. Cramped at first by the provincialism of Naxos, then by the provincialism of race, she is never able to find peaceful adjustment. At first Harlem is liberating. It has a more varied and open life than either Naxos or Chicago. And, at first, the unconfused blackness of Harlem is a welcome relief from the race specter in the South; it also frees her from the white-black tension of her mulatto consciousness. In Harlem, all one needs do is relax and be black, and yet that does not mean denying to oneself the finer things of living—civilized and cultural things. It is only a temporary pleasure, however, for Helga's white

consciousness makes her sense more keenly than other Negroes
the narrow provincial character of Harlem. The freedom from
self-consciousness that it allows black people evaporates outside the geographical and spiritual limits of Harlem. In Copenhagen, Helga is warmly received by her Danish relatives. She
becomes something of a phenomenon, dark and exotic. Here,
too, she finds pleasure in the comforts and ease of life of up-
per-middle-class Danish society. And she is honored by a pro-
posal of marriage to a highly regarded and handsome portrait
painter. She is disturbed, however, not merely because Axel
Olsen exposes, through his portrait of her, Helga's sensual and
primitive nature, but because she sees by this sudden insight
the key to her acceptance by the painter as well as her Danish
relatives. He senses a tiger, an animal within her which he
wants to possess—to ravish and to be ravished—through marriage if necessary. Even her relatives and their friends are a bit
breathless at the smell of the jungle, the savage, the primitive,
that they sense to be this almost-white girl's spirit. Helga
knows that she cannot be free—an honest self—and be a
lovely freak for cultivated Europeans. She begins to long again
for Harlem, where she can be herself. Her return, she tells herself and everybody, is only to be a short visit, yet she knows
that she will never go back to Copenhagen.

Harlem! What a relief, to be able to leave pretense, to be
free! But, now even more quickly, the narrowness of Harlem
life (and Negro life) begins to stultify, and Helga begins to
hate the black people around her, and hate that within her
that seems always to frustrate her. She wants, at least, to
accept—rather, to surrender to—the sensuality that she has always struggled against. She—submitting to her passion—offers
herself to Dr. Anderson, the president of Naxos College who
chances to be in New York, only to be rejected by this married
and wholly proper man. Helga's humiliation, shame, and self-
hate drive her to submit to Reverend Green, a just-literate

rural, southern preacher, who comforts her in her anguish. Helga tells herself that her marriage to Reverend Green, and her choice to live with him in the rural South, will give her a chance to do constructive and useful work. But this is a deception too, for she has surrendered more to her own sensuality than to him. She has rejected all pretense and has resigned to primal and uncluttered feelings. "And night came at the end of every day. Emotional, palpitating, amorous, all that was living in her sprang like rank weeds at the tingling thought of night, with a vitality so strong that it devoured all the shoots of reason." Thus, Helga's life ends in bed, semi-invalid from too frequent pregnancies and unattended deliveries, looking forward to death—the ultimate of all surrenders.

Miss Larsen's lesser novel, *Passing* (1929), also treats the schizophrenia which results from racial dualism. Two Negro women, friends from childhood, each light enough in color to be taken as white, choose different ways to direct their lives. Clare Kendry chooses to marry a white man (perversely a race bigot), while Irene Westover remains Negro, marrying a colored man who is to become a quite talented (but frustrated) physician. These different life-styles reflect different characters. Clare is adventuresome, risk-taking, exciting, and cosmopolitan. Irene, on the other hand, is safe, stolid, a bit frightened of adventure, and provincial. The choice to become white, while adventuresome and courageous on one level, turns out to be essentially sterile. The Bellews have no children, and Clare is drawn, as if by a magnet, to surreptitious trips into Harlem. The thrill of adventure, which partly motivated the "deception" in the first place, is kept alive by flirting with the risk of discovery. But her white life is sterile in another way. There is something essential to Negro life—the gaiety, the warmth—that she misses in her white world. Irene Redfield, on the other hand, has bought security and a family—including a child—at the price of adventure, daring, and risk. She is essentially conventional and conservative, which ultimately (and ironically) threatens her marriage. For her husband, cramped and confined by racial strictures in the United States, wants to take a chance of going to Brazil, where he might have the opportunity of opening new paths in medical practice. But that would mean physical danger and discomfort and, more frightening to his wife, an uncertain future. Her fears and lack of taste for adventure threaten to emasculate both her husband and her son. Clare's secret trips to Harlem bring her close to Brian Redfield; both respond to the other's thirst for adventure, risk, and desired freedom from the restraints of ordinary conventionality. And thus, a very real threat to Irene's life is thrust upon her. Her hysteria moves her almost to expose Clare's pretense. But Irene is even frightened of that, because Clare freed from her husband would be an even greater threat. Nella Larsen constructs a perfunctory and entirely unsatisfactory denouement. Clare's husband who has had her followed by private detectives, bursts into a Harlem party, and in the confusion Clare falls through a window and is killed. Clare, in fact, was relieved that her lie was discovered by her husband; she was then free. But that freedom was a threat to Irene, and the author broadly hints that Irene pushed Clare through the window.

In both novels, Miss Larsen moved away from the conventional genteel formula. There was something distinctive and attractive in Negro life, and it had nothing to do with Jessie Fauset's respectability. Yet, she was not able to abandon herself to an uncritical acceptance of black primitivism. The Negro had a special warmth, gaiety, and immediacy. But Nella Larsen also saw Negro life as peculiarly strict and confining. Harlem was provincial; it was pleasing only so long as one could envelop oneself into its geographical and psychic districts. The cosmopolitan had to be aware of its restrictions. Negro life was conservative and sterile; it had to devour itself to preserve itself. Contradicting, therefore, the faddism of Negro freedom, Miss Larsen exposed the psychological narrowness of Negro life, its avoidance of experiment, chance-taking, and daring. While she toyed with the notion of the Negro's basic sensuality, she could not let it overwhelm her credo. Perhaps, it was too difficult to project the female primitive to good advantage. And Miss Larsen, a nurse by profession, was too much of a realist to ignore the ugliness, pain, and deprivation which need result from a primitive life tamed only by the rhythm of one's blood. It is this sharp dichotomy of realist and romantic, etched in both her novels, that makes them seem schizophrenic.

No other Negro writer of the 1920s was more anxious to use primitive and atavistic motifs than the poet Countee Cullen. It is a bit ironic, because none of the Harlem writers was more formally schooled, none more genteel in inclination and taste, none indeed more prissy than Cullen. Educated at New York University, where he won the Witter Bynner poetry prize, and Harvard University, where he received his Master's degree, Cullen had consciously trained himself to be a poet. Most of his work was of a lyrical character, occasionally on racial themes. His *Ballad of a Brown Girl* was thought by Lyman Kittridge to be the best lyric written by any contemporary American. Cullen was clearly nineteenth century, and English, in his conception of poetic art; his strongest influence was Keats. The only contemporary poet to influence his work was Amy Lowell, but Cullen never appropriated her "Imagism." He always took it that poetry was truly one of the highest arts, that the poet's task was to say beautiful things, and that poetry, like all art, had moral intent. This formula made for the bland and bloodless verse which was characteristic of much American poetry around the turn of the century. So it is a bit strange to read those poems where Cullen—never with the abandon of Vachel Lindsay—seemed to step out of character and proclaim some deep primitive impulse of blood which threatened to command his mind and body.

Yet, according to Wallace Thurman, Countee Cullen was the most uncritical of the black writers in his acceptance of Alain Locke's instruction to turn to African and primitive origins as the source of new work. Cullen tried very hard to do that. In the rather long poem, "Heritage," [17] the poet engaged himself in a soliloquy which turns around the rhetorical question, *"What is Africa to me?"* The question is first posed in a simple historical context by *"One three centuries removed,"* and the question is repeated with the implied answer that Africa is nothing to the poet. But this is self-deception:

> So I lie, who all day long
> Want no sound except the song
> Sung by wild barbaric birds
> Goading massive jungle herds,
> Juggernauts of flesh that pass
> Trampling tall defiant grass
> Where young forest lovers lie,
> Plighting troth beneath the sky.

The thought that Africa is nothing comes from a willful denial, yet heritage is so primal that it will not be doomed by mind and will alone:

> So I lie, who always hear,
> Though I cram against my ear
> Both my thumbs, and keep them there,
> Great drums throbbing through the air.
> So I lie, whose fount of pride,
> Dear distress, and joy allied,
> Is my somber flesh and skin,
> With the dark blood dammed within
> Like great pulsing tides of wine
> That, I fear, must burst the fine
> Channels of the chafing net
> Where they surge and foam and fret.

But the denial of Africa continues following an assertion that it is merely "A book one thumbs/Listlessly, till slumber comes"; there is a catalogue of "unremembered" sights and sounds— jungle images. But, again, the poet finds "no slight release" from a blood-knowledge that makes him writhe to the rhythm of the rain. The rain's "primal measures drip/Through my body, crying, 'Strip'!" The soliloquy finds resolution in the statement that this black poet has become converted to Christianity, but even here he draws back from full commitment. "Wishing He I served were black,/Thinking then it would not lack/Precedent of pain to guide it." So the poet wanders between the primitive and the civilized, between the Christian and the pagan:

> Not yet has my heart or head
> In the least way realized
> They and I are civilized.

In "Fruit of the Flower" [18] Cullen reiterates some of the same themes. This time the poet contrasts himself with a father, "With sober, steady ways," and a "puritan" mother. Despite this the father's eyes bespeak "some still sacred sin." And, although, his mother longs for heaven, she is frightened of death. So the poet wonders

> Why should he deem it pure mischance
>   A son of his is fain
> To do a naked tribal dance
>   Each time he hears the rain?
>
> Why should she think it devil's art
>   That all my songs should be
> Of love and lovers, broken heart,
>   And wild sweet agony?
>
> Who plants a seed begets a bud,
>   Extract of that same root;
> Why marvel at the hectic blood
>   That flushes this wild fruit?

Of course, Countee Cullen was an orphan; the parents whom he knew most intimately were not of his "blood." Here, Cullen seemed to be confounding heredity in the romantic and racial way that was characteristic of those who applauded the primitive natures that they ascribed to Negroes.

Few of the notable Negro poets of the 1920s worked with the pagan-primitive theme as much as Cullen (indeed, it appears in only a few of his poems). The older generation, men like James Weldon Johnson, never touched it. While Langston Hughes was prepared to celebrate the beauty, spontaneity, and creativity of black Americans, his poetry of this period was clearly in the American folk tradition. He never used "primitive" or African characteristics to explain American Negroes. And Claude McKay's poetry is surprisingly devoid of these themes—surprising since his novels are not. Only "Harlem Dancer" comes close to approving atavism. And the sonnet "Africa" is simply a historical statement of that continent's grandeur which is no longer:

> Cradle of Power! Yet all things were in vain!
> Honor and Glory, Arrogance and Fame!
> They went. The darkness swallowed thee again.
> Thou art the harlot, now thy time is done,
> Of all the mighty nations of the sun.

And Cullen's efforts were confused as well, because they were not merely attempts to explore the source of African nativity, the wellsprings of Negro spirit and identity. But for that poet, Africa and "paganism" were instruments in his personal rebellion against the Christian church. His religious skepticism was always voiced as stemming from race consciousness: "Lord, I fashion dark gods, too." Cullen's attitudes about Africa and primitivism are enigmatic because they are only tools of this deeper revolt. "The Shroud of Color," which is free of primitivism, is a far more successful statement of his problem with Christianity than "Heritage." And while the latter is probably the author's best known work, the former is far the better poem for its clarity. Actually, even his struggle with faith was emblematic of a far deeper and more traumatic rebellion which his training in the genteel convention ill-equipped him to handle. Both as a person and a poet, Cullen tried to free himself of an unusually close relationship with his adoptive father, a minister. His personal rebellion was slight and genteel. Searching always—and futilely—for an adequate *persona,* Cullen toyed with the self-image of the pagan poet. Even so, his pretty diction never quite matched the desire:

> Where young forest lovers lie,
> Plighting troth beneath the sky.

For several reasons, some very personal, Cullen added his to the black voices that were suggesting the essential Negro spirit was to be found in Africa, in the jungle, in the primitive.

As one might imagine, the African influence was most immediately felt in the works of Negro painters and sculptors. Individual Negroes found a place for themselves, with great difficulty, in the plastic arts. Henry Tanner (1859–1937), for instance, after study under Thomas Eakins at the Pennsylvania Academy of Fine Arts and Benjamin Constant in the Académie Julian in Paris, became something of a master of the dying academic tradition. His contrived but disciplined treatments of the Holy Land won him some acclaim, and he became the "dean of American painters" in Paris. And Meta Warrick Fuller (1877–1968) received notice for her sensitivity to human suffering in sculpture which reflected the hand of her master, Auguste Rodin. Typical of their contemporary Negro artists, Mrs. Fuller and Henry Tanner stayed well within the bounds of studied, conventional, and conservative European imagination. Beginning in the 1920s, however, and continuing into the

1930s, Negro painters and sculptors attempted to incorporate Africanism and primitive motifs in their work. Except for William Johnson, sometime winner of Harmon Foundation awards, and Jacob Lawrence, who worked in the 1940s, they were not themselves primitives in art. Rather, some black artists, like some writers, were taken with the possibilities of Africanisms (as they understood them) and thought something profound in the Negro's life and spirit could be evoked by them.

Richmond Barthé's sculpture has covered a wide range of subjects, from the massive, heroic man-on-horseback representation of the Haitian General Dessalines to the simply representational head of Katharine Cornell. Beginning in the 1920s and extending into the next decade, Barthé's treatment of Negro subjects was not merely ethnic but he emphasized the primitive. His *Flute Boy*, which won a Harmon award in 1928, is typical. A standing nude—lithe, lean, adolescent—suggests freedom and innocence. The figure is quite angular—thin arms, pointed elbows, too-thin fingers holding the flute to the boy's lips. The hips are too small for the bony and upward-pointing shoulders. The figure's face continues these upward angles with boned cheeks and almond, almost feline, slanted eyes. All conspires to give this Pan-like figure a weightlessness, to make him a creature of air rather than earth.

Barthé continued to use these techniques to translate the primitive dance into sculpted form. *African Dancer* (1933) is a nude black girl. The slightest ornamentation at the hips accentuates the sensual and rolling movement of the dance. This figure has been caught as if in abandoned movement; the arms, legs, and head are poised, suggesting the controlled freedom of dance. The figure's sensuality, which is asserted by the contracted abdomen and nubile breasts, is climaxed by the dancer's upturned face, with closed eyes and slightly parted lips. A nude dancer, *Feral Benga* (1935), is a male counterpart to *African Dancer* and similarly expresses Barthé's primitivism. Here

Barthé's figure in front view holds in his right hand a long curved machete arched over his head. The sword begins a line continuing with the right arm which moves through a muscular and lean body to the legs—tightly closed, tensed, bent at the knees, and resting on the balls of the feet—to form a graceful S. On another plane, the left arm, curved downward, balances the figure and reiterates the line of the sword. Framed in the arc formed by the sword and the figure's arms is a small Negro head, eyes closed and face slightly contorted. Barthé exemplified this African influence in other ways. *Blackberry Woman* (1932) is something of a metaphor which relates the African to the Afro-American folk. One basket on her head, another hooked on her arm, this almost exotic figure hawks her wares through probable southern streets. In 1938, Barthé was commissioned to do marble reliefs for the Harlem River Houses in New York City. One of the panels, *Dance*, was a strange mixture which mimicked highly formalized Egyptian art, yet tried to depict the artist's conception of the rather athletic contemporary dance. The result was curious, but its debt to Africanism was clear enough.

Some artists did no more than include African objects in their works. Palmer Hayden, for instance, in his *Fétiche et Fleurs*, included in a still-life of western furnishings (a cigarette in an ashtray, table and chair, etc.), luxuriantly leafy plants, an African sculpture of a head, and a fabric (table cover) of distinctive African design. Charles Alston's mural for the Harlem Hospital, *Magic and Medicine*, which was commissioned by the W. P. A. Federal Art Project in 1937, included a panel which depicted that artist's conception of African magic. It has strong elemental and natural emphasis: animals, lightening, and the sun share the scene with dancing and conjuring Africans. Alston employed these obvious symbols—dancing, drums, fetishes, etc.—to embody the mural's message: modern medicine is better than primitive magic. Nevertheless, the African panel was more effective—more romantic and magical—than those which depicted modern doctors in white smocks.

The San Franciscan Sargent Johnson became a part of the Harlem scene through competition for Harmon Foundation awards: he made figures in terracotta, porcelain, and enameled wood. Johnson did heads of children, plain, simple, expressionless masks. These heads were strongly Negroid—full-lipped, broad-nosed. The eyes were large, open, and almond-shaped, and the heads were unadorned (except sometimes hair was stylized in the manner of Egyptian art). These open-faced, simple figures utilize the idea of mask to achieve an uncompromising purity and innocence. One standing figure, *Forever Free,* was so pleasing that Johnson did several renderings of it. The work is of an erect black woman, arms and hands straight to the side, face inclined looking up. The body—clothed in a long plain garment, with bare toes just visible from beneath the skirt—is almost cylindrical, having only slight definition of bust and stiff-straight arms and hands which are firm to the sides. Two children are mere reliefs on the woman's skirt, partly hidden and protected by her down-stretched hands. The figure's kerchiefed head is another Johnson mask, pure and open in its upward gaze. The figure is in stark lacquered black and white, except for the children who are brown. Of all the artists of the period, Sargent Johnson was most successful in taking a small suggestion from Africa and integrating it into his own unique statement.

None of the Negro artists of the postwar period was considered more promising than Aaron Douglas, and none was more influenced by Africanisms. Douglas was born in Topeka, Kansas, in 1898, educated in that city's public schools, and took a degree in fine arts at the University of Nebraska's School of Fine Arts. He came to New York City in 1925 and studied under Winold Reiss, who was famous at the time for his delineation of folk types and folk character. It was Reiss who encouraged Douglas to work with African themes to achieve a sense of the folk roots beneath the Negro people. Douglas' work found immediate recognition in such magazines as *Vanity Fair, Opportunity,* and *Theatre Arts Monthly.* His work also appeared in short-lived magazines like *Harlem* and *Fire,* Harlem's attempts at "little" magazines. *The New Negro* (1925) includes six Douglas illustrations, along with illuminations by his mentor Reiss. Of all the Harlem writers and artists, Douglas' work was most in view.

Aaron Douglas borrowed two things from the Africans. He thought that art should be design more than subject. And his personal predilictions for mysticism encouraged him to find racial unity and racial source in Africa. Music, the dance, that spirit beneath the substance—soul—were a connective tissue between the African and the Afro-American. In his art, he attempted to achieve that metaphor which would make that subliminal unity explicit.

His drawings were highly stylized designs: stark black and white silhouettes. What form appeared was part of the design; he used spear-like leaves; his human forms were flat silhouettes, angular, lithe, long-headed with mere slits for eyes. The effect was always savage: feline human figures crouched or moving as in dance.

This African phase of Douglas' work culminated in the unveiling of four murals in 1934, which had been completed under W. P. A. sponsorship. These panels attempted to work Douglas' ideas about design and Afro-American heritage onto canvas (in color rather than in stark black and white), and to infuse meaning into design. The first panel has his Negro figures in an African setting: dancing natives, spears, drums, and at the top center an African symbol of ancestry. The second panel treats the Negro's emancipation from slavery and subsequent subjugation under the threat of the Ku Klux Klan. Here, Douglas used symbols of cotton and labor to suggest slavery,

the reading of the Emancipation Proclamation to the jubilation
of music and dance, and at the extreme left of the panel the
hooded figures of the Klan ride on as Union soldiers march off.
The third panel protrays life for the southern Negro: at the
right, figures labor with hoe; in the center, subdued figures
sing but are grouped with a sense of sorrow and restraint, an-
ticipating grieving figures at the left under the horror of a
lynching. The final panel, "Song of the Towers," brings the
Negro into the industrial and urban world. At the right a
figure flees the clutching hands of serfdom. His escape, however, is over the steel cogs of machinery before belching smokestacks. Tall concrete towers angle at the background. But
one figure, a musician with his saxophone, dominates the center of the panel. At the left, the smokestacks do not bellow
smoke, however, and a heavy immobility seems to stifle life.
Thus the movement from right to left carries the Negro from
the clutches of serfdom into the machinery and sterility of the
industrial depression.

These four panels, then, attempt to depict the story of the
Negro from his origins in Africa, through slavery, emancipation, and oppression to the mechanized complexity of urban,
industrial America. Douglas worked within a narrow range of
color, tone, and value. The paintings were composed of relent-
lessly flat qualities of greens, browns, mauve, and black. His
human figures, always silhouettes, were unrelieved black or,
sometimes, darker shades of the dominant color. Hard line
dominates. The paintings achieve their illusion through symbol
rather than through representation. The African's head shape is
more spear-like than the Afro-American's, for instance. Douglas
not only maintains the flatness of color, but he, except for the
last panel, does not work in perspective. Not only his human
figures but his objects are two-dimensional. This serves to emphasize the design quality of the paintings, abandoning the illusion of three-dimensional reality. Because the human figures

are faceless and stylized, they are symbolic rather than representational, generic rather than personal, ethnic rather than individualistic. Douglas asks the Negro viewer to lose the particularity of ego in the paintings' generalized racial statement.

However flat and generalized these paintings were, they were surely not emotionally neutral. Among other things, Douglas used subtle gradations of color, at first glance undiscernible. Sometimes these were arranged in concentric circles, forcing the viewer's focus to particular points: the reading of the Emancipation Proclamation (panel two), the ancestral symbol (panel one). Sometimes they were arranged in broad wave-like bands, affecting a pulsating and emotional quality. In panel three, a thin shaft of light cuts a diagonal across the painting. Forsaking a wide range of color and fullness of form, Douglas chose to use these shafts and circles and waves for compositional ends—to arrange the work for emotional and aesthetic impact. It was a remarkable achievement. During this period when quite a few murals were being done under government support, Douglas' were surely as interesting as most. While some of these murals have earned public anonymity on the walls of U.S. Post Offices, Aaron Douglas' have been recently saved from obscurity and adorn the walls of the Countee Cullen branch of the New York Public Library.[19]

Aaron Douglas wanted, through his art, to interpret what he understood to be the spiritual identity of the Negro people. It was a kind of soul of self that united all that the black man was, in Africa and in the New World. Song, dance, image, poetry were to be united in the visual-emotional statement. Thus, the objects that he worked with could only suggest, they could not be something that was palpable. The more recognizable a thing was—the more particular—the less essential and universal. His work was, thus, necessarily abstract: mere design through which he wanted one to see a soul-self (an earlier age might have said over-soul) which united one with race, race with humanity, and man with God. Even today, Aaron Douglas talks about these paintings as stemming from his belief that art and culture are at the heart of life and can be the bridge between peoples. The abstraction, the symbol, should become the language in which men of disparate origins can speak to one another. Characteristically mystical, Douglas thought he saw in Gurdjieff's teaching (learned through Jean Toomer) and the "golden mean" the metaphor with which to make truly universal statements. He was abstract for philosophical not for painterly reasons. At the core of it all was the Negro, the primitive soul.

Of all the Harlem writers and artists none grasped the lure of Negro primitivism more eagerly and aggressively than Claude McKay. While the success of *Nigger Heaven* may have encouraged him to write his successful first novel, *Home to Harlem* (1928),[20] McKay subsequently transformed the idea of the Negro's spontaneity and vitality into something quite ominous. What had been for Van Vechten and even Rudolph Fisher exotic, naughty, and quaint was worked into a weapon in McKay's second novel, *Banjo* (1929). McKay crashed through into a statement of nihilism and new rebellion.

Ray, the West Indian intellectual from *Home to Harlem,* having left Harlem, has jumped ship in Marseilles. *Banjo* is a continuation of Ray's sojourn and an amplification of the educated man vs. natural man argument from the earlier novel. Ray has joined the company of black wharf-bums—an international riff-raff, the black residue of the shipping world. Banjo, so-called because he plays that instrument, is from the United States and has all of Jake's naturalness, instinctive superiority, and leadership. Banjo and Ray and the rest of the black men spend their time bumming and panhandling on the docks. They all hustle, and when one is especially successful, he shares at least part with the others. Life is easy and irresponsible. There is food enough, and they "bung-out" wine barrels for their free drinks. They connive for the favors of the district's vari-colored whores. But mainly they talk endlessly about the world (from their very special perspective) and the black man in that world. They are so much the scum of civilization that McKay asks the reader to believe they see life without self-deception—frankly and unadorned. Ray, still the intellectual of course, struggles against his growing sense that placelessness is his ultimate condition.

Banjo is subtitled quite accurately "A Story Without a Plot." McKay merely presents his characters (types really), announces that Banjo wants to lead a pick-up band for the sheer joy of it and that Ray is collecting authentic stories for a book that he is someday to write, and then leads the reader through more-or-less unrelated episodes. There is no development; there is no real change. Banjo gets a band together, and for a brief time they play ragtime and blues—relentless and unrestrained. Having served its purpose—instant joy—the organized band falls apart, but the music is always just beneath the surface ready to explode through Banjo, who is himself an instrument. And Ray thinks and talks, every episode an illustration or an argument about the black man's essence and his predicament.

Again and again, the message: the human and vital black man is alien in the sterile, mechanized European civilization. There was no qualification, despite superficial national differences. Although Frenchmen allowed black men to fornicate with white women, they were just as racist as Englishmen or Americans. Indeed, given the simple black-white dualism, the United States was much to be preferred. It was better, after all, to confront avowed racists than to be lured into the self-deceptions that Senegalese and other French subjects entertained because their white oppressors allowed them black representation in French government. Appearances to the contrary, all black men who were under the heel of European civilization had their essential character—spontaneity, rhythm, exuberance —mauled by the calculated and impersonal machine.

There was no way that black men could get into that dreadful mechanism without destroying their integrity. Ray had seen countless people try. He had found educated blacks in every European city carrying, always, "heavy literature under their arms. They toted these books to protect themselves from being hailed everywhere as minstrel niggers, coons, funny monkeys for the European audience." They needed symbols to be believable, even to themselves, as part of civilized respectability. "Some of them wore hideous parliamentary clothes as close as ever to the pattern of the most correctly gray respectability." Some black students wore glasses "that made them sissy-eyed," because they thought glasses were a mark of scholarship. And all the while the self was lost in the mad rush for costume and appearance. Of course, Ray's problem was how he could be a writer—an intellectual with necessarily universal standards— and at the same time maintain his ethnic self.

Nor was the problem wholly racial. McKay also states the issue as a tension between the machine and organization against humanity. Symbolic of dehumanized civilization was the quest for money. This was easy enough to see with Americans, but in a chapter titled "Everybody Doing It," McKay's characters illustrate how all the Europeans are being made slaves to the machine through money. One of the white bums, who occasionally shares drinks with the black boys, points out that he, too, is being tricked by white people. Although they sympathize, Ray concludes that it is the white man's world, after all.

The reader is made acquainted—too often through tedious discussions—with the differences of black people, one from another, and the variations in treatment of blacks by whites. The reciprocated prejudices of West Indian and American Negro, the variety of racial attitudes among Afro-Americans constitute some of the discussion. But the delineation of the white menace is the real flesh of the novel. Generalizations about people and nationalities abound: Arabs are dirty; Chinese make good pimps (Banjo finds none, however, better than Harlem pimps). There is always the assumption of national character and type. Some of these generalizations are mere clichés of experience: a well-dressed white bum can get large "raises" out of Europeans because they are embarrassed by him; southern "crackers" are more generous to black American bums in foreign lands than anyone else. But the generalizing web that holds the novel together is the idea that black men, wherever they are from, share a common "soul," a common instinct.

Most frankly put, McKay's characters, consciously or not, have chosen to drop out of civilization. In a conventional view, they would be failures, social rejects. But these are not men who have tried to succeed at something, they have had no wish to achieve. They just are—living wholly in the present and perfectly unconscious of a desired alternative within society. The characters themselves, as well as their speeches, represent frontal attacks on European civilization. They are no longer simply primitive-exotics, but they foreshadow the radical alienation of the mid-twentieth century. Indeed, as the novel ends, Banjo, who has agreed with several of the others to sign on to a British ship for the West Indies, draws a customary month's pay in advance and invites Ray privately to join him in flight to some other port. Ray protests that Banjo had signed his name and taken an advance in pay, "You can't quit now."

> "Nix and a zero for what I kain't do. Go looket that book and you won't find mah real name no moh than anybody is gwine find this nigger when I take mahself away from here. . . . I know youse thinking it ain't right. But we kain't afford to

> choose, because we ain't born and growed up like the choos-
> ing people. All we can do is grab our chance every time it
> comes our way."

The naïve romance, the simple anarchy of pleasure-loving people has been transformed. The assumptions behind the creation
of the Scarlet Creeper have been hammered into an aggressive
social force—criticism through rejection and denial.

The attack was broad-based and often confused. European
civilization (McKay included America) was aggressive, materialistic, and dehumanizing. It was hypocritical, making great
pronouncements about liberty and, in America, equality of opportunity, but it would not tolerate real individualism, and its
racism denied to non-whites any real chance. It excluded
blacks while it crushed their souls. Yet it was messianic and totally compelling; it could conceive of no people who would not
be improved and delivered by its blessings. McKay, like other
western blacks, had struggled futilely with identity and history. He was greatly impressed by Africans whom he met in
Europe. Ray, in *Banjo,* sat in awe of the Senegalese and other
West Africans who spoke their own dialects, who told tales
that bespoke a folk tradition that was timeless. European civilization had deracinated many blacks from that source and,
thus, deprived them of personality.

It is fancied that black men, because they share a spiritual
unity, could resist the whites and come together. They might
see through the façade of white culture into the fleshless machine within. They might see the desperateness of their plight,
join together to find the essence that had been lost, and say an
everlasting nay to the myth of whiteness and the costumes that
disguised that spiritual fraud. It was dreamed about and, in
the novel, talked about—a kind of Pan-Africanism, perhaps.
Yet, McKay's fellow Jamaican, Marcus Garvey, is always mentioned with contempt as a kind of buffoon. And by the end of
Banjo, all the talk and the dreams have dissipated into thin

air. There is no future, except to drop out as Banjo asks Ray to do, to bum around endlessly.

Ray wants to escape, but his mind, his intellect that ties him to that which he despises, makes him hesitate. The novel ends, and the reader is left to wonder what Ray decides. Whatever his decision, his attitudes were clear. The Africans gave him a feeling "of wholesome contact with racial roots. They made him feel that he was not merely an unfortunate accident of birth, but that he belonged . . . to a race weighed, tested, and poised in the universal scheme." They gave him a past, if not a future. "Even though they stood bewildered before the imposing bigness of white things, apparently unaware of the invaluable worth of their own, they were naturally defended by the richness of their fundamental racial values." He had no such feeling about "Afroamericans who, long-deracinated, were still rootless among phantoms and pale shadows and enfeebled by self-effacement before condescending patronage, social negativism, and miscegenation." And the black intellectual in the United States was the most enfeebled, vainly trying to move into white neighborhoods and to have "'white neighbors think well of us.'" Only among the "working boys and girls of the country" did he find integrity: "that raw unconscious and the-devil-with-them pride in being Negro that was his own natural birthright. Down there [among workers] the ideal skin was brown skin. Boys and girls were proud of their brown, sealskin brown, teasing brown, tantalizing brown, high-brown, low-brown, velvet brown, chocolate brown." It was clear that Ray had no place with the Americans. But whatever his pleasure, Africa gave him no viable choice. So he intended to escape with Banjo.

Reading *Banjo* today, one cannot help but be struck by the contemporaneity of its argument. It might well be the work of a present-day black militant or nationalist—racialist, aggressive, rhetorical, and provocative. One thing, of course, has changed; Africa is no longer a generality, an abstraction. There are particular black nations struggling with technological revolution. One can no longer think of Africa as simply the home of black men. There are Kenya, Ghana, Nigeria, and so on. We now must think of particular Africans with real economic and political challenges. One wonders what difference that would make to Ray. Whatever his reaction, some of the black intellectuals who helped articulate African nationalism —Aime Cesaire, L. S. Senghor, Sembene Ousmane, Ousmane Soce—felt themselves inspired by Claude McKay's *Banjo*. They found in it the challenge to produce black art and literature that had its own integrity, independent of white European norms.[21]

Claude McKay had finished both *Home to Harlem* and *Banjo* while in France, having completed a European tour which had included a visit to the newly revolutionized Russia, where he had been very well received. But McKay was not taken in by the new order; that socialist state was merely another variety of European civilization. He dismissed the Russians along with the French, British, Germans, and Americans. None meant the black man any good; all corrupted his soul.

McKay returned to the United States, continuing to write essays, an autobiography, a novel: *Banana Bottom* (1933). In 1943 he became seriously ill. He joined the Roman Catholic Church before he died in 1948. Two essays on his conversion emphasize his complete alienation from American Negro intellectuals, indicating his intense bitterness toward the impotent black American. He had come, at last, to despair of remedy other than white benevolence. "I maintain," he said, "that since in the United States we are a most special type minority, amid a majority of whites, the real issue for us is Adjustment and not Segregation. For when we come down to brass tacks, the Negro minority must depend finally on the good-will of white

America. We, more than any other people in the New World, need a Good Neighbor Policy." [22]

Africa and primitivism were a *cul de sac* for McKay, as frustrating as all other avenues to the self had been. While in *Banana Bottom* his heroine Bita—a black Jamaican who had been patronized by whites and was European educated—triumphantly and romantically returned to the rustic simplicity of Jamaican peasant life, the West Indies could never recapture him. So he died in a land where he had always felt taunted and despised.

Not all of the Harlem writers shared McKay's compulsion for Africa and the distant, black soul-land. Langston Hughes had traveled to Africa. It was fascinating, it was tragic, it was a mystery to him:

> So long,
> So far away
> Is Africa

Hughes could never, however, imagine himself as other than American. One of his difficulties with his patroness was that he had refused to be a primitive. "She wanted me to be primitive and know and feel the intuitions of the primitive. But, unfortunately, I did not feel the rhythms of the primitive surging through me, and so I could not live and write as though I did. I was only an American Negro—who had loved the surface of Africa and the rhythms of Africa—but I was not Africa. I was Chicago and Kansas City and Broadway and Harlem." Rather than search abroad for the essence of Negro identity, Hughes's conviction of his Americanness made him use the materials of his native land.

While Jean Toomer's remarkable *Cane* (1923) was written early in the decade, it was—more than other contemporary novels by black authors—a conscious exploration of Negro identity. Toomer was an artful and imaginative writer who found in symbolism a means of breaching the narrow constraints of conventional language. The people in *Cane* are grotesques rather than characters, and, in this sense, echo Sherwood Anderson's *Winesburg, Ohio*, and Edgar Lee Masters' *Spoon River Anthology*, *Cane* combines mysticism—a lifelong source of Toomer's inspiration—with a variety of literary naturalism; not the "scientific" reportage of Zola, Norris, and Dreiser, but, rather, the protrayal of human continuity with organic nature as in Turgenev. Toomer differed in many ways from the other Harlem novelists: indeed, his artistic associations were really in Greenwich Village. But mainly he was self-consciously *avant garde;* no other Harlem writer was. Toomer experimented with structure. *Cane* was a series of vignettes and short stories which were organically integrated by symbols. Its style moved freely from prose to prose-poetry to verse. At least in form and style, it was, with E. E. Cummings' *The Enormous Room*, among the truly innovative American novels of the decade.

Unlike Anderson and Masters, Toomer was not content in discovering for the reader the underlying warp in character; he was after a deeper meaning and a positive statement. *Cane* is a forthright search for the roots of the Negro self: the son to know the father.

Song of the Son [23]

Pour O pour that parting soul in song,
O pour it in the sawdust glow of night,
Into the velvet pine-smoke air to-night,
And let the valley carry it along.
And let the valley carry it along.

O land and soil, red soil and sweet-gum tree,
So scant of grass, so profligate of pines,
Now just before an epoch's sun declines

Thy son, in time, I have returned to thee.
Thy son, I have in time returned to thee.

In time, for though the sun is setting on
A song-lit race of slaves, it has not set;
Though late, O soil, it is not too late yet
To catch thy plaintive soul, leaving, soon gone,
Leaving, to catch thy plaintive soul soon gone.

O Negro slaves, dark purple ripened plums,
Squeezed and bursting in the pine-wood air,
Passing, before they stripped the old tree bare
One plum was saved for me, one seed becomes
An everlasting song, a singing tree,
Caroling softly souls of slavery,
What they were, and what they are to me,
Caroling softly souls of slavery.

The narrator, the son, returns to Georgia to capture and save forever the essence of the past that is himself. The soil is the everlasting source; the dusk—inevitable like time—threatens to enclose forever in darkness the past and continuity; pine trees stand as monuments of that organic continuity; the inorganic saw-mill which devours the pine trees, converting them into sawdust, foretells the civilized, mechanistic, inhuman fate of the deracinated; the pine-smoke from the sawdust piles drifts like ghosts—like the soul-songs of slaves—through the valleys and into the air. These are the dominating symbols of *Cane.*

Part I of *Cane* is a series of portraits of women—significantly, women—each in some way incomplete and stultified. Women, like fallow earth, wanting planting and generation. They are each potentially the generators of life, but only potentially. Absent is that which will quicken them into fruit. This want of wholeness and fruition sets the tone of pathos which pervades their stories. Men, children, and families are one step removed, always just out of focus. Men do act upon them, but always in some distorted way that emphasizes their essential impotency and detachment, which leaves these women empty. Karintha, for instance, "the soul of her was a growing thing ripened too soon," was taken before her time by young men, aching for her beauty. She buried her fatherless child in a sawdust pile, prostituting herself to repay them for her defilement. Becky was a white woman who had two Negro sons. Whites and blacks, too horrified to acknowledge this species of natural generation (evidence of covert miscegenation was everywhere to be seen), built Becky a cabin and left her for dead until the chimney of her cabin collapsed and buried her, making their fantasy real. "Carma, in overalls, and strong as any man," was responsible for her husband's being on the chain gang. She had deceived him twice. He had accused her of having other men, and she had feigned suicide in the cane-brake. Hysterical, he formed a gang to help find her. It had been a trick; she was alive. "Twice deceived,—and one deception proved the other. His head went off." He slashed a man, and now he is in the chain gang. Esther, the daughter of the town's richest Negro, translated her sexual wishes into fantasy about a very black itinerant preacher, King Barlo. In her adolescence, the light-skinned Esther imagined herself the mother of his child—a virginal hysterical pregnancy. When, at last, she offered her body to him, King Barlo rebuffed her, and she retreated into frigidity. Louisa has a black and a white lover. The black man kills the white man and is, in turn, lynched. All these feminine lives are cramped and limited; sex for them is mere ritual—habitual and sterile.

The general statement of Part I is brought into sharp focus in the story of Fern, whom you would understand if "you have heard a Jewish cantor sing, if he has touched you and made your own sorrow seem trivial." It was her eyes that hinted at the story. They were strange eyes in that "they sought nothing —that is, nothing that was obvious and tangible and that one

could see, and they gave the impression that nothing was to be
denied. When a woman seeks, you will have observed, her
eyes deny." Fern's eyes sought for nothing that one could give
her, so there was no reason why they should withhold. Men
were deceived by what they saw in her eyes; they thought she
was easy and would give herself to them. "When she was
young, a few men took her, but got no joy from it." Rather,
they became attached to her to fulfill some "obligation which
they could find no name for." They searched and hungered to
find the thing that she desired, that would satisfy her. "Men
were everlastingly bringing her their bodies. Something inside
of her got tired of them, I guess, for I am certain that for the
life of her she could not tell why or how she began to turn
them off." There was nothing a man could give her, no matter
how much he wanted to. She desired nothing, or she desired
something so grand and so profound and so essential that it
was, in fact, nothing. "'Let's take a walk.' I at last ventured."
So they walked into the cane-brake, followed by the eyes of
knowing people. And they sat, and he held her in his arms
until he looked into her eyes and was carried away by emotion.

> She sprang up. Rushed some distance from me. Fell to her
> knees, and began swaying, swaying. Her body was tortured
> with something it could not let out. Like boiling sap it
> flooded arms and fingers till she shook them as if they burned
> her. It found her throat, and spattered inarticulately in plain-
> tive, convulsive sounds, mingled with calls to Christ Jesus.
> And then she sang, brokenly. A Jewish cantor singing with a
> broken voice. A child's voice, uncertain, or an old man's.
> Dusk hid her; I could hear only her song. It seemed to me as
> though she were pounding her head in anguish upon the
> ground. I rushed to her. She fainted in my arms.

And after all of that, nothing really happened. "Nothing ever
came to Fern, not even I." But she remains, the narrator tells
us. She is still on the Dixie Pike, like the rest of these women,

like the soil: fallow, fecund with the sour-sweet odor of unfertilized festering seed. "Her name, against the chance that you might happen down that way, is Fernie May Rosen." Like the soil, stripped of its pines, saw-mills hum and at dusk the pine-smoke from sawdust piles drifts down the valleys and away—into nothing.

Part II shifts to the city and marks a different kind of sterility. The threat to humanity here is in people's attachment to inorganic objects and property, in their enslavement to abstractions like civilization and its conventions, and in their alienation from the past which spawned them. Inanimate symbols command most of these stories; objects dominate people, forcing a kind of death. "Rhobert [sounds like robot] wears a house, like a monstrous diver's helmet, on his head." Property owns Rhobert, and like a diver he sinks under the weight of it. "Let's sing Deep River when he goes down." Social position and convention stultify in several ways. Avey's parents want her to be a school teacher, but she has other ideas. Like trees planted in boxes on V Street, Avey strains against artificial confinement; her body and her womanhood defy social limits. In "Theater," John is inhibited by his sense of propriety and social status from telling Doris—a chorus girl whom he thinks moves her body with greater spontaneity and abandon than the other girls—that he desires her. So his desires remain dreams. Ironically, Doris wants John because she sees in him security, a home, and children. They dream; nothing happens. For the soul-health of one's being, one had to be tapped into the organic past—the South, slavery—that is the point in "Box Seat." Dan Moore, a young black itinerant preacher, illustrates it. He was born in a canefield. "The hands of Jesus touched me." He is one of the "powerful underground races," from whom will rise the next coming. He describes a heavy Negro woman who sits beside him in the theater: "A soil-soaked fragrance comes from her. Through the cement floor her strong roots sink down . . . and disappear in blood-lines that waver south." And all is denied to those who deny themselves. In "Bona and Paul," Paul is a Negro student who is "passing." Love is frustrated between Paul and a white girl, Bona—both are southern—because what she wants in him is his Negroness, which he denies.

"Box Seat" is a central story. Dan Moore loves Muriel, a school teacher, in whom he sees a "still unconquered animalism." But Muriel is a creature of convention and is protected by her landlady, Mrs. Pribby, who is her super-ego. Muriel's instincts are to emasculate Dan Moore by making him conform by taking a regular job. But Dan, the preacher, sees what he thinks to be the remnant of her soul and wants to love her, to save her. Muriel avoids Dan and goes with a girl friend to a vaudeville theater where she sits in a box seat, removed from the crowd but visible to all. Such is her social pretension and her enslavement to convention; she denies to herself free and honest human contact, for she is controlled by society's view of her. After a brutal boxing match between two dwarfs for the "heavyweight championship," the victor of this "act" presents to Muriel a blood-spattered rose. Repulsed, she refuses, then considers, and finally she accepts. But she has recoiled from the dwarf, as she recoils from reality, from her people, from her past. The dwarf's eyes search hers: "Do not shrink. Do not be afraid of me." Dan, who has observed, sees in this her profound self-hatred. "JESUS WAS ONCE A LEPER!" Dan the preacher screams and rushes free of her.

The aching futility of the fecund that cannot bear, the empty sterile pointlessness of uprooted lives—tumbleweed drifting across asphalt streets—is brought into sharp focus in the final story, "Kabnis." Ralph Kabnis is a northern mulatto who has gone to teach in rural Georgia. He is a pathetic figure who cannot accept his past, who has an unreasonable fear of being lynched, who cannot accept the reality of slavery and his relationship to it, whose fear and self-hatred prevent him from experiencing the "pain and beauty of the South." Kabnis is Toomer's ultimate statement of the rasping, withering, dying sterility of Negro self-denial, "suspended a few feet above the soil whose touch would resurrect him." Halsey is a blacksmith who has become a part of the southern community. His craft, and his limited aspiration, give him a superficially trouble-free life. He is a good nigger in that he expects no more than the white South will let him have. Kabnis, drifting with no sense of self, turns in his dependency from Halsey to others who have for him the appearance of definite place and purpose. The story culminates in a surrealistic debauch in the cellar of the blacksmith shop, where Kabnis has thrown himself for emotional support onto prostitutes. But there in this underground, like the hold of a slave ship, sits Father John, a leathery old black man. Father John, a former slave, like slavery is a mute witness, emblematic of the Negro's true and real past. He is hidden from view and almost forgotten. Lewis, a youth, tries to relate to Father John, while Kabnis characteristically denies him and claims that his ancestors were southern blue-bloods. Father John's only statement is to charge the white man with the sin of slavery. It is clear that redemption is to be found through Father John. Carrie Kate, a child who takes care of him, and Lewis who acknowledges him, promise that the new generation may find roots and sustenance, vitality and manhood.

Toomer's answer to the quest for Negro identity, then, is to find one's roots in the homeland, the South, and to claim it as one's own. It is to look into the fullness of the past without shame or fear. To be, and to relive the slave and the peasant and never be separated from that reality. It is to know Father John, the black, gnarled, ugly, brutalized slave. To know and to accept slavery: the horror of it, the pain of it, the humiliation of it. To absorb it all, this living and dying past, as part of blood and breath. The Negro has to embrace the slave and the dwarf in himself. He, like a son, despite all, must learn to love his father—flesh of his flesh, blood of his blood—to be a man.

Of all of these efforts to define a Negro identity, Jean Toomer's seems the most profound and provocative. Attempts to find black models in convention and the Protestant Ethic were unsatisfactory because they had to ignore the reality of actual black people. They inferentially placed an onus on Negroes to conform to standards of behavior and "civilization" which were beyond the wisdom of normal life. They contained within themselves ready-made failure and necessary self-depreciation. But the reversal of conventional standards offered no better choice.

The Negro intellectual's fascination with primitivism was filled with ironies. Contrary to assertions of the soul-community of blacks, the American Negroes had to *learn* to appreciate the value of African art and culture. Too often they were taught by Europeans for whom Africa had a powerful, but limited, significance. When post-impressionist painters, sated with the tradition of the academies and despairing of fresh insights and statements, viewed African sculpture, they discovered a wind that would blow through the galleries, museums, and academies; it opened windows. It was liberating for these men who stood squarely on a tradition and who would never wholly abandon it. But when the black American intellectual got the news, he wanted to be able to identify completely with Africa, to find his tradition there. Now that was quite fanciful. Consider, too, the Negro Aaron Douglas learning techniques of African art from the Bavarian Winold Reiss. While Douglas used the techniques he learned in this association, African art had little lasting influence.

No less ironic is the stimulating effect that American "primitives" had on Africans. If we are to believe the testimony of African intellectuals like President Leopold Senghor of Senegal, Harlem writers (particularly Claude McKay in *Banjo*) gave them a sense of direction. They looked to Americans for cultural leadership at the same time that Americans like McKay were searching abroad. What the African intellectuals got from books like *Banjo* was the injunction to assert ethnic integrity. This was not a unique message in that age of self-determination and proliferating nations. It was special, however, in that it rejected the natural supremacy of European civilization and championed the superior humanity of African culture. This message could mean far less to American Negroes than it could to Africans, because the Senegalese, the Ibos, the Ashanti, though colonials, had some cultural integrity and a tradition from which to work. That was precisely what Americans were looking for; lacking it, they were thrust back upon themselves.[24] The white expatriates of the 1920s had a remarkably similar experience in Europe. For as they explored Europe for meaningful culture, European intellectuals were turning to America.[25]

The primitivism of Countee Cullen and Claude McKay was very romantic and rested on very superficial knowledge of African life. Cullen's "Heritage," with rain beating incessant rhythms on his "body's street," is only slightly more intelligent than Vachel Lindsay's "Congo." Whatever McKay's fantasy was, African tribal life is in reality very formal and obligatory to its members. Jake or Banjo could not survive, fornicating at their pleasure and serving no social function. McKay's personal irony is that in the last years of his life, his mind and body deteriorating from disease, he threw himself on the most traditional institution of his despised European civilization, the Roman Catholic Church.[26]

For the purpose of ethnic identity, primitivism is peculiarly limited. It is especially a male fantasy. It is easier to imagine men as roustabouts, vagabonds, bums, and heroes, harder to draw sympathetic females whose whole existence is their bodies and instinct. It is also difficult to create the illusion of development and generation; there are no children anywhere in these works. Perhaps women, whose freedom has natural limitations—they have babies—are essentially conservative. In the last paragraph of the novel, Banjo answers Ray, who breathed regret that Banjo's woman could not be taken along. "Don't get soft ovah any one wimmens, pardner. Tha's you' big weakness. A woman is a conjunction. Gawd fixed her different from us in moh ways than one. And theah's things we can git away with all the time and she just kain't." It was a difference that was hard to deal with. McKay could imagine his English-educated Bita willfully committing herself to Jamaican peasant life (he could not). Nella Larsen, on the other hand, a professional nurse as well as a woman, could not shake off the reality of the often-too-slow death by continuous child-bearing of peasant women. Without women, and without children, there could be no race or race consciousness.

The real power of Jean Toomer's conception and its superiority to the romanticisms of McKay and Cullen was that *Cane*, though symbolic and mystical, dealt with the past as a palpable reality. It faced the fact of the South and slavery. The final, and perhaps supreme, irony of the primitives was that they were, in their quest for Africa, in their fancy of Timbuctoo and Alexandria, forsaking their actual past. They were in effect denying that which was immediate, personal, and discernible for something which was vague, distant, half-myth. Toomer asked to embrace the slave father, while Countee Cullen fancied "spicy grove and cinnamon tree." For all of its search for ancestral roots, the quest for Africa denied the soil in which the particular plant had sprouted. It is a supreme irony because it is so characteristically American. Black Americans, like white Americans, dissatisfied with and unfulfilled by the selves that they had, sought escape in exotica.

5 🎨 Art:
The Ethnic Province

The depression brought an abrupt end to the vogue of Harlem. Hard times made people concentrate on the immediate, the mundane, the essentials of living, rather than on cultural concerns. The end of prohibition deprived Harlem of some of its exclusive appeal: nightlife, cabarets, illicit amusements. That could be had anywhere if one had the purse and spirit. The demise of the vogue of the Negro also ended that promoted culture called the "Harlem Renaissance." Self-conscious culture had to struggle for relevancy at a time when physical survival was a notable achievement. The industrial apparatus, the capitalistic system, the white man's machine, however much despised, had never been doubted as the agent of automatic progress—the promise of American life. Economic collapse was, thus, far more shocking than could have been imagined. The intellectual dispossessed—white or black—could not avoid the mixed feelings of horror and glee that the monster was fallible after all. But the shock destroyed the easy optimism that had been assumed even among social critics. The naïveté that nurtured the belief that black poets and writers, painters and sculptors, would emerge from the pages of *Crisis* and *Opportunity* or from the Harmon Foundation competitions as the new and genuine American culture seemed pathetically innocent as bread lines lengthened. It appeared that the Harlem Renaissance had been a false labor. Of course, Negro artists and writers continued under different sponsorship and promotion—sometimes by the W.P.A. and sometimes the Communist party.

In the year of Franklin Roosevelt's first presidential victory, 1932, Wallace Thurman published his second novel, *Infants of the Spring*. Thurman had been one of those most deeply committed to the birth of culture in Harlem. A very dark man, whose nervous and apparently cynical laughter only imperfectly disguised deep inner tensions and anxiety, Thurman had published one novel (*The Blacker the Berry*, 1928, about a very black girl's struggle with color prejudice among Negroes) and two plays. He had worked as business manager for *Messenger*, had read for Macaulay's (Langston Hughes guessed he was the only Negro reader for a large publishing firm), had ghosted for *True Story* and well-known white writers, and had almost single-handedly produced *Fire*. *Infants of the Spring*, which was to be his last and most important work, was really an obituary of the Harlem Renaissance.

That novel's Euphoria Blake, an energetic woman with a sense of purpose and uplift, came from the South charged with the compelling duty to do something for her race. She moved from one disillusionment to another—the Negro leadership, the Communist party, etc.—but all the while she had converted her great drive to make money through business success. She had become convinced that the race's real future and salvation lay in art; whenever she might find time from her business, she too would become a writer. In the meantime, however, she turned her rooming house over to a group of Negro artists. Raymond Taylor, the novel's protagonist, a writer, is a resident of what he calls Niggeratti Manor. The other lodgers are Eustace Savoy, "actor, singer, and what have you"; Pelham Gaylord, a very infantile semi-literate who has illusions of becoming an artist and poet; Paul Arbian, a decadent who was very talented; an actress lady with daughter; and the "Pig Woman," a non-artist and permanent fixture in the house (a kind of Caliban in the world of ideals). Other characters—white and black—drift in and out of Niggeratti Manor, its parties and orgies.

Eustace wants to sing Schubert but is denied the chance, because white people, he thinks, want Negroes to sing only spirituals. Refusing, he remains unemployed. But he is strangely content, wandering in his rooms filled with cloisonné bric-a-brac, resolutely singing Schubert. But Eustace Savoy is persuaded to take a chance at an audition singing spirituals. It would be a way to begin; later he could do as he pleased. Once convinced, he eagerly enters the project, learning the soul-songs. He proves, however, not good enough even at what he considered an inferior art; this failure destroys his only illusion.

Pelham Gaylord is pathetic. He traces illustrations out of magazines and writes childish love poems to the actress lady's adolescent daughter. That is his art. Sadly, Pelham takes his maukish sentimentality seriously, and this sexual innocent is seduced by the rather experienced little girl. For his pains, he is convicted of statutory rape largely to gratify the mother's desire to play a courtroom scene and the Pig Woman's compulsion to be the voice of God.

So there is not much art to speak of in Niggeratti Manor. There is a great deal of pretense and innocence of the hard work and talent that good art requires. Paul Arbian's brilliance gives him facility in several arts. But he is a sensualist and given to experiments with sex, drugs, and the exotic. Through it all, Raymond Taylor attempts to find solid ground, in terms

of the Harlem Renaissance, for his own artistic integrity. He
wonders through the maze: the Negro as artist or advocate, the
writer as individual or race man, art as self-expression or expo-
sition of ethnic culture. Explicit or not, these were the problems of Afro-American artists then and now. Wallace Thurman, more than any other writer of the period, tried to address
himself to these issues.

Coming at the end of an episode in Harlem culture, *Infants
of the Spring* was intended to be a critical evaluation—a
roman à clef—of the Harlem Renaissance. At one point in the
novel, Raymond Taylor hosts a gathering of Harlem literati;
their names are thin disguises. Dr. Parkes (Alain Locke)
wanted a permanent salon (Taylor's party might initiate it)
where black intellectuals and artists could share ideas and
stimulate one another. The group—Sweetie May Carr (Zora
Neal Hurston), Tony Crews (Langston Hughes), DeWitt Clinton (Countee Cullen), Dr. Manfred Trout (Rudolph Fisher),
Cedric Williams (Eric Walrond), Carl Denny (Aaron Douglas)
—will meet only this one time, however, for their attempt to
share ideas explodes into a fight.

Dr. Parkes wants to discuss the primacy of beauty over
truth: art should come before propaganda; the Negro should
devote his energies to producing art rather than arguing about
race relations. He also despairs of the post-Victorian decadence that he detects in Negro as well as white writing. The
Negro artist must avoid the "post-Victorian license" at all
costs. " 'You have too much at stake. You must have ideals. You
should become . . . well, let me suggest your going back to
your racial roots, and cultivating a healthy paganism based on
African traditions.' " DeWitt Clinton agrees with Dr. Parkes,
but he insists that the " 'young Negro artist must go back to his
pagan heritage for inspiration and to the old masters for
form.' " This encourages Raymond to imagine Harlem's "poet
laureate" in his creative hours—"eyes on a page of Keats, fin-

gers on typewriter, mind frantically conjuring African scenes.
And there would of course be a Bible nearby." But the discussion disintegrates rapidly. Paul Arbian claims that it is impossible (and unrealistic) to find his African roots when his African blood is mixed with German, French, and other blood.
The West Indian, Cedric Williams, argues against any stan-
dardized art. Then he claims that American Negroes are too
diluted culturally to find any link with Africa. Unlike West Indians, he says, " 'I have yet to see an intelligent or middle class
American Negro laugh and sing and dance spontaneously.
That's an illusion, a pretty sentimental fiction.' " Anyway, the
spirituals are " 'mediocre folk songs, ignorantly culled from
Methodist hymn books.' " And white men are as good at singing and dancing as the American Negroes. At this, everyone
begins to scream, while the inarticulate and stammering Carl
Denny tries to express some new insight he has into the nature
of art.

The dispute clearly illustrates Thurman's own despair at the
idea of artificially imposed norms for art—Dr. Parkes's curious
mixture of Platonic idealism and paganism, or DuBois's theory
of uplift by the talented tenth, or any compelled obligation for
ethnic art all share the same fault. The writer, painter, poet,
sculptor, musician is in the final analysis a single sensibility attempting to master a craft with personal insight. It is the
height of folly to believe that you can cultivate Negro art in a
hot-house. The fate of Niggeratti Manor is Thurman's statement of that ultimate futility.

After several disappointments and some notoriety from wild
parties and Pelham's trial, Euphoria Blake has a change of
heart. She does not want to run a "miscegenated bawdy
house." Slanderous gossip gives the house that fame, but as a
business woman she cannot afford a bad reputation. " 'I must
make money. That's all a Negro can do. Money means freedom. There's nothing to this art stuff. I've given up the idea of

writing stories. I only want to make money.' " So Euphoria unwittingly points her finger at the artistic limits of the promotional personality. It must have results, success. But she has
not totally lost her idealism and her will to do good. Euphoria
intends to convert the house into a dormitory for Negro working girls between the ages of eighteen and thirty. " 'It is something that has long been needed, a very serious enterprise.
Where is there a place that's decent for young girls, bachelor
women rather, to stay?" The vogue had past as easily as that.
Convert from culture-making to money-making, from artists'
"digs" to bachelor women's dormitory. But Raymond Taylor
knew, as Wallace Thurman knew, the deeply troubling problems of Negro art had never really been touched. They had
been there all along—noticed but unresolved—and the Negro
with artistic pretensions would, each one in his turn, have to
face them and solve them.

Whatever the difficulties of art for the white man, the American Negro has his special burdens. The Harlem art of the
1920s shows the strains that he lived under. The Negro artist in
the United States lives in a peculiar province—a spiritual geography. His art is self-consciously national while, at the same
time, special—ethnically regional. It attempts to speak with
two voices, one from the stage of national culture and the
other from the soul of ethnic experience. Nor is this condition
wholly a matter of the artist's will or intent. It is his ethnic
fact. It is as if it were defined in the eternal constitution of
things that to be a Negro artist in America one must, in some
way, be a race-conscious artist.

In the first decades of the twentieth century especially, the
phenomenon of Negro art was forced to signify far more than
poetry, art, and fiction are ordinarily obliged to do. This was
partly due to the conventional view of the role of art and culture, and partly to the Negro's slave past. It was assumed by

the "Custodians of Culture," to use Henry May's phrase, that the translation of human ideals into verse, drama, or novel was really the highest human achievement; thus it was emblematic of civilization. It is an understandable anamoly that the United States—that epitome of materialism and utilitarianism—should in its art be Platonic and value idealism and inutility. Conservative critics, men like Stuart Pratt Sherman, Paul Elmer More, and Irving Babbitt who presumed to speak for the cultural establishment, knew that it was not the mason or industrialist, the carpenter or financier, who was the measure of society's excellence. Rather, society's ultimate man was he who could produce that which had its value in idea—in abstraction —thereby elevating human experience. And since that art which illuminated pure beauty and morality was almost wholly free of practical use, was most universal and uplifting, it was the finest mark of civilized man.

Negro art, in such an environment, bore the special weight of proving racial civility. Most people, black and white, conceptualized Negro history as the story of a progressive climb from slavery to freedom. At issue, always, was whether the Negro had achieved, since emancipation, the level of civilization of other Americans. Thus, it was merely conventional wisdom that James Weldon Johnson echoed when he prescribed as the best remedy for racial prejudice the "demonstration of intellectual parity by the Negro through the production of literature and art." That Paul Laurence Dunbar had written poems and novels, that Charles W. Chestnutt had written novels, that the expatriate Henry Tanner was an important painter in Paris, and that Meta Warrick Fuller was one of Auguste Rodin's promising students were precious milestones in that imagined trek which would end when Negroes were rightfully placed in the pantheon of American civilization. Whatever the art was, its existence was its significance. Each such evidence of refinement and culture was another argument against bigotry, was proof of black humanity. Surely, W. E. B. DuBois believed that, as he defended the art of beauty against modern decadence. The *Crisis* and *Opportunity* magazines supported this idea in their promotions of Negro artists. Some writers, like Countee Cullen, never ignored this special calling.

This attitude produced a racial rather than a regional provincialism. But saying that, one wonders at the difference. For Henry James's surprise that Nathaniel Hawthorne (with all his faults) could have flourished in New England's thin soil is akin to Witter Bynner's, Lyman Kittredge's, and W. E. B. DuBois's pleasure that Countee Cullen's lyrical and classical artistry came from a Negro. There was a general American artistic provincialism that caused the celebration of James Whitcomb Riley, whose poetry is remarkable more for the fact that it came from Indiana than that it was good verse. Indeed, Riley and Dunbar nicely illustrate the racial-regional parallel. Probably, Dunbar had higher aspirations than Riley. It was the sorrow of his life that he could find no critical appreciation for his verse in literary English; Negro dialect was commercial. It is no small irony that Dunbar had to learn the techniques of dialect verse from Riley. So both men achieved their fame and defined their art in a versified "local-color realism." Critics, editors, and publishers were more to blame than the writers. Henry James was quick to say that it takes a lot of history to make a literature, and he might have added that one needs to be fairly steeped in literary tradition to make courageous critical judgments. American critics, intimidated as they were by the English tradition, would find it easier to encourage Negro, Hoosier, western, southern, Creole, and Yankee voices—which would not be taken seriously as good art—than to question the essentially European basis of their values.

Here, too, music was an exception. The practitioners of the newly developing jazz found artistic standards within the art itself, rather than in academic edict. Men like Louis Armstrong, Bubber Miley, Jelly Roll Morton, Fletcher Henderson, Don Redman, and so on were too engaged in essential artistic definition to think much about civilization. And their art came from their own ethnic context. Everywhere they looked they found white men mimicking them, trying to master their blue notes, their slurs, their swing, their darting arpeggios, their artistic concept. It was as if black jazzmen, from the very beginning, sensed that they were creating an art, and the whole world would have to find them the reference point for critical judgment. Unlike Alain Locke, few black jazzmen of the 1920s would have found more than indifferent satisfaction in the knowledge that Milhaud, Stravinsky, and Ravel used jazz in their European music. Although some highly schooled black musicians, like the pianists James P. Johnson and Fats Waller, were frustrated in their desire to compose and play "serious" music, they were drawn into the vortex of this powerful new art in which they had a distinctive voice.

Significantly, while those men who promoted the New Negro and the Harlem Renaissance would give credit to jazz and the dance, it was often because they evidenced qualities in the Negro character that might be converted into something important. Jazz was definitely not the "high art" that James Weldon Johnson and Alain Locke were hoping for. Thus, these literary men were encumbered by a self-consciousness that crippled art. They were provincials within a provincial America. But whatever their white contemporaries might do, black artists could not be content with such condescension. Bret Harte and Thomas Hart Benton might happily commercialize the West, Hamlin Garland might not ask more than to be the plaintive voice of the Middle Border, but a Negro artist had more than his region to think about. He was also a race, an issue. He had to be more than a curiosity. Between the aspiration and the achievement, however, fell the frustrating and doubt-ridden effort.

The burden of race was heavy. It was the weight of doubt —societal doubt that one saw in white men's eyes and the self-doubt it kindled. As the twentieth century opened, even the Negro's best white friends might well have wondered how a people almost fifty years out of slavery could produce an art which would speak to all men, everywhere; after all, they were not convinced that white Americans could. It had taken, they would say, centuries for Europeans to distil their experience into the purity of a fine poem. Beyond the ominous doubt which worries all works of imagination and craft, the Negro had to overcome another doubt too—that imposed by history and race. The black artist had to convince himself that he had something to say worth saying, and that he had the skill to say it; then he had to defy the white eyes which were too often his eyes as well. All so that he could end with a work of art. Then the world might say, "hats off! Hats off to you, black man, for the courage of your journey. Hats off to you, black people, that, against all odds, you have achieved beauty."

Such doubt, however, takes a heavy toll from the traveler. For what is art and beauty, after all, except what other men have applauded? And' the world will only salute you, one thinks, when those who make judgments and pronouncements discover you. The more profound one's doubt, the more his work is likely to be recognizable echoes or reflections of past greats. This explains why Phyllis Wheatley's voice was that of a feeble Alexander Pope rather than that of an African singer, why Henry Tanner's art was of the French Academy and Meta Fuller's a derivative of Rodin's rather than part of the new wave of impressionism and post-impressionism that was swelling all around them in Europe. Such deep doubt makes conservatives and, sometimes, mimics. What a cruel paradox that such a troubled traveler's labor should at best celebrate the past, the already acclaimed. Dead men!

The Negro writer also had a problem defining himself as an

artist. Was he something special because of race? Did he have
a primary commitment to his ethnic group, or was he a free
agent? Academic questions, perhaps. But they expose practical
and theoretical questions that have perplexed black writers.
And the answers have not been exclusively theirs to give.
Charles W. Chestnutt wrote about Negro characters and, except for *Sport of the Gods,* Paul Lawrence Dunbar used white
subjects. But neither author was free to depart from conventional attitudes toward color. Their mulattoes followed formula
and were as tragic as any. But did they have any choice other
than to reiterate the message so often expressed in American
ficiton, that the true American tragedy was to be less than pure
white? Chestnutt's editor at Houghton Mifflin still hesitated to
make public the author's race. Some writers, like Wallace
Thurman and Rudolph Fisher, ghosted stories about whites.
But it only served to intensify Thurman's already ample sense
of guilt. It was something akin to "passing" for a Negro author
to disguise his race in the choice of white subjects. The com-
pulsions of racial loyalty were too real; the goad was internal.[1]
White writers have always been thought able to move back
and forth across the color-line without sacrificing loyalty or detachment. It was as if white were a neutral color. The psychology of blackness has made it hard to entertain such an illusion.

There is no quarrel that great literature is generated by
ethos. Immigrants in the United States, as well as blacks, found
their special condition a natural source of literature. Immigrants, however, seemed to feel more free than blacks to write
about themselves. Judging by Mary Antin, Abraham Cahan,[2]
and Michael Gold, they could believe that the process of their
Americanization was really the American story. Blacks, on the
other hand, were plagued by a sense of being anamolous. The
artistic question remained whether a work of art was a window opening onto an ethnic province—peculiar and curious—
or whether through it the viewer could be drawn into a geog-

raphy of his own humanity, regardless of ethos. Recent writers —Bellow, Ellison, Malamud, Tolson—exemplify the possibilities. Through their works, the reader is taken through the "province" into the world at large. Also, art as craft defies parochialism. For there is pure pleasure in the discovery of a brilliant artistic conception, well constructed so that it holds together and works. Melvin Tolson's *Harlem Gallery* gives us such delight, independent of its ethnic center. The jazzmen of the 1920s seemed to understand all of this perfectly well. But for the contemporary black writer to do the same, he would have to lose the self-consciousness that made him a black man who wrote poems and novels (the same could be said for the Hoosier, the Yankee, the Jew, the southerner, the woman, or what have you). One had to lose that self-consciousness, or, rather, transform it into the very instrument that could slice through the boundaries that defined it.

Negro experience in the United States has been inseparably tied to issues of social reform, so one would naturally expect a Negro art with a message. This, too, was a problem for the Harlem writers: how could a black man write about his deepest inner feelings artistically rather than sociologically? Carl Van Vechten had been anxious to warn Negro writers against trying to use literature as a means of arguing social issues. He sensed, quite accurately, the reading public's disdain for overt discussions of race in novels and poems. Since before World War I, there had been much discussion of the proper role of art, and though the argument had often been heated there was much agreement. The old guard wanted to see literature that was uplifting and pointed to some moral center, while the younger and more rebellious leaned toward an art-for-art's-sake position which would be unburdened of judgment external to itself. Neither of these conceptions could be comfortable with what the war had taught men to call "propaganda." Nearly everyone would have joined Alain Locke in condemning that already contemptible word. In "Art or Propaganda?" [3] Locke insisted that the Negro had too many prophets and preachers. "My chief objection to propaganda . . . is that it perpetuates the position of group inferiority. For it . . . speaks under the shadow of a dominant majority whom it harrangues, cajoles, threatens or supplicates." Art, on the other hand, "is rooted in self-expression and . . . is self-contained." It was with the inward and personal creation that "David" could confront the "Philistines." "The sense of inferiority must be innerly compensated, self-conviction must supplant self-justification and in the dignity of this attitude a convinced minority must confront a condescending majority." A minority's conviction and self-esteem, he felt, would come from its art, which distilled and illuminated its beauty. For Locke, beauty was to be in the front rank. "After Beauty, let Truth come into the Renaissance picture."

Locke's position may well be taken for the view of those— white and black—who wished to promote Negro art in the 1920s. It was no simple thing, however, to follow this neo-Platonic ideal, to deal with oppression so indirectly, to let the abstraction stand for the concrete experience. The disillusioned public of a new period, the depression decade, would welcome a social realism in art that would relieve the Negro artist of a perplexity which demanded that his self-expression avoid his deepest racial experience.

In the same article, Locke unwittingly glossed over another profound problem of the Negro artist. "In our [Negroes'] spiritual growth," he wrote, "genius and talent must more and more choose the role of group expression, or even at times the role of free individualistic expression. . . ." This rather casual juggling of the group and the self ignored a fundamental dilemma of creative work. Here, as in all of his comment about the Harlem Renaissance, Locke was quick to define normative models for Negro art, justifying Wallace Thurman's characterization of him as Dr. Parkes. Nevertheless, he was equally agile in claiming that art was a deeply individual and personal expression. Beginning in the core of the self, but knowing one's necessary debt to history, to condition, and to group, one can indulge his private voice. If one's most honest statement does not appear to contribute to "our spiritual growth," does some group loyalty argue for a higher honesty? Indeed, at what point in the artist's subservience to the race, and similar non-personal abstractions, does his statement cease being individual and become propaganda? If one begins with the highly idealized view of art that Alain Locke shared with many of his contemporaries, he must wrestle with the definition of a Negro artist; what stress should be placed on the adjective and what on the noun? Irish literature attests that this is not a peculiarly American or Negro problem.

Like Irish writers, the Negro artists had to resolve the question of whether there was a special Negro voice and art. Langston Hughes was convinced that beneath the artifice of middle-class Negro life there was an authentic and pure voice which the black artist would do well to interpret. It was this special well-spring of culture that should feed the Negro genius. Hughes argued against the notion that all things white were good and that the Negro should emulate white art and taste.[4] "One of the most promising . . . Negro poets said to me once, 'I want to write like a white poet'; meaning behind that, 'I would like to be white.'" Hughes's breathtaking logic exposes the quite treacherous path of race loyalty that the black artist had to traverse. Because Hughes had a mind that tended to simplify—to reduce or ignore complication—it was a fairly easy matter for him. For poets like Claude McKay or Countee Cullen, or a novelist like Wallace Thurman, the racial mountain was far more threatening.

As Hughes saw it, part of the problem of Negro art was the

attitude of the black middle and upper classes. Of course, any
art needs an audience, and it is in the nature of things that
paintings, poems, and stories are sustained by the patronage of
those with money and leisure. Regrettably, affluent blacks
tended to identify with white culture. "In the North," Hughes
wrote, "they go to white theaters and white movies . . .
[adopt] Nordic manners, Nordic faces, Nordic hair, Nordic art
(if any), and an Episcopal heaven." There was no source of art
in such artifice.

By romanticising the lower classes, Hughes claimed to find
the stuff from which art was made. The "low-down folks" who
"do not particularly care whether they are like white folks or
anybody else. Their joy runs, bang! into ecstasy. Their religion
soars to a shout. Work maybe a little today, rest a little tomor-
row. Play awhile. Sing awhile. . . . These common people are
not afraid of spirituals . . . and jazz is their child. They furnish
a wealth of colorful, distinctive material for any artist because
they still hold their own ividividuality in the face of American
standardizations." Hughes expected that the truly great Negro
artist would be produced by these people; he would not be a
son of black, race-denying privileged class. The lower classes
would produce art because "they accept what beauty is their
own without question." Hughes insisted that there was enough
material for the Negro artist without his going outside the race.
And "in spite of the Nordicized Negro intelligentsia and the
desires of some white editors, we have an honest American
Negro literature already with us."

Hughes's article was a solicited answer to George S. Schuyler's "Negro-Art Hokum," which appeared in an earlier number
of the *Nation*.[5] Schuyler also tended to view things in simple
absolutes. For him, an artist can only use the equipment fur-
nished him by education and environment. "Consequently, his
creation will be French, British, German. . . . The work of an

artist raised and educated in this country must necessarily be American"; he did not say what that was. Schuyler was too cynical to be taken in by lower-class romanticism. "It is the Aframerican masses," he claimed, "who consume hair-straightener and skin-whitener. . . ." He could find very little sense of race beauty in that. Many years later, in an interview for the *Columbia Oral History,* Schuyler reaffirmed that view, and he went on to report that "this idea of a special and separate Negro art and literature was very current in those days, and a lot of people were profiting from it. In other words, they were making it a sort of a racket, and I felt that this was unscientific and unsound."

Beyond what Schuyler's cynicism exposed, another problem with Hughes's conception was that his beautiful people would hardly sustain an artist, nor would they provide a critical exchange that would help define and refine the art. Thus, the folk artist was especially on his own. He was forced to create his own audience and to generate almost wholly from within himself the critical terms on which his art would rest. Like it or not, Hughes would have to admit judgment from outside his folk base. If one wanted to be acclaimed an artist, he could not depend on a particular ethnic province. Countee Cullen, thus, aspired to be "a poet, not a Negro poet."

By the end of his life, Countee Cullen had acquired all of the marks of a poet. He had published five books of original poetry, not including *On These I Stand* (1947), which collects his already published work. In addition, Cullen had edited a book of Negro verse, written a novel and two books about his cat, and collaborated on two theatrical works. He had won prizes: the Witter Bynner award for the best poetry by a college undergraduate, the *Opportunity* magazine contests, the Harmon Foundation competition, and a Guggenheim Fellowship. From the writing of his earliest verse, in high school, to the end of his life, he had always received favorable critical comment, pointing to him as exemplary of one whose art had transcended race.

This kind of judgment was especially pleasing to Cullen, because he believed that art—especially poetry—should transcend the mundane, the ordinary; be elevating. His view of art was quite conventional—indeed conservative—in the postwar years. He believed poetry should deal with higher emotions and ideals; it should avoid sensuality—its language more pure than ordinary speech, more elevated than prose. While this convention had been under attack in the United States since before the war—many of Cullen's white contemporaries had long since thrown over their obedience to it, and were experimenting not only with form but with poetry's proper subject and common diction—Cullen, himself, held quite tenaciously to the genteel tradition.

This conservative idealism was educated into the poet. In high school and college, Cullen took the traditional path to the art of poetry: languages, classics, English literature. He helped to edit as well as contributed poetry to the DeWitt Clinton High School literary magazine, *The Magpie*. While an undergraduate at New York University, Cullen published in several literary magazines, including *Bookman* and *Poetry*, and in his senior year Harper contracted to publish his first book of poems, *Color* (1925). His acclaim in his college years was for poems which varied in subject if not style: "Simon the Cyrenian Speaks" as well as appreciations of John Keats. His "Ballad of the Brown Girl" won the Witter Bynner award and was considered by Harvard's Lyman Kittredge to be the finest literary ballad by an American he had read. So Countee Cullen was already published and praised (a Phi Beta Kappa graduate) when he went to take his Master's degree at Harvard. He found Robert Hillyer's seminar in versification just to his liking. Hillyer had asked for exercises in various traditional forms of English verse; that poet-professor later was to publish one of Cullen's exercises as a rare American example of the Chaucerian rime royal. Cullen was forever committed to the formalism that this education implies. His biographer attributes to him the assertion that his poetry just "came out" in metered lines and rhyme. In any case, he never experimented with anything else, and that is quite remarkable considering what other poets were doing in the 1920s.

Formalism was not the only mark of Cullen's conservatism. He understood Art to be a slave to Beauty (he would capitalize those nouns). Poetry more than prose was the pure essence of the literary art; as essential beauty it should allow the human imagination to soar, to live with the gods. He was encouraged in this by the influence of Alain Locke, and by W. E. B. DuBois, whose views on art and uplift would vie with any other New England Yankee's for gentility and conservatism. Furthermore, Countee Cullen had tied himself spiritually to the Romantics, particularly John Keats, who continued to serve as models for his verse as well as inspirations for his vision. He cultivated in himself that emotional temperament that expected to find poems in graveyards and palm-pressed palpitations on hillsides, and which saw the body and human condition as inconvenient harness to the spirit; the muse, genius, the imagination, and art transformed man into a kind of immortal, into a kind of god. He visited Keats's grave in Rome and read the epitaph that Keats had chosen for himself: "Here lies one whose name was writ in water." Later Cullen wrote his own.

For John Keats, Apostle of Beauty [6]

> Not writ in water, nor in mist,
>> Sweet lyric throat, thy name;
> Thy singing lips that cold death kissed
>> Have seared his own with flame.

One could hardly find a more perfect example of a twentieth-century poet marching to a nineteenth-century drummer: the subject, the title, the diction, the stiff period of the first two lines, the conceit of the poet, the "lyric throat" and the kiss of "cold death." Like most of Cullen's poetry, this epitaph leaves the reader with little doubt about what it is. It looks like a poem, it sounds like a poem, and it is about what poems are supposed to be about.

With all of his sense of idealized art, Countee Cullen was, nevertheless, very conscious of the obligation that race placed on him as a poet. Given his view of the art of poetry, his race consciousness was quite a dilemma. The problems of Negroes were real, too real. They were a part of this world, the mud, guts, and stuff of life. Lynchings, murder, discrimination, poverty inevitably would be the subjects of Negro life. Yet how could this be translated into verse that would be elevating and truly poetic? Furthermore, Cullen believed that the art of poetry, like all art and true culture, was abstracted from race or any other condition of life. It was Cullen who told Langston Hughes that he wanted to be a poet, not a Negro poet. For him, there was no such thing as Negro poetry. How, then, could he remain true to his sense of art and, at the same time, to his strong racial feelings? His conservative critical judgment told him that he must write poems that were at least once removed from the source of his strongest emotions. No wonder that he thought God had done a curious thing: "To make a poet black and bid him sing."

Cullen also was never free from his sense of being exemplary. Like so many Negroes whose achievement catapults them into the public eye, he was a public Negro. He was not merely a poet, he was a "credit to his race." No matter how much he achieved or how little it depended on race, it was inevitable that his blackness would mark him. Of the ten initiates into New York University's Phi Beta Kappa chapter, it was Countee

Cullen who was singled out for extensive press coverage—an example of Negro achievement. While he consciously wrote to ensure his acceptance as a good American poet, and while critics often remarked that his true achievement was as a poet and not as a Negro poet, he never could avoid being defined by race. *The New York Times* of January 10, 1946, amplified the irony with its headline: "Countee Cullen, Negro Poet, Dead." Nor can one say that the poet would have really wanted it otherwise. Langston Hughes's simplistic logic did not recognize that the motive to write like a poet (a white poet) could be indeed quite the opposite from wanting to be white. Cullen wanted to be acknowledged as a poet so that he would not be condescended to as a Negro, so that he could be an example of Negro potential, successfully competing on the white man's ground. As an exemplar, he could point the way to others, he could be a symbol of possibility, and he could turn other black boys' eyes to poetry and art so that the muse might allow them to transcend their condition as he had. Such a conception was problematic, yet Cullen was sustained by important Negroes —Booker T. Washington, W. E. B. DuBois, James Weldon Johnson—in this view of racial uplift through culture, achievement, and example.

In writing love poems it was easy enough for Cullen to handle the problem of race and art. In his art, love, like spring, was color-blind, and for the most part those poems could be addressed to a lady of any hue. Cullen sometimes wrote poems about brown girls and brown boys, but for the most part the color was only in the title; the poems themselves were characteristically devoid of concreteness and specificity. In "A Song of Praise," Cullen answers a poet who praises his lady for being fair, by alluding to African beauty. The same theme is suggested in "Brown Boy to Brown Girl." But, as with most of his poems, the reader is left in the realm of idea, far from palpable reality. "Ballad for the Brown Girl," however, does point to the difficulty of emulating, for racial purposes, works of an alien era and culture. Cullen mistakenly thought the brown girl in the medieval ballad was Negro, whereas, in fact, the balladeer meant a peasant girl. This tale of a struggle for the affections of a handsome lord by a country girl and a fair London maiden had different meaning from what Cullen intended. Tied as he was to the story as well as to form, the poem is only slight and confused comfort to the Negro reader who might hope to be elated by it.

When Countee Cullen wanted to write seriously about Negroes, his aesthetic forced him to couch his meaning and intent in classical or religious context. The reader would have to infer the racial significance, and it was thought that the classical context would elevate the particular to the universal. He wrote "Simon the Cyrenian Speaks" to show the courageous dignity of a humble black man's answer to the Christian call. He obliquely wrote about prostitutes in "Black Magdalens," thus dignifying Harlem whores with biblical reference. The predicament of the black man, deprived of justice and possibility, is worked out in "Shroud of Color," a poem of passion in which the narrator challenges God to tell him why he must go on living. God gives him a series of visions, but it is the final chorus of all black men's hopes and aspirations that gives him courage, will, and determination to live as one of these.

· · ·

> And somehow it was borne upon my brain
> How being dark, and living through the pain
> Of it, is courage more than angels have.

· · ·

Lynching is the subject of "Black Christ," his long narrative. Whereas the same subject moved Claude McKay to bitterness and James Weldon Johnson in "Brothers" to expose the brutality of murdering mobs and their kinship to the victim, Cullen

Aaron Douglas and Arthur Schomburg
before Douglas' mural, "Song of the Towers."

"African Dancer."
Bronze by Richmond Barthé.

"Feral Benga."
Bronze by Richmond Barthé.

"Forever Free."
Lacquered wood sculpture
by Sargent Johnson.

"Head of Negro Woman."
Terra cotta by Sargent Johnson.

"Negro Woman."
Terra cotta by Sargent Johnson.

Bob Cole, James and J. Rosamund Johnson.

Bert Williams and George Walker.

James Weldon Johnson and Walter Damrosh present the Spingarn
Medal to Roland Hayes aboard the S.S. *Aquitania*, April 7, 1925.

Paul Robeson.
Photograph by
Carl Van Vechten.

Charles Gilpin
in *The Emperor Jones*.

Rose McClendon in *In Abraham's Bosom*.

Fletcher Henderson.

Bessie Smith.
Photograph by
Carl Van Vechten.

Edward "Duke" Ellington.

Two kinds of pretense: top, the Cakewalk;
bottom: performers at the Bradley Martin Ball.

characteristically chose another statement. Bitterness was not beautiful or elevating, neither was the bestiality of men; these could not be the voice or theme of a poem. Cullen used the lynching as a test of faith. The brother of the lynched man lost his faith in God, despite his mother's unswerving devotion. But the lynched brother rises from the dead, redeeming his doubting brother. The resurrection also, completing the analogy to Christ, ennobles the murdered man and the murder. And even when Cullen wanted to explore the question of his African heritage, he chose in "Heritage" to bind the problem to the religious question of pagan vs. Christian belief.

These were never very satisfactory ways of dealing with the themes that prompted the poems. Sometimes, one suspects, the work would have been more successful as prose. Always the reader—the modern reader at any rate—wonders why the poet does not say what is on his mind. The obliqueness surely does not help. Yet Cullen, forever true to a genteel straightjacket, seldom if ever ventured to tell it as it was, or better yet, to tell it as he felt it.

I quote here the four stanzas of "Harsh World that Lashest Me" because it illustrates Countee Cullen's persistent Romantic vision, and it serves as a sharp contrast to Claude McKay's treatments of the same themes in "America," quoted earlier, and "Baptism."

Harsh World that Lashest Me [7]

Harsh World that lashest me each day,
    Dub me not cowardly because
I seem to find no sudden way
    To throttle you or clip your claws.
No force compels me to the wound
    Whereof my body bears the scar;
Although my feet are on the ground,
    Doubt not my eyes are on a star.

You cannot keep me captive, World,
      Entrammeled, chained, spit on, and
         spurned.
More free than all your flags unfurled,
      I give my body to be burned.
I mount my cross because I will,
      I drink the hemlock which you give
For wine which you withhold—and still
      Because I will not die, I live.

I live because an ember in
      Me smoulders to regain its fire,
Because what is and what has been
      Not yet have conquered my desire.
I live to prove the groping clod
      Is surely more than simple dust;
I live to see the breath of God
      Beatify the carnal crust.

But when I will, World, I can go,
      Though triple bronze should wall me
         round
Slip past your guard as swift as snow,
      Translated without pain or sound.
Within myself is lodged the key
      To that vast room of couches laid
For those too proud to live and see
      Their dreams of light eclipsed in shade.

There is, here, no real evidence that the poet is black, yet one
has to know that fact to have the romantic sentiment make any
sense. Cullen like McKay speaks of torment in the world
(McKay calls America a "cultured hell"). Cullen and McKay
alike echo the late Victorian stoicism of W. E. Henley and
Kipling which finds comfort in an indomitable soul.

Countee Cullen had a genuine talent for lyric verse, and he
did manage to write pretty lines. William Grant Still put "If
You Should Go" to music.

If You Should Go [8]

Love, leave me like the light,
        The gently passing day;
We would not know, but for the night,
        When it has slipped away.

Go quietly; a dream
        When done, should leave no trace
That it has lived, except a gleam
        Across the dreamer's face.

There is a prettiness here that wants to live in all of Cullen's work. He liked softness and liquid sounds. Seldom did he write anything harsh. "Incident" is the one exception. For in this poem a white boy of about eight years calls the narrator "Nigger"; nevertheless, the tone is plaintive and innocent.

Countee Cullen liked form, he liked words, and he liked rhyme, but he never experimented with any of them. One looks in vain in his poems to find departures from convention. The rhymes are regular, and the reader is never startled by a strange or new one. He never forgot his formal exercises from his Harvard seminar. He was content to be good at them, so his poetry remained exercises in verse, never experiment or play. And the same for words. Cullen did not serve that function of poetry which molds the language into something new. Surely, he would never write in vernacular, and even his precious diction is never marked by freshness of usage. Poetry was a very serious business to Countee Cullen; he might be light but never funny. Significantly, he left his slight poetic humor for short verse epitaphs.

In 1935, just ten years after his first book of poems, Countee Cullen published *The Medea and Some Poems,* which was to be his last book of new poetry. He did write some children's stories and two books about his cat, but to all intents his life as a poet had ended. He taught in the New York City public schools, working very hard to interest young boys in poetry. This was time-consuming, but it fails to explain why a young man who was dedicated to poetry early in his youth should have lost the will to write. Since his days in high school nothing else had mattered. But, despite what he told himself, his dedication was not to the art; he did nothing toward advancing the art. As he told Langston Hughes, he wanted to write poetry, not Negro poetry; he wanted to be a poet, not a Negro poet. It was akin to his wanting to be first in his class, and being Phi Beta Kappa (which he was). It was a means of excelling and being exemplary. Having several volumes of poetry to his name, several awards, and critical recognition as a poet among Negroes, the real incentive was gone. He already had what he wanted. Of course, his health began to deteriorate; he was troubled with ulcers and hypertension—common ailments of exemplars. Remarkably, in 1945, when he was just forty-three, Cullen began to arrange with his publisher for a collection of his poetry. He did not plan to publish another book of verse, and he wanted a single volume to contain the work on which his reputation should rest. *On These I Stand* appeared in 1947, just about a year after Countee Cullen's death.

No one could have been less afflicted by poetic prettiness than Claude McKay, yet his poetry, like Countee Cullen's, was crippled by a tradition not truly the poet's own. Max Eastman was surely excessive when he wrote in a biographical note for *Selected Poems of Claude McKay* (1953) that the poet "will live in history as the first great lyric genius that his race produced." At least Eastman did discern McKay's real talent to be lyric. The Jamaican writer is best known, however, for his popular novel, *Home to Harlem*, and—to that special audience who has followed Negro literature—as the writer of militant, race-conscious poems. A balanced view of McKay's art would judge him a good lyric poet and in *Harlem: Negro Metropolis* (1940) an essayist of consummate skill.

Claude McKay began writing dialect verse in the West Indies. He had acquired something of a reputation there—the Bobby Burns of Jamaica—before coming to the United States. He briefly attended college, worked about at odd jobs, and finally joined the staff of Max Eastman's *Liberator*. McKay published his verse, now in literary English, in *Spring in New Hampshire* (1920) and *Harlem Shadows* (1922). Both of these volumes contained many lyrical poems, often reminiscent of the West Indies. They were often fresh, poignant, and revealed the poet's deep appreciation for nature. McKay, himself, disclaimed influence of any literary school. "I have adhered to such of the older traditions as I find adequate for my most lawless and revolutionary passions and moods." Like Countee Cullen, this poet was very preoccupied with what he thought to be his wildness of character. But unlike Cullen, McKay denied any artistic commitment to form for its own sake. "I have not used patterns, images and words that would stamp me a classicist nor a modernist . . . I have never studied poetics; but the forms I have used I am convinced are the ones I can work in with the highest degree of spontaneity and freedom." He chose to give latitude to his own taste: "I have chosen my melodies and rhythms by instinct, and I have favored words and figures which flow smoothly and harmoniously into my compositions." [9] In so far as he remained true to these intentions, McKay was effective. When he wrote of his longing for home, he could do nice things.

After the Winter [10]

Some day, when trees have shed their leaves
    And against the morning's white

> The shivering birds beneath the eves
>   Have sheltered for the night,
> We'll turn our faces southward, love
>   Toward the summer isle
> Where bamboos spire the shafted grove
>   And wide-mouthed orchids smile.
>
> And we will seek the quiet hill
>   Where towers the cotton tree,
> And leaps the laughing crystal rill,
>   And works the droning bee.
> And we will build a cottage there
>   Beside an open glade,
> With black-ribbed blue-bells blowing near,
>   And ferns that never fade.

There is a pleasantness about this poem that helps one to ignore rhyme problems (love-grove, there-near) and even to
overlook that dead "poetry-word" rill. But McKay was not consistent.

In *Harlem Shadows*, there appeared a number of quite formal fourteen-line sonnets. While the poet claimed never to
have studied "poetics," and while he disclaimed the inclination
("My intellect is not scientific enough. . . ."), nevertheless, he
tried to write in this very formal and "classical" verse form and
persisted in regular, studied rhyme patterns, despite claimed
lawless passions and moods. It is interesting that these sonnets
comprise almost all of his poems that have any claim to militance and racial protest.

Few of these sonnets, however, directly discuss race or race
experience. Their imputed militancy is in the defiance and the
bitter tone. The poet occasionally wrote of hatred for civilization, meaning European-American culture. But the remarkable
thing is the persistent egocentrism of his poems. Except for one
or two, the defiance and bitterness are personal—the poet's
own against the world. This, again, reiterates the strongly stoi-

cal character of his work. It also points to the important influence on McKay of that late Victorian, James Thomson, and his *City of Dreadful Night.* Seldom does McKay direct the reader into some emotional or visual reality that belonged to race experience. Occasionally, he was explicit about white-black conflict.[11]

To the White Fiends [12]

Think you I am not fiend and savage too?
Think you I could not arm me with a gun
And shoot down ten of you for every one
Of my black brothers murdered, burnt by you?
Be not deceived, for every deed you do
I could match—out-match: am I not Africa's son,
Black of that black land where black deeds are done?
But the Almighty from the darkness drew
My soul and said: Even thou shalt be a light
Awhile to burn on the benighted earth,
Thy dusky face I set among the white
For thee to prove thyself of higher worth;
Before the world is swallowed up in night,
To show thy little lamp: go forth, go forth!

Ignoring the rather large question of art in this poem we can note some of the characteristic features of McKay's sonnets. The defiance, the militance, is rhetorical and argumentative rather than substantive and palpable. While in this poem McKay assumes the *persona* of the Negro people, his use of first person can hardly be extended beyond his personal self. Whatever God's design, one reads this poem as rather hollow rhetoric.

McKay, like Cullen, seemed to think that serious poetry (poetry with a message) had to be lifted out of the ordinary, the recognizable experiences of man. Such poems needed to be couched in designs that were grander than life. Powerful poetry was hyperbole.

Baptism [13]

Into the furnace let me go alone;
Stay you without in terror of the heat.
I will go naked in—for thus 'tis sweet—
Into the weird depths of the hottest zone.
I will not quiver in the frailest bone,
You will not note a flicker of defeat;
My heart shall tremble not its fate to meet,
My mouth give utterance to any moan.
The yawning oven spits forth fiery spears;
Red aspish tongues shout wordlessly my name.
Desire destroys, consumes my mortal fears,
Transforming me into a shape of flame.
I will come out, back to your world of tears,
A stronger soul within a finer frame.

The title and the last four lines of this sonnet tell the reader
that the poem is about a trial by fire, from which the fearless,
stoical narrator emerges purified and redeemed. The sense is
made awkward by the trial being put in the future, making it
the faith or fancy of the first-person narrator. Furthermore, the
trial is uncertain, since we are never told what it is. Line
eleven serves to confuse the vagueness, because it appears that
desire is the fire which consumes and destroys. His own desire
—such a vague word, desire for God, for sex, for purity, for
virtue?—has given the poet a stronger soul and a finer frame.
McKay is characteristically indifferent to as well as careless of
image. A furnace in one line becomes an oven in another.
Since bones hardly quiver, line five claims little. The use of
"flicker" in line six is confusing, since flame is supposed to be
the content of the furnace (if not the oven). Nor is this looseness of style peculiar to this poem, it is characteristic of
McKay's sonnets. One need merely observe the collision of disparate images in the previously quoted "America" to sense the

limitations of this poet's craft when he struggles with rigorous form.

Nor can it be argued that McKay should not be judged by conventional standards since he disclaimed any intent to be a "classicist." He tried to adhere rigorously to the iambic line and to regular rhyme. He was not careful enough as a poet to work within such a harness with grace and style. Form forced him into strange syntax. It did not make him spontaneous and free. Rather, it pushed him into impossible inversions: "My heart shall tremble not its fate to meet." This formal problem, coupled with his characteristic treatment of racial themes by means of self-inflation and rhetoric, subvert the power of these poems. It is hard to believe his statement that "in all my moods I have striven to achieve directness, truthfulness and naturalness of expression. . . ."

McKay's racial attitudes and militancy are further confounded. "If We Must Die" is undoubtedly the poem for which he is best known. Also, as a demand for resistance against oppressors, it has always been taken as a call for Negro militancy. Yet, when the poet read that poem for Arna Bontemps' recording of Negro poets, he insisted that the sonnet had universal intent. The poem, he recognized "makes me a poet among colored Americans. Yet, frankly, I have never regarded myself as a Negro poet. I have always felt that my gift of song was something bigger than the narrow confined limits of any one people and its problems." [14] How strange a statement from the voice of black defiance and bitterness! McKay had learned that a white American soldier, who had died on the Russian front in World War II, had this poem among his belongings. "I felt profoundly gratified and justified. I felt assurance that 'If We Must Die' was just what I intended it to be, a universal poem." Thus, race conscious, yet torn between the particularity of race and the assumed universality of poetry, McKay resorted to form which he could not manage and vagueness which obfuscated and blunted his statement. Whatever his claims about form, McKay was, in his own way, as tied to the English tradition and conception of poetry as was Countee Cullen. Formal matters as well as personal attitudes inhibited McKay from transforming his bitterness and disillusionment—which no doubt many Negroes felt—into memorable or powerful art. The Negro-as-artist dilemma is nowhere better exemplified than in what James Weldon Johnson called the "sonnet-tragedies" of Claude McKay. Failing in the poetic demand—to reduce to crystaline purity the emotional center of experience—they are strangled by the arbitrary restraints of form which McKay could not master. What emerges is a tone of personal defiance—echoing late Victorian attitudes, too often a braggadocio—depending almost wholly on rhetorical and argumentative style. It may be too precious to say, "a poem should not mean but be," nevertheless a poem should be its own validity. None of these "sonnet-tragedies" achieve that.

Nor is this an argument to deny artistic merit to poems because they are not great. Rather, it is to point to these particular failures as due to a slavish devotion to questionable (and poorly mastered) form and attitude, confusing art as well as meaning. Those who were more contemplative than McKay—who wrestled more ruthlessly to sharpen and define their insights and who struggled to give their statement its proper form—came closer to artistic success, even though they like him might not have produced great poetry. "Reapers," a quite modest poem by Jean Toomer, attempts to evoke emotion (not sentiment) that could not be better done in prose.

Reapers [15]

Black reapers with the sound of steel on stones
Are sharpening scythes. I see them place the hones
In their hip-pockets as a thing that's done,

> And start their silent swinging, one by one.
> Black horses drive a mower through the weeds,
> And there, a field rat, startled, squealing bleeds,
> His belly close to ground. I see the blade,
> Blood-stained, continue cutting weeds and shade.

The regular rhyme scheme is so natural and unforced that its influence is subtle and unnoticed. Toomer's "Song of the Son" (previously quoted) also may be admired for its effort to combine symbol and rhythm to express an emotion of search and prodigal return. That poem, too, has its failings; the first two lines echo a rousing Methodist hymn which clatters, unfortunately, against the plaintive tone the poet wants to set. Granting limitations, such poems approach success precisely because they attempt to express themselves rather than an abstraction called poetry.

Langston Hughes had a view of art and the role of poetry different from both Countee Cullen and Claude McKay. The poets who influenced him were Carl Sandburg and, in a limited way, Vachel Lindsay. He, along with Sterling Brown, shared the American poetic vision that ran from Walt Whitman through Sandburg—its belief in the validity of the intuitive sense and the spontaneity of art. Hughes not only believed that art should be the immediate expression of the self, but he also shared with Whitman, Sandburg, and Lindsay an open, optimistic faith in the common man. Hughes and Brown were democrats, accepting, without question, the rightness of the unadorned and unpretentious expression of ordinary people.

The acceptance of an intuitive truth and a spontaneous art freed them from any commitment to a necessary form. Experimentation was possible. Any arrangement of words could be poetic if it captured the mystical essence of the human voice. The measure of rightness had more to do with the closeness to real human experience than it did with rules of verse or rhyme. Hughes never studied versification in any formal way. Indeed,

he prided himself that he did little rewriting. He remembered
finishing "The Negro Speaks of Rivers" on a train crossing the
Mississippi.

> No doubt I changed a few words the next day, or maybe
> crossed out a line or two. But there are seldom many
> changes in my poems, once they're down. Generally, the first
> two or three lines come to me from something I'm thinking
> about, or looking at, or doing, and the rest of the poem (if
> there is to be a poem) flows from those first few lines, usually
> right away. If there is a chance to put the poem down then,
> I write it down. If not, I try to remember it until I get to a
> pencil and paper; for poems are like rainbows: they escape
> you quickly.[16]

Hughes believed the poet should not wrestle with rules of poetics; they distorted the freshness and trueness of the poet's vision. A poem was an instant life-song frozen into words.

This belief in instinct gave Hughes a great respect for the
common man; to him, even when the most ordinary person
sang, or danced, or worked, or suffered, he was likely to be
making beauty. Hughes's absolute faith in the dignity of the
lowest human being skinned his eyes and unstopped his ears to
folk art. That very faith, however, touched him with an optimism which subtly colored all he wrote, even when it was sad
or tragic. Thus Langston Hughes and Sterling Brown were folk
artists in that they exploited the wealth of material that was
provided by the common people; and for both writers that
meant Negroes, workers, farmers, bums, pimps, gamblers, musicians, anyone who lived his life without intentional deceit.
Langston Hughes really believed that these people were producing art and culture all of the time, rainbows that had to be
captured before they vanished.

Hughes envisioned the poet as a kind of troubadour, bringing experience into art and music. He thought himself quite
akin to the jazzmen and the blues singers he found about him.

Like them, he had faith in the extemporaneous expression; art was innovation. Hughes saw himself as analogous to the blues singer, with his guitar and repertoire of songs—standard themes—to which he added innovations and new verses as they came to him. Analogous too was the street language of black boys in their verbal games—"dozens" and "capping"— which also honored the virtuosity of those who could innovate from standard and remembered verses. An oral tradition tied together the street boys, the folk preachers, the blues singers, and the jazzmen. Hughes's poetry exploited that tradition in which stories are told again and again, singers creating their own style through innovation. While freshness was prized, ownership was not. Once a blues singer had "published," it belonged to everyone. Because Hughes used this model, much of his poetry appears common, in the public domain, like folk art. But his effort, from his own testimony, was to capture vagrant rainbows of life experience and freeze them into a lasting form.[17]

As the title of his first book of poems *Weary Blues* (1926) would indicate, he wanted to use blues themes as poetry. Many of his poems are nothing more or less than blues lyrics, which cannot be properly sensed without familiarity with the blues patterns and refrains. The a, a, b, a pattern is obvious, but a good ear can often detect falsetto breaks and other blues characteristics.

Black Maria [18]

Must be the Black Maria
That I see,
The Black Maria that I see—
But I hope it
Ain't comin' for me.

Hear that music playin' upstairs?
Aw, my heart is

Full of cares—
But that music playin' upstairs
Is for me.

Babe, did you ever
See the sun
Rise at dawnin' full of fun?
Says, did you ever see the sun rise
Full of fun, full of fun?
Then you know a new day's
Done begun.

Black Maria passin' by
Leaves the sunrise in the sky—
And a new day,
Yes, a new day's
Done begun!

Poems appear that are surely parts of the blues-man's repertoire:

Hope [19]

Sometimes when I'm lonely,
Don't know why,
Keep thinkin' I won't be lonely
By and by.

By giving these lines—so often sung in one way or another—a
title and the form of poetry, Hughes attempted to give the
blues a new dimension.

No Negro folk matter was exempt from Hughes's treatment:
sermons, gospels, spirituals. Sometimes his poems were tales
told in street language and in a loose rhythm and rhyme, a
kind of doggerel like the "Ballad of the Landlord." Others are
street verse and street wisdom.

Advice [20]

Folks, I'm telling you
birthing is hard
and dying is mean—
so get yourself
a little loving
in between.

Nor did Langston Hughes have to reach far to find form to express the horror and terror of Negro life in America. He could combine call-and-response patterns with traditional Christian symbolism.

Song for a Dark Girl [21]

Way Down South in Dixie
(Break the heart of me)
They hung my black young lover
To a cross roads tree.

Way Down South in Dixie
(Bruised body high in air)
I asked the white Lord Jesus
What was the use of prayer.

Way Down South in Dixie
(Break the heart of me)
Love is a naked shadow
On a gnarled and naked tree.

The openness of folk modes freed poets from the arbitrariness of form. Anything that was authentic could be written. Undiluted race feeling could be expressed more directly in this genre. Sterling Brown's poem "Memphis Blues," [22] for instance, is telling and remarkably modern. The poem is a sermon-song in three parts. Part I relates Memphis to ancient and ruined cities:

Nineveh, Tyre
Babylon,
Not much lef'
Of either one.
All dese cities
Ashes and rust,
De win' sing sperrichals
Through deir dus' . . .

The poet remembers Memphis on the Nile, and suggests that the modern city on the Mississippi might drown in flood or blow away in wind. Part II is a series of verses asking, in turn, the preacher man, lover man, music man, working man, drinking man, and gambling man what they will do when "Memphis on fire," and each responds that he will do what he does, only better. Then Part III concludes:

Memphis go
By Flood or Flame;
Nigger won't worry
All de same—
Memphis go
Memphis come back,
Ain' no skin
Off de nigger's back.
All dese cities
Ashes, rust. . . .
De win' sing sperrichals
Through deir dus'.

This is not much different from what Claude McKay would write, but Brown's statement rings more true, especially to the reader today.

Such poems of Langston Hughes's and Sterling Brown's defy criticism because they lack pretension. They do not ask for academic acclaim; thus they are exempt from its contempt. In truth, Hughes was not writing to be approved as a literary poet (Brown sometimes did). While his poems appealed to an audience which included whites, Hughes created for himself a black audience, especially school children. And he expected his poems to be taken on the simple and unpretentious level on which they were written. One would be right in saying that Langston Hughes backed out of the Negro-artist dilemma by choosing not to deal with art as serious "high culture." His casual and almost anti-intellectual attitude about art permitted him a wide freedom of subject and a personal honesty. It allowed him to make the very important point that the people's language, and voice, and rhythms were legitimate stuff of poetry. But this same freedom deprived him of the control and mastery that might make each (or indeed any) of his poems really singular. Langston Hughes avoided the Scylla of formalism only to founder in the Charybdis of folk art.

The dilemmas that gripped Negro writers were not mere sophomoric arguments over the primacy of form or content. They were much more profound than that, having more to do with the racial urgency to be "culturally" recognized. James Weldon Johnson put the matter most cogently in the preface to his *Book of American Negro Poetry* (1922). A people, he thought, might choose many paths to greatness, but "there is only one measure by which its greatness is recognized and acknowledged." That final and indisputable measure is the "amount and standard of literature and art they have produced." Without it, a people's quality and stature would be hidden from the world; while, on the other hand, no "people that has produced great literature and art has ever been looked upon by the world as distinctly inferior." [23]

There are many difficulties with this argument; the assumption not only throws the burden of creation on the artist, but it also gives him the onus of race image. And the judge of achievement is the "world," or more immediately an American critical establishment. Presumably, at some moment the critics and pundits would say, "look, some of our best poems, and pictures, and stories are being done by black people, there must be something to them." But who were these judges, and how could you please them? On the one hand they were editors, critics, and professors who made it their business to comment on culture. On the other hand, they were ghosts from the past: writers and artists whom the "world" had acknowledged as great and who held the ring for the neophyte to grasp. Unsubstantial, but real, it was tradition at which these black artists were groping. Both Countee Cullen and Claude McKay set their eyes on the Romantics. Langston Hughes and Sterling Brown, on the other hand, desperate to be the voice of their people and impatient with formalism, paid homage to tradition by playing innocent and disclaiming intention of *serious* art.

But this tradition had nothing to do with these writers, it had nothing to do with Negroes, and, in fact, it really had nothing to do with Americans. Nothing, that is, other than the clothes fitted in the schools and colleges to costume a "cultured man or woman." Real or unreal, relevant or not, it was awesome to one who wanted to prove that he belonged. Literary tradition is like an exclusive social club; a candidate's certainty of belonging permits a casualness about details; questionable credentials, on the other hand, encourage minutest observance of manner and style. The notable thing about American literature from 1900 through the 1920s was its apparent coming of age. Poets and novelists were departing from slavish dependence on nineteenth-century English models. The period was alive with innovation. Yet, except for Jean Toomer and, in a very special way, Langston Hughes, there was no evidence of literary inventiveness in Harlem.

Henry May, in writing about the prewar cultural rebellion, notes the large and important contingent of rebels to come from the bastions of conservative culture: eastern colleges, especially Harvard and Columbia. It was precisely because men like Wallace Stevens, Witter Bynner, Arthur Davison Ficke, John Gould Fletcher, T. S. Eliot, Conrad Aiken, E. E. Cummings, and Malcolm Cowley knew that they "belonged" by birth and training that they could dare adventure. It was also, perhaps, because they were steeped in a stodgy, historical literary training (which stood for tradition) that they were moved to rebel. The same Lyman Kittredge who sent Countee Cullen a prized letter praising the "Ballad of the Brown Girl" was filling Harvard heads with a great deal of historical literature and boring some young men enough to revolt. Innovative though these young men were, their work grew out of a deep, persistent, and cross-generational immersion in the standard English booklist. To know it well might be to admire it, but to know it well would also be to recognize its formal irrelevancy to modern needs.

But one needs this intimacy with the historical literature in which one wishes to work in order to make innovations—calibrated and discrete—which become style. And, here, Negro writers up to the 1930s were at a distinct disadvantage. Fifty years out of slavery by the end of World War I, harassed and restricted (both North and South), limited in educational opportunity, few (if any) Negroes could boast a continuity of intellectual engagement beyond their immediate generation. Surely, no one was so steeped in the English literary canon that he could risk change.

Afro-Americans, however, for many generations shared in America's oldest "literary" tradition, the sermon—characteristically rhetorical, didactic oratory. But the black tradition developed its own peculiar oral tradition that extended far beyond the folk sermon. Of probably African origin was the call-and-response pattern which engaged the audience in the speaker's art. Sometimes the response was little more than an amen (right-on), but often whole remembered phrases would come in unison. This call-and-response pattern has been worked into the blues, and the attentive ear can detect it as a primary feature of jazz instrumentation. The black tradition is also marked by the purposefully repeated phrase. The folk preacher used the repeated phrase to give focus, an organizing principle. Here, too, are parallels in the blues and in the jazz riff. It served the common function of allowing the artist to mark time while he "composed" his next innovation. Speech and music also shared the characteristic a, a, b, a pattern of lines. The repeated second line gives emphasis and allows for innovation in the third and fourth lines.[24]

All of these characteristics are elements of an oral tradition that the Afro-American sustained. These devices originally served to make the performer independent of written words or music, but eventually even the written words and music of black Americans resonated to this powerful tradition. The art and techniques of this "literature" were never formally taught in school. Yet, they were "natural" with black people. The pre-adolescent boy acquired them in verbal combat on the street, and they became his music and his speech as an adult.[25] These techniques became part of the Negro's written language as well. Sometimes it is a fault; nothing can be more deadening to imaginative literature than preaching. But sometimes it worked well.

Surely some of the most satisfying work to come out of Harlem in the 1920s was James Weldon Johnson's *God's Trombones* (1927), in which he tried to capture, in the poet's words, "the genuine folk stuff that clings around the old-time Negro preacher, material which had many times been worked into something both artificial and false."[26] Some of the most moving bits of Cullen's poetry also are generated from this source. "Shroud of Color" still has much of the Romantic tradition in its concept, but Keats is less present in this dialogue between God and the narrator than the church people who were inti-

mates of Cullen's life. And one of the best bits of prose writing
to come out of Harlem during this period occurs in Wallace
Thurman's *Infants of the Spring* when Euphoria Blake tells her
story. Like a good sermon, it is pungent, forceful, and very
moving. Whatever the limitations, what came out of the Negro's own life and experience had the best chance of being
effective art.

Again, James Weldon Johnson voiced the problem. What the
Negro poet needed to do, he said, is "something like what
Synge did for the Irish; he needs to find a form that will express the racial spirit by symbols from within rather than by
symbols from without, such as mere mutilation of English
spelling and pronunciation." Dialect, which had been the
mode, was merely manner, genre; there was nothing in it to
take one to the soul-center of Negroes, or Italians, or Jews, or
anyone. Johnson asked for a form which would be freer and
larger than dialect, yet "still hold the racial flavor; a form expressing the imagery, the idioms, the peculiar turns of thought,
and the distinctive humor and pathos, too, of the Negro." But
this form would also have to be capable of expressing the
deepest and highest emotions and aspirations, and allow the
widest range of subjects. He knew that dialect verse, with the
stereotype that it promoted, could not serve. Yet, he hoped
that there would be a form adequate for Negro literature. But
one wonders, if there had come a literature such as Johnson
dreamed, would a world and a white nation which viewed
black men with contempt or pity have recognized it as an art
and culture to be honored? And would Johnson, himself, recognize it as the great art that was to deliver the race?

The alienation from respected tradition, to which I have
been pointing, might easily be understood as one of the many
other burdens peculiar to Negroes in American life. But the
problem is more complicated and more interesting than that.
This uncertainty was a problem of all Americans. One need

only recall the almost perverse preoccupation of Americans
with the travel literature of Europeans, especially when it was
not congratuatory: Alexis de Tocqueville, Mrs. Trollope,
Charles Dickens. The question was always being asked, "what
do you think of us?" It mattered what Europeans thought, because it was their civilization and their culture and their tradition (improved, of course, by democracy) to which white
Americans aspired to belong. Any number of white Americans
could have used James Weldon Johnson's edict about art when
referring to the general American predicament. A number of
names come to mind, but consider merely James Fenimore
Cooper, Ralph Waldo Emerson in his journals, Henry Adams,
and even Walt Whitman in *Democratic Vistas*. All Americans,
white as well as black, were provincials of a European tradition, Anne Bradstreet no less than Phyllis Wheatley, Thomas
Nelson Page no less then Charles Waddell Chestnutt. But Negroes, being one notch further removed from "belonging," were
less likely (or less quickly) to gain the perspective that would
show the way to transform their own experience into art, free
from the corpselike clutch of past formalism and manner.
Negro literature and art, of course, was to free itself, just as the
general American art and letters had during the war years, but
that would come in the 1930s and after.

While we are on the subject, it is worthwhile remembering
how deep and troubling a problem tradition and provincialism
have been to American letters. Cooper and Emerson discuss it,
but nowhere is the issue spelled out more clearly than in Nathaniel Hawthorne's preface to *The Scarlet Letter*. He keenly
felt himself to be the product of an austere New England past;
his ancestors had been substantial Puritan divines. Yet, here he
was, in this world that honored only the useful and the good, a
writer of stories. And he felt the gaze of that Puritan past on
him. "Either of these stern and black-browed Puritans would

have thought it quite a sufficient retribution for his sins that after so long a lapse of years the old trunk of the family tree . . . should have borne, as its topmost bough, an idler like myself." Hawthorne feared that no thing he had ever done, no value he truly cherished would his fathers have recognized. " 'What is he?' murmurs one grey shadow of my forefathers to the other. 'A writer of story-books! What kind of a business in life, what manner of glorifying God, or being serviceable to mankind in his day and generation, may that be? Why, the degenerate fellow might as well have been a fiddler!' "

Had Hawthorne been a writer of sermons or their offspring, history, or the didactic, expository essay, he would have been less troubled. But the writer of imaginative literature could find it hard to explain his efforts as business or worship, the two stops in traditional Yankee music. Hawthorne also felt an ambivalence and restiveness in Salem, the town where he spent most of his writing years. He had a filial attachment for it—his family had lived there for one hundred and seventy years—but he was also overwhelmed by the cultural, spiritual, and emotional flatness of the place. Its "long and lazy street, lounging wearisomely through the whole extent of the peninsula, with Gallows Hill and New Guinea at one end, and a view of the almshouse at the other—such being the features of my native town, it would be quite as reasonable to form a sentimental attachment to a disarranged chequer-board." Aside from these problems, Hawthorne was harassed by other, even more aggravating, conditions of provincial American life. He had great trouble getting himself into print and receiving intelligent critical judgment. In the 1840s, the few book publishers, with their still primitive methods of promotion and distribution, and magazine editors were understandably more willing to publish history (which had become the American epic) and to reprint substantial European authors than they were to ex-

periment with first flowers from American soil. There was not
the guarantee of audience, nor was there the critical environment necessary for the development of a literature.

Some fifteen years after Hawthorne's death, Henry James
published a biography of him. James's sympathy for and appreciation of Hawthorne stemmed from what he saw to be
their spiritual union in the struggle with the provincialism of
American life and its divorce from literary tradition. As James
saw it, the very things that made America great—its newness,
its rawness, its identity with change, its innocence—were what
made it poor soil for imaginative literature. The culture was
too thin. It had not had the time or the experience to build up
the institutions and conventions that had to be taken for
granted in literary works. The American setting, in which
character rested, was itself too remarkable and changed too
abruptly and fundamentally to permit the writer to ignore it.
Context, James felt, absorbed the American novelist's energies
and stole focus from character, where it ought to be. He wrote
of Hawthorne, "it is only in a country where newness and
change and brevity of tenure are the common substance of life,
that the fact of one's ancestors having lived for a hundred and
seventy years in a single spot would become an element of
one's morality. It is only an imaginative American that would
feel urged to keep reverting to this circumstance, to keep ana-
lysing and cunningly considering it." [27]

What appealed to Henry James about Europe was exactly
what tradition had provided—richness and thickness of institu-
tional elaboration, manner, style, which made for stability as
well as corruption. In such a setting, the context could be
taken for granted—it was known, anticipated, not involved in
convulsive change—thus the writer could focus on the people
of his novel rather than their circumstances. The novelist
could, as James thought he should, explore the inner regions of

character: psychology and motivation. In the European setting, the slightest variation of context could be enough to deeply affect human motivation. In the United States, on the other hand, change being so much a part of the environment, to affect similar deep human reaction one had to alter the circumstances so radically as to overwhelm character altogether. Such artistic considerations influenced James in his decision to become, like Cooper before him, an American expatriate writer in Europe. His affection for Americans and America was profound, thus Americans so often are the subject of his explorations into character. Europe made the task possible, he thought, whereas the United States did not.

In 1919, T. S. Eliot wrote his famous essay, "Tradition and the Individual Talent." Eliot was troubled in a slightly different way about literary tradition. He felt that the writer himself would not be able to develop into a mature artist without a dedicated apprenticeship to tradition. The work of the typically talented writer, without such devotion, was bound to be erratic and unfinished. As Eliot saw it, literature was a slow accretion onto tradition, like a seashell or a tree, each generation developing its new self from within. Artists and writers grow into maturity and fineness by making themselves the growing edge of their culture—working themselves through and out of the past. Without such adherence to tradition, Eliot thought, one could hardly expect finished artists. And, by inference, one could not expect a literary tradition where such apprenticeship was impossible. Eliot, himself, despaired of the United States providing him the environment for his own art, and he became more than an expatriate: he became an Englishman.[28] Eliot, too, had recognized the essential provincialism of the United States; it was forever to be external to the English tradition which he felt to be essential to his art, so he went where he could "belong." I wonder, however, if his agony

over Anglo-Catholicism does not suggest a continued alienation from the tradition that he wanted to be a part of. The
provincial who dwells within is a hard spirit to convert.

Hawthorne's and James's agony about audience was echoed
in some way by everyone who dreamed of contributing to a
black literature in the 1920s. It is not merely a commercial
matter, although that is important; a writer has to live, and a
publisher must have his certainties. But deeper than that, a
writer must sense that he is being understood. Ideally, his
readers should know enough about his subject so that he need
not explain the obvious. Or, lacking that, he needs the confidence that his readers will work to learn enough to understand
his meaning. Black writers were learning that there was a
readership for Negro matter. But what was it? It surely was
not even substantially made up of Negroes. What did the others know of Negro life? How much did they want to know?
What could you tell them? But a better question, really, was
how much could you risk not telling them?

The fact was that none of these questions were really an-
swerable. A writer could never know, so he had to probe, and
feel, and try. None of the novels that came out of Harlem in
the renaissance took its audience for granted. Actually, Toomer's *Cane* is an exception, and if you stretch a point Thurman's
Infants of the Spring can be excepted too. But for the rest—
including Van Vechten's *Nigger Heaven*—they were all novels
of circumstance, of context rather than of the characters that
peopled them. Nella Larsen came as close as any to treating
human motivation with complexity and sophistication. But she
could not wrestle free of the mulatto condition that the main
characters in her two novels had been given. Once she made
them mulatto and female the conventions of American thought
—conditioned by the tragic mulatto and the light-dark heroine
formulas—seemed to take the matter out of the author's hands.
For the rest, environment seems the subject of the works. Jessie

Fauset delineates middle-class Negro life, contrives problems to generate the stories. Claude McKay, whether writing about Harlem or Marseilles, writes about a style of life which is really external to character. Jake, or Banjo, or Ray could be anybody. They are not characters, they merely stand for points of view, or styles of life. Ray talks more about his inner tensions than most of the people in these novels. Yet, his talk gives no insight into him, it does not serve to make him more than two-dimensional. It is merely explication of impersonal dilemmas that would likely be shared by any intellectual Negro.

Imagination that might have been used to explore the inner regions of character was spent explaining to the reader the special circumstance of being Negro, or living in Harlem, or being mulatto, or "passing." These novels are filled with set speeches by characters, which have no other purpose than to place in the record a particular fact or nuance of Negro life. In Claude McKay's *Banjo,* the reader is faced with long expository statements that might well be essays in themselves. Even Carl Van Vechten—white, an experienced and sophisticated author, presumably as certain as anyone could be of his audience—was reduced to telling the "facts of Negro life" in *Nigger Heaven.* He dared not assume that his readers knew that there were intelligent, "cultured," and well-mannered Negroes. He could not suppose that this audience would know of the wide spectrum of life and character in Harlem. So he had to sprinkle his novel with reproductions of the "Mona Lisa"; he had to make his characters speak French and talk about literature and art as one might suppose intelligent people would. And he had to have formal discussions of major racial preoccupations lest the nuances of ethnic attitude be lost. No art can bear such a burden of the obvious and the banal. No important character or truly artistic creation can survive in such an atmosphere of preachment. Without the certainty of audience, or

preferably without the luxury of indifference to it, black literature like any literature or art would be stifled in its own atmosphere.

I mentioned that Jean Toomer's *Cane* was an exception. It
was because the author chose as his focus the essentials of
Negro identity rather than the circumstances of Negro life. He
worked in symbols that served as the metaphors to allow a
reader, whether white or black, to enter into the crux of those
tensions that tugged at the Negro self. *Cane* stands apart because it was a self-conscious artistic achievement; the same
cannot be said about any of the other novels associated with
the Harlem Renaissance. It is a mark of the problem of audience that *Cane* sold less than five hundred copies in the year
that it was issued. Art and literature, whatever James Weldon
Johnson had hoped, need not win the acclaim of the world.

While some may argue that America has lacked a literary
tradition, few can say that American literature has lacked
greatness. Unlike the great literatures of Europe, America's can
not be measured by the galaxies of competent to excellent artistic work that cluster in historical periods. Nor has American
greatness in literature been the mark of adherence to tradition,
or as T. S. Eliot would have it, a devoted apprenticeship to
tradition. Rather, as I have argued, tradition has been a laby-
rinth through which only the most singular talent can come
into his own distinctive art. One thinks of Herman Melville,
Walt Whitman, and Mark Twain. Their achievement was in
their ability to wrap up essentials of the American experience
(the human experience) and with colossal imagination and
boundless energy break through the provincial bounds of
American life and literature to produce works that stood apart.
This is characteristic of the more artistically successful of
American letters. Anyway it suggests that the Negro writer, in
creating a Negro literature, had to be confident enough to be
free of slavishness to tradition. The creation of an *American*

literature and the creation of a *Negro literature* may have been futile efforts from the start. The provincial character of American art and life may demand that truly significant art exist as individual expression rather than in the constellations or "schools" of art Henry James and T. S. Eliot searched for.

As time passed, beginning in the 1930s, it became more and more possible to anticipate an audience that would know enough about Negroes not to be told everything. In *Native Son* Richard Wright did not feel compelled to explicate Negro life in Chicago in order to move Bigger Thomas through murder and his trial. Wright did, however, like other naturalists, use the courtroom speech as a device to tell the reader what to conclude from the evidence systematically laid before him. But Negro writers in the 1950s and 1960s have been able to assume that they have an audience that can understand (or wants to understand) their subject. Or, better yet, perhaps Ralph Ellison, LeRoi Jones, and others may not care; what they say is important enough, and so the audience will come to them. People, black and white, may have to work to understand, but they will. This confidence is partly due to these men's sense of artistic mastery. But it is also due to a more sophisticated and cosmopolitan general readership than existed in the 1920s. And finally, it is due to a constellation of sociological and political developments that have changed the attitude of whites and blacks toward Negroes. People will read about Negroes and struggle to understand them, if they will do nothing else. None of the writers in the 1920s could have had such confidence, either in themselves or in their society. Thus, they were severely limited in their attempts to strike free.

Wallace Thurman sensed these problems. One might say, that he, of all the Harlem literati, contained within him the paradoxes of Negro art. Robert A. Bone, whose book on the Negro novel is often faulty, is nowhere less perceptive than in his treatment of Thurman. Bone dismisses *Infants of the Spring* perfunctorily as the vehicle of Thurman's personal bitterness, self-hatred, and suicidal impulses directed to the critical destruction of the entire renaissance generation. "No one who has read *The Blacker the Berry* will doubt that the source of this self-hatred was his dark complexion." [29] Actually, Thurman was critical of the renaissance because it was naïve, innocent, optimistic, and engaged in the promotion of art. After all the talking was over, Thurman knew that it would take a lot of hard work and skill to write good novels and short stories and poems. And he knew that little truly good art had come from theorizing.

None of the people connected with Harlem in these years was as dedicated to art and its excellence as Wallace Thurman. His trouble was that he had a critical mind. He had read everything, and, as Langston Hughes reports, could find something wrong with even the things he liked. "He wanted to be a *very* great writer, like Gorki or Thomas Mann, and he felt that he was merely a journalistic writer. His critical mind, comparing his pages to the thousands of other pages he had read, by Proust, Melville, Tolstoy, Galsworthy, Dostoyevski, Henry James . . . found his own pages vastly wanting." He could also see that what was appearing in the pages of *Crisis, Opportunity,* and the *Messenger* was not worthy art. Because he had keen critical judgment, he was less vulnerable than many to the optimistic rhetoric that promoted Negro art. That did not mean that Thurman was indifferent; he was probably more deeply committed, emotionally, than any. When the little magazine, *Fire,* was produced, it was Thurman who insisted on its perfection. "It had to be on good paper . . . worthy of the drawings of Aaron Douglas. It had to have beautiful type, worthy of the first Negro art quarterly. It had to be what we seven young Negroes," Langston Hughes recalls, "dreamed our magazine would be—so in the end it cost almost a thousand dollars, and nobody could pay the bills." [30]

It was Thurman who persuaded the printer to release the copies. And it was Thurman who, after *Fire* had burned and been reduced to ashes—a total loss—had his salary attached to pay the bills. Hughes remembered that "Wallace Thurman laughed a long bitter laugh. He was a strange kind of fellow, who liked to drink gin, but *didn't* like to drink gin; who liked being a Negro, but felt it a great handicap; who adored bohemianism, but thought it wrong to be a bohemian. He liked to waste a lot of time, but he always felt guilty wasting time. He loathed crowds, yet he hated to be alone. He almost always felt bad. . . ." Once Hughes told him that, feeling so bad all the time, he should surely produce wonderful books. "But he said you had to know how to *write* as well as how to feel bad." And that was Thurman's complaint about the vogue of the Negro. He thought it "had made us all too conscious of ourselves, had flattered and spoiled us, and had provided too many easy opportunities for some of us to drink gin and more gin. . . ." And of what he read and saw, little would he judge good literature.

It is on this ground that Thurman satirized the Harlem Renaissance in *Infants of the Spring*. It was not merely bohemianism which was at fault, but the very self-conscious promotion of art and culture typified by Alain Locke and the "New Negro." He knew, or at least some part of him knew, that artistic production was an extremely personal, individualistic thing, not to be turned on or off by nationalism of any kind. And as he looked over the results of a decade of Negro art, his perhaps too critical mind could find very little to applaud, his own work included. So he wrote *Infants of the Spring*, one of the best written and most readable novels of the period, to bury the renaissance once and for all. Paul Arbian, a decadent and one of the few truly talented characters in the novel, serves that symbolic end. He had been thrown out of Niggeratti Manor by Euphoria Blake, and he had moved in with

Greenwich Village friends. One evening, Paul locked himself in the bathroom, put on a crimson mandarin robe, "wrapped his head in a batik scarf of his own designing," hung a group of his spirit portraits on the wall, "and carpeted the floor with sheets of paper detached from the notebook in which he had been writing his novel. He had then, it seemed, placed joss-sticks in the four corners of the room, lit them, climbed into the bathtub, turned on the water, then slashed his wrists with a highly ornamented Chinese dirk." Raymond Taylor thought that this was Paul's idea of delightful publicity to precede the publication of his exotic novel: *Wu Sing: The Geisha Man.* But, ironically, the water had overflowed the tub and rendered the inked pages illegible. Such grand display. Such futile gesture.

Only the title page and dedication remained. It had been dedicated:

To

Huysmans' Des Esseintes and Oscar Wilde's Oscar Wilde
Ecstatic Spirits with whom I Cohabit
And whose golden spores and decadent pollen
I shall broadcast and fertilize
It is written

Paul Arbian.

Wallace Thurman buried the Harlem Renaissance—or Niggeratti Manor—with Paul Arbian. One might say, the manner was appropriately exotic and decadent. The novel ended, however, on a positive note. Raymond Taylor had struggled through his own self-doubt; he was a writer. His novel was almost done; he would finish it. Thurman's message was delivered more by Raymond than by Paul. It was not talent mixed with fad that made art. Neither was art to come from the endless philosophical arguments about race, ancestry, form, propaganda, and so on. Rather, art would be produced by individuals of talent who were willing to work hard with the self-consciousness that defied crippling doubt. Those conditions could not be promoted merely because it was thought Negroes had come of age. Nor would it come because the race needed a self-image. It would come when the individual artists made it come. That is what Wallace Thurman wanted his work to say of him. And because it could not, he might as well destroy himself along with the façade of Niggeratti Manor.

One week in December 1934, Harlem intellectuals were sadly reminded that the era of casual art had passed. In that week both Rudolph Fisher and Wallace Thurman died. Surely, they were two of the most talented writers of Harlem's twenties. You may as well know that Thurman—"who liked to drink gin, but *didn't* like to drink gin"—died of tuberculosis in the charity ward of Bellevue Hospital.

6 🎭 Personae:
White/Black Faces – Black Masks

Wallace Thurman's tragedy was that he saw himself only too well through the eyes of those who could not really give him an accurate measure of his true talent. W. E. B. DuBois described this dilemma of Negro identity most clearly in his *Souls of Black Folk*. The Negro, he said, was a kind of seventh son, "born with a veil, and gifted with a second-sight in this American world." It is a strange, prismatic vision because that world "yields him no true self-consciousness, but only lets him see himself through the revelation of the other world." As if in a room of mirrors, the Negro stands among a collision of images such that reality is indistinguishable, impalpable, not self-determined. "It is a peculiar sensation," DuBois continued, "this double-consciousness, this sense of always looking at one's self through the eyes of others, of measuring one's soul by the tape of a world that looks on in amused contempt and pity." This remarkable and profound statement fails only to make explicit an important corollary: this "double-consciousness" opens to the Negro—through his own quest and passion —a unique insight into the vulnerable and unfulfilled soul of that other world; a possibility which, once grasped, liberates one forever from the snarls of that other world's measuring tape.

DuBois's point was that the Negro was forever looking at himself through the eyes of white men, trying to be what he thought they were, or trying to be what he thought they wanted him to be. Self-consciously on view, the Negro's sense of achievement—his manhood—depended ultimately on the white man's view of him. Carl Van Vechten misplaced the theatrical image when he titled his Harlem novel *Nigger Heaven.* Harlem was no segregated balcony to Manhattan's "theater," where black people sat up high to watch the show of life go on. Rather, it was a stage; the performers played for all they were worth to a white world. Dance as no one can; sing with the humor or pathos no one else has; make jokes about oneself (make oneself into a joke), anything, everything but with style; turn to the audience and bow deeply and smile broadly and live in that rare luxury of applause, approval, love. If the figure of theater is appropriate, then the Negro was the performer in a strange, almost macabre, act of black collusion in his own emasculation. For that white world, itself unfulfilled, was compelled to approve only that view of the Negro which served its image. The theatrical stage itself, more than any other cultural phenomenon, opens a perspective into the pathology of American race relations. It exposes the white-black dependency which has defined race relations in the United States and which persists despite all reform.

It has been a commonplace among blacks and whites that Negroes have had a special theatrical genius. And if we broaden the definition of theater to include the general entertainment professions of sports and music, recognized Negro achievement has most often occurred there. Perhaps this tells us nothing more than that entertainment has been one of the few culturally acceptable avenues to Negro accomplishment.

Nevertheless, Negroes as well as whites have long assumed that blacks could make it in the world of entertainment. And since theater has been one of the few paths, it has not only provided ready opportunity for public adulation to those few black men and women with talent and tenacity, but it has also served to delimit the terms of Negro identity within the popular culture and to ensure the persistence of those limits. We must be prepared to consider not only the black artist's willingness to work within limits that were often demeaning but also the cultural conditions which made the audience tolerate, only with the greatest anxiety, breaches of those boundaries.

In what is normally understood as the theater, in this entertainment world broadly conceived, there has been no truly Negro ethnic theater until the last decade. There have been efforts to sustain Negro acting groups within black communities, but these, as far as one can tell, have not been ethnic in the sense that the Yiddish theater was. This failure is quite instructive. But we should first recall what were the characteristics of ethnic theater in America. The Yiddish theater will serve as an example.

Following the American Civil War, during the same years that Negroes were making a place for themselves on the American stage, the Yiddish theater blossomed in New York City. It had been founded in Rumania in 1876, but it achieved its fullest flower in Bowery theaters around the turn of the century. Although the vernacular of the Eastern European Jew was depreciated by many—Jew and non-Jew alike—Yiddish was a means of maintaining ethnic authenticity. Yiddish guaranteed that the plays would be written by Jews and, being in a near argot, would reach the ethnic audience rather than a sophisticated critical establishment. Often the plays were treatments of themes from Jewish history. But the Jewish sense of community—common history, present experience, and shared symbolic and imagistic language—permitted some playwrights, who condemned what they called "historical plunder," to exploit, in "realistic" plays, the shared experiences and emotions of the audience. Such realism, though often melodramatic, touched deep emotions. The themes were familiar to those new Americans: the shock of adjustment for the "greenhorn," alienation of the newly uprooted, woeful loneliness from untimely death, economic and social hardship in a society that had set one free of traditional associations, self-sacrificing parents with ungrateful children. All was within the reach and comprehension of everyone. New plays were often no more than variations on stock forms and ideas. Indeed, the audience might be so familiar with the ideas that they might contribute or criticize from their seats. (This was a characteristic of the Russian theater, where the critics might be so vocal as to prevent a performance from proceeding.) But the audience was a vital part of the Yiddish theater, not because they laughed or wept on cue, but because they felt obliged to improve the performances. Finally, what made the Yiddish theater succeed was that it had an audience that would support four houses and four companies in New York City at one time, seven days a week. When one considers that language excluded most non-Jews from the audience, that was remarkable. These theatrical efforts remained so vital to the Jewish community that, by themselves, Jews sustained them.[1]

The culture-conscious black intellectuals of the 1920s were as anxious to produce a Negro theater as to promote the Harlem Renaissance. While there were notable efforts to develop a viable ethnic theater in Harlem—efforts which helped to catapult some individuals to commercial success—an authentic black drama never emerged. Many writers have shared Harold Cruse's confusion and anger over the frustrations of dramatic enterprises that might have done for Afro-American imagination, culture, and language what the Yiddish theater did for the Jews. The 1920s seemed the right time, and New York seemed the right place, but it did not happen. Actually, this failure is understandable enough if one considers the history and traditions such efforts were contending against.

Jews, and other immigrants coming into the United States starting with the end of the nineteenth century, were essentially alien to the American culture. Whatever hostility they might have encountered, there was no strong tradition for them in America, thus they were more free than Negroes to continue (or to develop) popular culture according to their own needs and traditions. Blacks, on the other hand, had been alienated within the American experience; alienation presumes no alternative culture. Furthermore, Negroes who attempted to relate to American popular theater from the Civil War on were faced with a very strong tradition of "black theater" extending at least into the early nineteenth century. The blackface minstrel reached far back into the past, fed the most popular imagination, and served very deep emotional needs. He had gone far toward defining, for the American mind, the characteristics of Negro personality and Negro theatrical type. This tradition was crippling to Negro ethnic theater in two ways. It provided a ready avenue to commercial success for those blacks willing to accommodate themselves to it. And the very powerful hold it had on American imagination and emotion narrowed the limits of social tolerance for black deviation.

Of course it will be said that Negroes were only incidentally related to the origins of blackface minstrelsy. That is true. It developed out of early nineteenth-century circus performances by white men who blacked their faces, and it was formalized in the 1840s by white performers like Thomas D. Rice and Daniel Decatur Emmett. Despite standard explanations that these white showmen were mimics of southern plantation Negroes, there is very little evidence to support the claim. Close analysis of the minstrel shows reveal very little Afro-American influence in the music, dance, or inspiration. In fact, the two

principal character types who define this theater—Jim Crow
and Jim Dandy (or Zip Coon)—are unlike any concept of the
plantation black or even the Sambo stereotype. Rather, Jim
Crow (the rough, coarse, barbarian) is clearly a part of the
backwoods and riverboat tradition, a blackfaced Mike Fink or
Davy Crockett. Jim Dandy (urban, dandified, almost effeminate), on the other hand, is the blackfaced counterpart to Yankee Doodle. In short, these supposed mimics of slaves were
really standard American comedy types underneath the burnt
cork.[2]

The fact that the "Negro theatrical tradition" which black
performers encountered in the late nineteenth century was of
white creation made it, in many ways, all the more formidable.
This very popular cultural phenomenon pervaded the American imagination and served important emotional needs. To understand the failure of Negro ethnic theater in the early twentieth century, it will be necessary to consider how this
tradition had used the "Negro" to serve the white psyche and
why that tradition would circumscribe Afro-American theatrical development to allow only grudging deviations from the
model.

By the end of the Civil War the minstrel show had become
fixed into a rather elaborate form which persisted with white
performers down into the twentieth century. The curtain rose
on blackfaced performers playing a rousing opening. They sat
in a row, facing the audience, costumed in the extremes; on the
one hand, the careless abandon of Jim Crow, while on the
other, the ruffled, ultra-stylishness of Dandy Jim—and all faces
made up in the most grotesque burnt-cork caricatures of Negroes, with painted-on huge red clownlike lips. Usually, the
center man, the interlocutor, remained in whiteface. The minstrels played and sang an opening, such as "There'll Be a Hot
Time in the Old Town Tonight," while their legs and bodies
moved in defiance of all rules of stage decorum. After the

opening, the interlocutor would play the "straight man" to the humor of the "end men," Mr. Bones and Mr. Tambo. He would engage them in a series of short conversations where the end men's twists of meanings or crudeness would force the joke back upon the pompous and pretentious interlocutor. Jokes and conundrums would give way to "serious" sermons, speeches, or lectures on the most weighty moral, political, or scientific topics by the blackfaced comedians. And this would be broken by the "specialty" songs of members of the group. After the "first part," there would follow the "olio," in which a mixed bag of individual and ensemble song and dance would be presented. Wild banjo music and abandoned dance would give way to sentimental ballads and dances of slow, rhythmic, insinuating shuffle. The "olio" over, the "third part" would be a grand finale: rousing music—perhaps a medley—in which the ensemble performed, culminating in a "walk-around."

It was this highly stylized variety show with which Negroes made their first appearance in the commercial theater. Afro-Americans were thus faced with a "Stage Negro" who had become a dominant type for more than forty years. Black entertainers played this white creation rather than themselves. Charles Hicks, a Negro, organized the Georgia Minstrels in 1865, but he found the hostility to a Negro business manager so great among theater people that he turned his troupe over to a white man, Charles Callender. Callender's Georgia Minstrels became the first successful all-black theatrical group. It featured entertainers like Billy Kersands and Sam Lucas, who were to become great names in Negro minstrelsy. This company, and black entertainers who followed in the late nineteenth and early twentieth centuries, remained very close to the traditional model, even to the extent that black men blacked their faces into grotesque masks in the way the white originators had. Negro entertainers had little commercial choice. They did make changes in the model, but the limits within which they worked were very crippling to their art.[3]

The discerning eye and ear can detect the minstrel tradition in present-day white comics (Jack Benny, Rowan and Martin, the Smothers Brothers) and black comics ("Pigmeat" Markam, Moms Maberly); indeed, the minstrels have deeply affected American commercial humor. But whatever the tradition's contribution, it was hardly a vehicle to create an ethnic theater for blacks; not only was it white-created but the audience that made it commercially viable was also white. Blacks were permitted into this theater only to serve that audience. It became a place for Negro achievement and thus siphoned off black talent that might have developed an authentic ethnic theater.

The audience (one should say the popular culture) had ingrained in its imagination a view of the Negro that was comic and pathetic. The theatrical darky was childlike; he could be duped into the most idiotic and foolish schemes; but like a child, too, innocence would protect him and turn the tables on the schemers. His songs were vulgar and his stories the most gross and broad; his jokes were often on himself, his wife or woman. Lazy, he was slow of movement, or when he displayed a quickness of wit it was generally in flight from work or ghosts. Nevertheless, he was unrestrained in enthusiasm for music—for athletic and rhythmical dance. Likewise, he was insatiable in his bodily appetites; his songs and tales about food would make one think him all mouth, gullet, and stomach. Indeed, performers gave themselves grotesque lips, creating the illusion of cavernous mouths. The stage Negro went into ecstasy over succulent foods—pork, chicken, watermelon—"lip-smacking," "mouth-watering." Whether he played in the Jim Crow or the Jim Dandy tradition, he never left these bounds. This caricature was patently the antithesis of the Protestant Ethic, as was the Negro stereotype. We must wonder why white men would have created this character and resisted alternatives.

In the early nineteenth century, when the blackface imitator was emerging from the circuses into wide public appeal, the United States was experiencing dramatic expansion not only in physical territory but also in individual economic opportunity and personal political power. The American, who saw himself as a man characterized by risk-taking, enterprise, and achievement, was defining the American Dream in terms of individual success and upward mobility. But crisis was built into such a concept. For as the American Dream denoted success, it implied the possibility of failure and since success meant individual achievement any failure was personal. It could be a frightening and lonely road. But the way was definitely marked by formula, from Benjamin Franklin's prescriptions for character through the moral preachments of McGuffey's reader. No properly reared American boy or girl could doubt the essentials of character and success: industry (dedicated work in some useful calling), order (decorum, good manners, the avoidance of excess in emotions and all other things), cleanliness (the honoring of one's own body and possessions but also the deference to the good taste and sensibility of others), punctuality (industry and order combined for efficiency and in deference to the opinion of others), frugality (negatively, not wasting, but positively, accumulating by deferring present consumption for future benefits).

The dogma told everyone to work hard, to restrain, to deny pleasures for future success. But there was a complication that made for great anxiety. It was not all saving. One had to know how and when to spend. For economy and hoarding, on the one hand, merely anticipated the proper occasion and opportunity for risk and speculation. Everyone knew that great achievement required great risks. A man was allotted only so much in a lifetime; he had to make it count.

The stinting was not only in things, but also in human substance. Of course, one saved money by patching and handing down old clothes; surely it helped also to serve cheaper foods, stretched for several days. But it was also necessary to husband one's passions so that impulsiveness would not dissipate energy in frolics. The wise man knew that his opportunity would come, and he must be ready for it. He should be like a coiled spring—energy and resources hoarded—ready to unleash his full, preserved power at his target, at his chance. A young man might wisely choose to remain in his mother's home a few years beyond adulthood. Perhaps, without a girl (or with the right one) he could defer marriage a few years. Failing in that, however, there was twisted a new knot of tension. For although controlling the size of families was essential, it was troublesome—technologically as well as moralistically. Sexual abstinence, not even moderation, was the surest policy, because mistakes—unwanted children—would be continuous drains on his well-husbanded potential. The incontinent or careless man might, at last, find himself spent, never having had a chance to strike out at his opportunity and now, if he were to see it, too encumbered to do so. Could the fantasies of such men have been other than the loose and undisciplined creatures of appetite—Sambo, Jim Crow, Jim Dandy? [4]

What would be more likely and more natural for men who were tied up in the knots of an achievement ethic—depending almost wholly on self-sacrifice and self-restraint—than to create a *persona* which would be completely self-indulgent and irresponsible? White men put on black masks and became another self, one which was loose of limb, innocent of obligation to anything outside itself, indifferent to success (for whom success was impossible by racial definition), and thus a creature totally devoid of tension and deep anxiety. The verisimilitude of this *persona* to actual Negroes, who were around to be seen, was at best incidental. For the white man who put on the black mask modeled himself after a subjective black man—a black man of lust and passion and natural freedom (license) which white men carried within themselves and harbored with both fascination and dread. It was the self that white men might become—would become—except for those civilizing restraints of character and order that kept the tension real. How much better it was to have that other self in a mask, on stage, objectified as it were. How that tautness of fear and self-doubt could be released in explosions of laughter once one saw that the fool—the animal, the corruption one feared most—was nothing more than a prancing darky on a stage. The entire theatrical "darky" character—from the actual face-mask itself with its grotesque mouth and lips and eyes, its wool for hair, the colorful and ridiculous clothing, to the actual style of song and dance— was calculated to achieve the effect of character and personality antithetical to respectable taste and manners.[5]

It was a cultural doubt, as well as personal, that compelled white Americans to use a black theatrical *persona*, defining themselves in contrast to it. Americans anxiously measured themselves through European eyes. And the nineteenth century was filled with contemptuous and condescending observations of American character and manners by Europeans. No one was more critical of Americans than Mrs. Frances Trollope. Nor was anyone more taken to heart than she.[6] She delighted in describing the coarseness and vulgarity of men and their wives, who, within a few short years, had made fortunes or high rank in the military. But Americans bought her book, read that they were crude and vulgar, and were deeply affected by what she said. It was shortly after the publication of *Domestic Manners* that the *New York Evening Post* reported an incident which occurred at a theatrical performance. Between acts, it seems, a man in the audience, in order to talk, assumed a sprawling posture on a box railing:

> Hissing arose, and then bleatings, and then imitations of the lowing of cattle: still the unconscious disturber pursued his chat—still the offending fragment of his coat-tail hung over

the side. At last there was a laugh, and cries of "Trollope! Trollope! Trollope!" with roars of laughter, still more loud and general.[7]

Americans were aware that civilized eyes were constantly appraising them. Americans were conscious that what was really being risked in the new world and its adventure—after all of the material achievement, the possibility, the opportunity, the individual freedom—what was in jeopardy was civilization itself. Americans, from the seventeenth century on, at least those of European origin, had never lost sight of the threat of chaos once the restraints of traditional order were undone. Democratization and expansion in the early nineteenth century seemed to be sweeping away propriety and order faster than people could accept. Nothing could be done to stop the revolution (surely nobody would have wanted to), but it made one wonder if the new American in the making was civilized enough to measure up to traditional judgments of culture.[8]

Here, too, the blackface minstrel provided a surrogate whose character combined the grotesques of manners that would be offensive to civilized taste. Jim Crow's ragged costume, Jim Dandy's dress which was always beyond the height of fashion, were both vulgar. Illustrations of performing minstrels—indeed, directions of stage action down into the twentieth century—always demanded that the performers break all of the rules of stage decorum. Not only were their bodies to move in very exaggerated ways—arms and legs flailing, head bobbing and rocking—but the performers were to sit with their legs spread wide apart, vigorously tap their feet to the music while making their faces grimace and contort beyond imagination. The minstrel's dialect, whatever its relationship to true Negro speech, was coarse, clumsy, ignorant, and stood at the opposite pole from the soft tones and grace of what was considered cultivated speech. Whatever else, the minstrel's dance utterly obliterated the highly formalized dance that was familiar to fashionable society.

The black mask that white men put on was the antithesis of proper character and proper manners. These white faces in black masks were, one might say, their own alter-egos. Having Americans of African origin in the South and in northern cities was a great convenience to white men. The black-white polarity was too dramatic a symbol to ignore. By objectifying one's horror through blackness one attributed to whiteness a quality of rightness, but it could not remove the self-doubt that had caused the anxiety. Personal and societal doubt was deep and required continuous reassurance. Yet, if there had been no black men around, white Americans, like their English cousins, might have found distant models to serve. The English, after all, delighted in the American blackface performers; they had their "Little Black Sambo," their Indian niggers, their African niggers, their Polynesian niggers—all, with slight variations of the same stereotype. But the American whites, with the black man in their own home, so to speak, found themselves with the additional anxiety that their black countryman should not destroy his objectified fantasy. Negroes, in real life as well as on the stage, should not get out of character. If Negroes were men like other men, what then?

But as long as everyone knew his role and kept within it, the blackface minstrel was not merely a kind of catharsis but he was also a pleasurable escape into naturalness. It was surely much easier to be a fool—to let oneself go—from behind the mask, from within one's blackness, than as a white man. It was also easier for the audience to escape into the grotesqueness of a black *persona* at a circus or on the stage than to identify with an undisciplined white man for whom no such stereotype existed.[9] The Negro stereotype and the blackface minstrel provided performer and audience with a way of being themselves —part of themselves at least.

Thus the blackface minstrel objectified and therefore created a distance between white men's normative selves (what they had to be) and their natural selves (what they feared but were fascinated by). With such a creation, one could almost at will move in or out of the blackface character. It is not hard to believe that the white performers did find remarkable freedom behind their black masks.

When black men put on black masks it was not really a different affectation. After all, American Negroes were no different in their values and expectations than their middle-class, white countrymen. If anything, black Americans in the late nineteenth century, with slavery in their recent past, were more anxious to prove themselves—to achieve—than were whites. And the formula for them was the same as it was for other Americans. Booker T. Washington is only a darker Benjamin Franklin, a poorer Andrew Carnegie. If anything, there was more at stake, for the black man carried not only the burden of self but also that of race. It was thought, and expected, that every individual success was exemplary. By the same token, every failure was not only an individual tragedy but evidence of racial limitation. One's surrender to appetites—self-indulgence—might thus seem more frightening and guilt-producing, or it might seem inevitable, in the blood so to speak. Thus, Negroes might be more compulsive in their reining the animal within them, or they might be resigned to the inevitable: "We'll never get anywhere," or "Black men are more natural; we have more fun." Whether striving to achieve or surrendering to racial inevitability, whether submitting to "blood" with elation or despair, black men accepted the Protestant Ethic and its terms for achievement.

So the black masks that black men wore, placed on stage—externalized, objectified—those very qualities which certified failure in a commercial and industrial society. Black men, like white men, could use the theatrical grotesques as ways of

marking distance between themselves and their horror. But
since these were racial delineations—white fantasy's conscrip-
tion of black men to serve its needs—the problem of maintaining distance for the Negro was crucial and difficult. Bert Williams and George Walker, probably the most talented team of
black theatrical performers at the turn of the century, tried to
push beyond the limits of the minstrel character. They tried to
use the stereotype as an instrumental satire. Or, when this
team billed themselves as "Two Real Coons," they were not
portraying themselves or any other Negroes they knew. Rather,
they were intending to give style and comic dignity to a fiction
that white men had created and fostered and with which black
men (on and off stage) conspired, being one of the few public
selves that they were permitted.

Some black performers attempted to achieve the distance between the stage character and themselves by the very extremi-
ties of the exaggeration. Grotesques, themselves, could allow
black men, as they did white men, the assurance that the foolishness on stage was not them. Thus Billy Kersands, popular
with Negro as well as white audiences around 1911, made himself into a freak entertainer. Claiming to have the largest

NEW EPOCH IN NEGRO MINSTRELSY

UNDER THE MANAGEMENT OF R. VOELCKEL

The Famous and Original   America's Oldest Minstrel

"BILLY"   KERSANDS

The Minstrel King   Under Spacious Canvas

MINSTRELS

Home Office:
Times Building

mouth in the world—"If God ever wanted to make my mouth
any bigger, He would have to move my ears"—did a dancing
act with two billiard balls in his mouth. And the very popular
Ernest Hogan pushed the darky characterization to the limits
of unction and denigration. Neither he, nor anyone he could
have known, ate watermelon the way his stage character
claimed to. Hogan and Kersands prided themselves on playing
at its most extreme what the audience wanted. That could be a
personal insulation.

"You have to be one to know one" goes the common *riposte*
in name-calling games. Much humor, indeed, assumes this, together with the opposite insight that to recognize a fool makes
one not a fool any longer; and that is very pleasing. Surely this
is true of ethnic humor, whether on or off stage, especially as it
is performed by members of the characterized group. For the
comic accepts a demeaning characterization of his group, assuming to improve upon it with his claim of authenticity.
Thus, he becomes superior because his perspective allows him
to judge himself and his people and because his pose places
him above even those who had disdain for him to begin with.
Such a posture is common to both the professional ethnic hu-
morists and the amateurs who intend merely to amuse others
and put them at their ease. Jewish, Negro, Italian, they are as
much as saying, "Yes you are right about us, but even you
don't know how right. Let *me* tell you." Nor need one be a
performer to play that game; the ethnic audience is served as
well. To watch a slow-witted blackfaced incompetent on stage,
or a Negro who stumbles through foolish predicaments, is at
once to recognize an identity and to assume a superiority as
viewer and critic. In this regard, there was no difference between a Negro whose anxieties were released through laughter
at a blackfaced simpleton who cannot manage his life and a
Jew who laughed himself into tears at a "greenhorn's" incom-
petences as portrayed on the Yiddish stage. It is all a kind of

masochism which converts self-hatred—through its indulgence
—into gratification and the pleasure of self-esteem. But the rub
is that the contempt for self and race on which such humor
turns must be ever-present to make it work. Lurking beneath
the surface of amused accommodation was the uneasiness—
"you have to be one to know one"—which might at any moment bubble up, twisting the smile into a grimace of hurt.
Truth to tell, it was laughing to keep from crying.

The black mask of the minstrel—its most figurative representation of the ethnic stereotype—was a substantive shield pro-
tecting more than self-esteem. The mask was a means of
survival—only by wearing it in some form could black entertainers find work—and, even more, it was a defense against
violence. The veteran comic Tom Fletcher recalled that many
of the small southern towns his company performed in were so
hostile to Negroes that violence was always threatening, murder seemed in the shadow of white men's eyes. Signs which
warned, "Nigger, Read and Run" chilled the hearts of Negro
performers who played there. Yet, they hit upon a way. They
would enter such towns in private Pullman cars, which were
parked at a siding. Then, with their band, the entertainers
would parade from the railroad car to whatever served as the
theater; and after the performance, they would strike up the
band and parade back to their Pullman. Whatever the number
of shows—if there was a matinee or two-day stand—they
would march to rousing music or they would not be on the
streets of that town. And they seldom had doubt, Fletcher reports, as to what tune would do them the most good. "As soon
as all the members of the company were on the ground we
would start playing '*Dixie.*' No matter how many different
tunes we had in our band books, we could play that song in
any key." [10] It was as if the *modus vivendi* depended on the
Negroes continuing to play their parts, off stage as well as on.
And these black performers knew that their very existence de-

pended on their never pretending to be other than their stage characters. Such an experience is emblematic of the great charade that whites and blacks joined in. The stereotype—the mask—defined the Afro-American as white Americans chose to see him; outside the mask the black man was either invisible or threatening. Negroes, accepting the pretense, wore the mask to move in and out of the white world with safety and profit. Tom Fletcher knew, without understanding, that the magic of the mask would work. He tells of entertaining alumni gatherings for Princeton University. He was barraged with hot-dog buns by the hostile audience in his first appearance in 1902. But Fletcher held his ground, played and sang, and was asked back every year after he had "broken the ice." He never had trouble playing for white people, once they knew what he could do.

What Tom Fletcher describes—finding accommodation within the role that was acceptable to whites—was little different from what other black people were doing throughout American society. The duality of self was everywhere commented on by Negroes. The domestic servant—soul of deference at his employer's Long Island estate—swung in the Harlem cabarets on weekends; the placid-faced cook broke into shrieks of ecstasy in the store-front church; everyone played a role. Paul Laurence Dunbar had said it:

> Why should the world be overwise
> In counting all our tears and sighs?
> Nay, let them only see us while
> We wear the mask.

And the theme is echoed in the blues:

> Got one mind for white folks to see,
> 'nother for what I know is me;
> he don't know, he don't know my mind.

But as much as it was a passport into the white man's consciousness, as much as it was an assurance of safety for that private self behind the mask, it was also a dissembler to one's own eye. For to feel forced to parade in disguise before men who are hostile to all but their charade cannot but distort the hidden face. There is a danger of corrosion of the self in this pretense, and surely a rending of integrity. How, and when does one call upon the real self to dispel the make-believe and claim humanity and dignity? How could one make it clear that the public self was only a façade that covered a real man or woman?

Ernest Hogan, just before his death, told Tom Fletcher of an incident when his characters became confused. Forgetting he was in the Deep South, Hogan went to the wrong (white) box-office to collect money owed to him. He was accosted by a white man; Hogan recalled, he " 'started cursing at me and raised his fist but I beat him to the punch and knocked him down.' " Hogan was smuggled out of the town and remembered, " 'I didn't get myself together again until I was in Australia with my own company.' " [11] Hogan not only forgot *where* he was, but more importantly, he forgot *who* he was. And that is the point of the story—the point that Hogan wanted to make. Because, apocryphal or not, it was meant to assert the reality of that self which, indeed, was most often forgotten. In the later years of his life, Tom Fletcher had come to believe that his characterizations were of authentic Negro "folk." He saw efforts of "reformers" to eliminate the racial stereotype from show business as simply hurtful to black entertainers. Criticism came from "outsiders" who did not understand. In fact, Fletcher insisted, these men and women who had done darky characterizations for a living, had done their part in changing conditions affecting Negroes:

> All of us knew what we were up against but we just kept plugging along, minding our own business, doing our work

and always letting the other fellow open the conversation rather than forcing ourselves upon him. When the other fellow did the asking, our answers were always direct, and polite. This tended to make him forget a lot of things he had read or heard and to take us as we really were. As a result, season after season we could see barriers being let down, and in a way which would insure that they would not be raised again.[12]

Doubtless, Tom Fletcher and others who had joined in the charade could answer questions so that the white man would "forget a lot of things he had read or heard," forget what he feared. The white man could be put at his ease, "to take us as we really were." At least, so it would appear, but the profound question was never asked and never answered: who were these black men *really?* It was just possible that the trick had been too perfect; *legerdemain* had undone itself in a disappearance act where the self had vanished, but also the incantation to call it back again.

This was the atmosphere in which a Negro theater would have to survive in the first decades of the twentieth century. James Weldon Johnson was right when he observed that the theatrical Negro was reduced to two voices, comedy and pathos. This convention, too, defined the limits of possibilities. Actually, travesty was the single comic mode in the minstrel tradition. And travesty, broadly speaking, continued to describe the Negro theatrical comedy. Travesty, recall, turns on the disparity between the actor and his costume which thinly disguised pretense. The small girl with her face powdered and rouged, in the high heels, furs, and baubles of her mother; the jester wearing the king's crown; the peasant in the robes of nobility; transvestites (men in chorus lines, women acting as "toughs") are classical sources of comedy. To make travesty work, however, the disproportion must be obvious. No matter how she stretches and struts and preens herself, it is impossible for the little girl to be her mother. Knowing that, the audience finds the pretense funny. It is possible to laugh at a jester's antics as he wears the crown of his king, but were he to have more than the symbol of authority, were he even for a moment to be the actual sovereign that the crown represents, his actions would be something other than comic. So, too, the female impersonator whose maleness is in doubt may be a comedian but his humor will depend on something other than travesty.

American Negro humor [13] has been mainly travesty, if the term is considered in its most figurative sense. For it is not only clothes and other such costumes which symbolize classes. Language, or even a name, might do. In the South before the Civil War, for instance, slaveholders found a common source of amusement in the naming of their servants. Black butlers or waiters, haphazardly liveried, slow and inefficient (a common complaint), might be named Cicero or Caesar. A small black child, collecting wood for the kitchen, might answer to the name of Pompey or Maceo. Black slaves with such names were walking, living travesties even to those who knew Roman classics imperfectly. Such exaggeration deftly emphasized the rightness of the servant's condition. For what distorted mind could place African slaves on a parity with white men, heirs of that grand civilization those Roman names denoted? Lest there be doubt about that august heritage, white Americans had borrowed other names from the Roman republic—"congress," "senate," and "republic" itself—these, of course, without humorous intent.

On stage, the names given to Negro characters have been important to comedy from the earliest blackfaced minstrel down into the twentieth century. Borrowing names from classical antiquity, from the Old Testament, or from the heroic national past, blackfaced comics pranced about drawing laughter every time their names were spoken. Sometimes the pretentiousness of the names was simply due to the pomposity of sound. Rastus is such a name, but also Old Testament names such as Rufus, Amos, and Moses had the same effect. So common, as humorous characterizations of Negroes, did these names become, connoting the stage personality more readily than the historical character, that they became embarrassments for genuine bearers and almost fell out of use among Afro-Americans. Bert Williams and George Walker, with characteristic inventiveness, went beyond simple travesty in their stage names. *In Dahomey,* for instance, they played private detectives Shylock Homestead and Rareback Pinkerton respectively. In the same play, the president of the Dahomey Colonization Society carried a name, Cicero Lightfoot, which rested as much on well-known southern aristocracy as on classical Rome. Surely, the point was made when Rosetta Lightfoot (Mrs. George Walker) sang "I Want To Be a Real Lady."

Language—a symbol of civilization and social class—was another cloak of travesty for the stage Negro. The use, or misuse, of ponderous latinate words, the stiff, formal, pompous diction of the minstrels' interlocutor (that name itself, indeed) served the pretense and exposed it all at once. The audience was asked to look at blackfaced performers (Ethiopian Delineators as they sometimes called themselves) occasionally pretending to be civilized, and they laughed because the frequent malapropisms and misunderstandings made the pretense ludicrous. The language of the minstrel was, throughout, the language of social pretense. The first thing that happened, in fact, was that all the blackfaced characters were called "Gentlemen," and told to be seated. The conundrums and the repartee that flowed between the interlocutor and the end men were almost wholly plays on words, figures of speech, etc. Mr. Interlocutor might ask Mr. Bones if a sentimental ballad just sung had not touched him. Mr. Bones would give a series of answers, always missing Interlocutor's specific metaphorical use of touch. "The man next to me touched me, and I'll hit him if he does it again." "Tambo touched me for five dollars, and he'd better pay me back." Interlocutor would then shift to other sentimental figures—to be moved, to have a heart—with the apparent hope that Bones would somehow catch his meaning. But, of course, Bones would always lead him through intricate verbal frolics, never touching the point, and leaving the audience in stitches while Mr. Interlocutor shrugged with exasperation and relief as the next musical number started.

The minstrel tradition always included a parody of formal oratory, again pointing up the importance of language. From the very first of his minstrel performances, Dan Emmett included long disquisitions on a collection of topical, political, and religious subjects. A man in the grotesque of blackface make-up would stand center-stage, and, with the most serious expression and intent, deliver a speech which might toss together the Mexican War, women's dress styles, and the need for sound leadership in Washington. And despite the posture of seriousness, the oration would be laden with all of the malapropisms and jarring collision of images that would at once emphasize the distortion, and ridicule the genuine political or clerical orator. This form of humor, too, was quite traditional in American culture, reaching into the backwoods, Davy Crockett tradition. Americans had always seemed to find great amusement in the elegance and inflation of language and posture. And here, too, was something of travesty, for the language and speech of great oration coming from the mouth of a blackfaced minstrel was humorous in its disproportion.[14]

Significantly, much of American oratory in the early years of the nineteenth century came very close to self-ridicule when it was most serious. Orators like Daniel Webster were using speech and formal rhetoric to clothe their meaning (as well as their personalities) in greatness. The long rhetorical periods, the flourish of elegant figures were stylistic emblems of grandeur—put-on in republican pretense—just as those pre-

tentious names of senator, congressman, and president lifted
quite ordinary men out of the pedestrian. Much was in doubt
in a new republic that was trying to live the greatness of its
idealism. Often it was language, posture, pretense that stood
for the difference between the conventionality of everyday political life and the epoch-making (nation-making) challenge of
their historical moment—that stood for the difference between
the common-man origins which everyone jealously remembered and the statesmanlike postures politicians anxiously assumed. Oratorical style made the difference. Daniel Webster,
that Yankee who was born in rustic New Hampshire and lived
to serve New England banking and textile interests, found it
important to sound like a Roman orator sounded. He had the
language and the style to make tariffs and most mundane selfish
interests sound grand and monumental. Oratory for Americans was like the names they chose to give their political
institutions and the Greek columns they placed on their banks
and other public buildings, costumes for greatness. Parodies of
Webster's speech in blackface not only ridiculed the posturing
of the political orator but the fantastic pretense of black men
playing the role of statesmen. The minstrel orator could satirize current events through the assumed ridiculousness of
black pretense. The most popular speech of Byron Christy
of the famous Christy Minstrels was a direct parody of Daniel
Webster's Seventh of March speech which supported the Compromise of 1850:

> What do de folks mean talkin' 'bout de Norf and de Souf?
> Do dey want to separate us from our brederin in de sun-
> shiney Souf? Do dey? Eh? umph? Do dese people (whats
> roamin' round like hungry lions seekin' whom dey may de-
> vour) want more? Eh? umph? It dey do let 'em hab New
> Jersey, Hardscrable, or—or—or any other man.
> Do dese people want to tear up dat magnificent and mag-
> niglorious American flag what's ravelin' out in de breezes ob
> de atmosphere on de top ob de St. Nicholas Hotel? Eh?

umph? Do dey want to strip it up and gib de stars to de
Souf, and de stripes to de Norf? I answer you in clarion
tones dat I hope may be heard from de risin' place ob de sun
to de cheer in which he sets down. Dey can't do it, nor—nor
any other man.[15]

Of course, often the travesty of the minstrel and his heirs
was more direct, less figurative. Blackfaced characters, dressed
as policemen, businessmen, politicians, by the 1920s had become standard material for stage comedy. The humor always
depended on the disparity between the black man and the costume he wore as much as on the comic situation itself. Present-day popular comedy has revived this kind of travesty in
television performances of "Pigmeat" Markham (an old
trooper, whose career goes back into the active days of Tom
Fletcher) and his recording success of "Here Comes de Judge."
It would seem that the "camp" vogue has discovered a new
humor in a parody on a parody.

But the cultural phenomenon of the minstrel travesty
reaches deep into the racial pathology of Americans. For what
white men in blackface objectified on stage was the conceptualization of the Negro as naturally foolish in roles that white
men envisioned themselves playing in real life. A black man as
mayor, senator, policemen, or clergyman was utter fantasy.
But more, one step beyond the backwoodsman, the black man as
human was fantasy too; or so it would seem from the performance of the theatrical Negro.[16]

Lest we ignore the tragic aspect of this psychology, we
should remember that the compulsive racism in this travesty
suggests potential crisis in white men's identity. His own feasi-
bility as human, eloquent, and grand depended on the farce.
The white common man, whatever his distance from power,
could sense his belonging to a civilized, democratic society to
the degree that he could see the Negro as ludicrous in it. Notably, the white consensus about the tragedy of Reconstruction

in the South following the Civil War (a concensus of historians, novelists, and journalists, which no amount of contradictory scholarship has managed to destroy) has it that radical Republicans forced upon southern society that very travesty which had been unthinkable—Negro rule. The sin was to have imposed, in real life, what because of its absurdity was comic on stage. One need only recall D. W. Griffith's *Birth of a Nation* (1915) to understand the power of the minstrel myth. All of the white men in blackface who played in that film were merely playing minstrel types. It would have been funny to those white audiences had it not been distorting *real* history and had it not provoked horrible fantasies about the political future of northern communities following the migration of southern blacks. Reconstruction was simply the other side of the minstrel coin. Nor were black men free of the effects of travesty and the minstrel myth. Intellectual blacks were horrified at Marcus "Aurelius" Garvey [17] in the 1920s (his uniforms, titles, bombastic rhetoric, and seemingly wild fantasies about Africa) precisely because they saw him through the eyes "of others, who looked on in amused contempt and pity." Men like DuBois saw Garvey as a minstrel; perhaps white men did too.

One further characteristic of travesty will complete this consideration of the theatrical Negro as part of American popular culture. So far, it has only been suggested that travesty, aside from keeping the pretender in his place, may be a vehicle for social satire of the audience's betters. That is clearly within this comic mode. For as the child preens and postures like an adult, and as the jester swaggers and bellows like the king, each, through exaggeration, is discovering the latent pretense and assumption of those they mimic. So, travesty often cuts both ways, making comment on the higher as well as lower order.

This is easy enough to see in the Jim Dandy character. Always a stable part of the minstrel, he was an obvious travesty of urban Negro elegance, always in his "long-tailed blue." He apparently had his real-life model. For, one traveler recorded seeing in Boston a black dandy "lounging down the street. He was a Sable Count d'Orsay. His toilet was the most elaborately recherché you can imagine. He seemed intensely and harmlessly happy in his coat and waistcoat, of the finest possible materials; and the careful carelessness of the adjustment of the wool [hair] and hat was not readily to be surpassed." [18] The ultra-elegant, almost effeminate Jim Dandy was as much a ridicule of the pretensions of the gentleman of fashion, particularly the parvenu, as he was of the urban Negro. Frank Dumont, the famous Philadelphia white man who did blackfaced minstrels, exposed the dual satire of his performances. Demonstrating to a reporter his costuming technique, dressed finally in white ruffled collar and cuffs, bright blue velvet pants, and red velvet jacket, Dumont said with a grand gesture, "This is very genteel, dressy and in keeping with minstrelsy. It is also full evening dress as adopted by the 'Four Hundred,' so you see we are 'in it' so to speak." [19] It was this possible, yet incredible, juxtaposition that provided the broad format of theatrical Negro humor.

In the last decades of the nineteenth century, upper class Americans were very vulnerable to ridicule. Many who had only recently acquired wealth tried, through conspicuous consumption and borrowed taste, to draw social distinctions which would define them as the American aristocracy. The very social fluidity that had permitted their rise made the task difficult; there was little satisfaction in an aristocracy based on money alone. Therefore, as the century came to a close, American society (especially New York City) witnessed the most grandiloquent spectacles, orchestrated by impresarios like Ward McAllister. Social distinction needed promotion and show.[20]

Without the "families" of European society, the Americans

had to create an elite as they went along; Ward McAllister set himself that task for New York. During the flush and expansive 1880s and 1890s, New York society defined itself by giving parties of fashion and dinners of exquisite (mainly expensive) taste. The social events were patterned, as much as they could be, after English society. But social definition rested on public acceptance; people had to know what was going on, not merely those playing the game but the general public as well. McAllister's genius (as well as his downfall) was in his willingness to exploit popular interest in the upper classes by holding press conferences and providing news for society pages. Thus, he gave public definition to the American aristocracy (according to his design) by making their antics a spectacle. It was from McAllister that a New York *Tribune* reporter mined the gold of the Four Hundred label. "Why, there are only about 400 people in fashionable New York Society. If you go outside that number you strike people who are either not at ease in a ballroom or else make other people not at ease. See the point? . . . When we give a large ball like the last New Year's ball for 800 guests, we go outside of the exclusive fashionable set, and invite professional men, doctors, lawyers, editors, artists and the like." [21] The label stuck. The general public seemed to have an insatiable appetite for this kind of social news. Society was doing all that it could to prove itself fashionable with grand balls and grander dinner parties. And everything was given great coverage by the press, so that it would not be too much to say that "society" was on stage.

The most notorious of the social displays was the Bradley Martin fancy dress ball of February 10, 1897. Dixon Wecter, writing about the event long after, estimated it cost $369,200 by the time it was over. The Waldorf Hotel had to be boarded up to keep the curious from looking in. Couturiers in New York and Paris were engaged for months designing costumes from the Renaissance or the Elizabethan period, or following

the styles of Van Dyck, Madame Pompadour, or Marie Antoinette. Mrs. Bradley Martin herself came as Mary Queen of
Scots. She wore "a bodice of black velvet lined with cerise
satin, an overdress opened over a white satin petticoat, a
richly jewelled stomacher, and a pointed cap of silver, together
with a massive ruby necklace worn by Marie Antoinette and a
cluster of diamond grapes which had belonged to Louis XIV."
Mr. Bradley Martin came as Louis XV. But probably August
Belmont outdid the men in a full suit of steel armor inlaid
with gold which cost him $10,000. Excitement was kept high
when there were reports of crises: James Van Alen decided
that mourning a relative's death would prevent his dancing the
quadrille d'honneur "which had been rehearsing for days at
Mrs. Astor's under the scrutiny of Professor Karl Marwig." But
all the problems of production seemed minor; the Ball came off
as scheduled and very much as planned. It was such a success,
indeed, that the Bradley Martins removed themselves perma-
nently to England under the pressure of the notoriety that followed.[22]

Surely, there was no greater travesty, on or off stage, than
the Bradley Martin ball. I suspect that it was this quality that
excited the public interest and amusement. Yet, that affair was
only an exaggeration of what "society" had been doing since
the Civil War. Significantly, there are several parallels between these social functions and the minstrel theater: the costuming, the pretense, the excess, and the gluttony. And like the
minstrel, the public performance of "society" was important.
Whereas Ernest Hogan made public the connoisseur techniques of watermelon eating—the right sound when thumped,
the right smell, the right way to savor it—Ward McAllister
was no less public in his expertness about the mouth-watering,
lip-smacking delicacies at Delmonico's. It was more a difference in class than style. Like the minstrels, the upper classes
had abandoned some of the most compulsive features of the

Protestant Ethic. So when looking at "society" and the minstrels in the 1880s and 1890s, they seem to be parodies of one
another. At least, "society's" pretenses are no less grotesque
than those of the blackfaced minstrels, and it seems to me
more than likely that the lower middle-class white audiences
made the connection. Frank Dumont's expansive association of
minstrelsy and the Four Hundred reveals a dimension of the
minstrel as social commentary. Certainly, the blackface minstrels' origins in the Yankee Doodle and Mike Fink characters
would support such an idea and help to explain the contagious
popularity of this theatrical form.

The fad of the Cakewalk is just another facet of the same
idea. This dance was the finale of Sam T. Jack's *Creole Show*
(1890), which was the first notable instance of its performance
on stage. It became something of a craze for the remainder of
the decade. All Negro shows featured the dance; towns and
cities throughout the country had Cakewalk contests. Madison
Square Garden, indeed, held the annual national championship, where very large prizes were given, and the top performers could be assured of a professional theatrical future. The
traditional explanation of the origins of the dance tell of slaves
prancing before the "big house" on Christmas or similar holi-
days to win the prize—a cake. There is doubtless some truth
to this—such dances probably did occur on large plantations
—but the dance of the 1890s is related only in name and idea.
The Cakewalk featured Negro couples in fancy dress in large
numbers (50 to 60 couples at Madison Square Garden). The
couples pranced and strutted and twirled to lively music. It
was spectacular. The winners were those who had style, flashi-
ness of manner, elegance of costume, and could execute intricate figures and strutting steps to the rousing music. Whatever
the dance's origins, surely in the 1890s, this dance parodied the
quadrille d'honneur that climaxed the fancy dressed balls of
the Four Hundred, as the Cakewalk climaxed the minstrel

show. And the contemporaries did not miss this point. For the Cakewalk was being done by "society," and reported on the society pages of the daily press. Bert Williams and George Walker made advertising capital out of a report that William K. Vanderbilt had done the Cakewalk at a ball. With due publicity, the comedians, "dressed a point or two above the height of fashion," left a letter at Vanderbilt's Fifth Avenue mansion as a formal challenge to a "cake-walking match." Their letter placed the stakes at $50 because, as Williams said, "It's a shame to take the money." Of course, the match never came off, but an appropriate point was made. They were, after all, performers on a public stage—all pretenders.[23]

Americans were No-Man and Everyman; the newness and the openness of society created its special anxieties. White men's selves depended on blacks being less than men; the wholeness of the black person too often rested on his accepting that white judgment and achieving applause through self-denial and self-depreciation. But real achievement for white men, too, meant an acknowledgment of a superior European culture, and, thus, a self-denial and self-depreciation of a different kind. All was a jumble of masks and costumes covering naked uncertainties. White men pretended to be black men of their fantasy, black men pretended to be the grotesques that white men had created, while other white men and women pretended to be aristocrats, court jesters, knights in $10,000 armor, Mary Queen of Scots, and so on. The deep realities from which they were all fleeing were doubtless more horrible than the acts that they put on. It all was a theater of the absurd.

Certainly the theatrical Negro was a formidable act to follow. Black performers accommodated themselves to the tradition, while at the same time they tried to innovate and find more room for their talents within the convention; they moved toward the musical review. Sam T. Jack's *The Creole Show* opened at Boston's Old Howard Theater in 1890. It featured girls for the first time in a major minstrel. They were light-skinned dancers whose dance and burlesque accommodated the style of the "olio" to standard variety acts. Following a very successful run in Boston, *The Creole Show* played in Chicago through the World's Fair in 1893.

John W. Isham's *The Octoroons* (1895) was billed as a musical farce in minstrel pattern. Isham transformed the "olio" (which also featured a girls' chorus) into a burlesque sketch; specialty numbers were strung on a thin thread of plot. The rousing minstrel finale remained a Cakewalk jubilee, minstrel drill, and chorus march. But in the following year, Isham abandoned the minstrel finale *In Oriental America* for one in which singers performed operatic selections: solos and choruses from *Faust, Martha, Rigoletto, Carmen,* and *Il Trovatore.* And in the same year, two white producers engaged Bob Cole to write a review around the singing talent of Sissieretta Jones, who had made something of a singing sensation in 1892. Mme. Jones was quickly promoted as "Black Patti," after the white operatic star Adeline Patti. In *"Black Patti's" Troubadours* (1896) the minstrel form was still discernible, but the finale was called an "Operatic Kaleidoscope" and featured Mme. Jones (who took no other part in the show) and a chorus; they sang selections from operas. Comedy and blackface remained, but the form and some part of the content of the minstrel was giving way to innovative Negro talent.

In 1898 Bob Cole produced *A Trip to Coontown,* which had several path-breaking features. It was the first show to have been organized, written, produced, and managed by Negroes. The show had a story and continuity, with a cast of characters who worked out the plot from beginning to end. In truth, therefore, this was the first commercial Negro musical comedy. Also in 1898, *Clorindy—The Origin of the Cake-Walk* was produced, combining the musical talents of Will Marion Cook with the lyrics of Paul Laurence Dunbar, James Weldon Johnson reported that "*Clorindy* was the talk of New York. It was the first demonstration of the possibilities of syncopated Negro music. Cook was the first competent composer to take what was then known as ragtime and work it out in a musicianly way. His choruses and finales in *Clorindy*, complete novelties as they were, sung by a lusty chorus, were simply breath-taking. Broadway had something entirely new." [24]

But these changes, notable as they were, remained essentially formal; the stage characterization—the theatrical Negro—improved only slightly. Many black performers were content to add only style to the caricature. Indeed, some seemed to have discovered that the formula for success was Negro depreciation, and they capitalized on it. Ernest Hogan was an extremely talented blackface comedian who reached the height of his career in the last decades of the nineteenth century. He is described by James Weldon Johnson as having been a genuine rival to Bert Williams. "He had greater unction than Bert Williams and by that very token lacked Williams's subtlety and finish." [25] Indeed, his most notable and lasting contribution was the introduction of a new genre of popular music. In the late 1880s, Hogan lifted a tune from a ragtime piano player in a Chicago brothel, gave it new lyrics and a new name, and profited from what became one of the most popular songs of the 1890s. "All Coons Look Alike to Me" was not only popular, it introduced true ragtime to theatrical music, and it was the first of what came to be known as "coon songs." Ragtime was still associated with brothels and "low-life," and it was thought something of an event to make it part of Tin Pan Alley. "Coon songs" were merely ragtime songs that had lyrics about Negroes, called coons. Apparently, it was the derision of the Negro that seemed magically to make the music acceptable. They were very popular. "All Coons Look Alike to Me," Hogan claimed, earned royalties second only to "After the Ball Is

Over." His other favorites were "Rufus Rastus Johnson," and "Won't You Come Home Bill Bailey"; the latter, with modernized lyrics, is still sung today.

Aside from "coon songs," Hogan leaned heavily on another pillar of the Negro stereotype. Creatures of appetite, black people were always presented as slaves to food, particularly watermelon, chicken, pork chops, and ham. Ernest Hogan not only wrote songs about these foods, but his routine always consisted of songs like "Watermelon Time." While the orchestra would play the melody, Hogan would pantomime the eating of that fruit, and he would explain to the audience the best way to eat it. And Hogan's success inspired others to write such songs as "Who Is Dat Said Chicken In Dis Crowd." [26]

Apparently, Hogan had misgivings about this kind of performance and, especially, his role in the "coon song" phenomenon. If not misgivings, at least he had been made sensitive enough by the criticism of other black performers that he felt moved to justify himself. Tom Fletcher reports a conversation with Hogan in 1907, the year before Hogan's death. He was seriously ill and convalescing. "All Coons Look Alike to Me," Hogan admitted, " 'caused a lot of trouble in and out of show business. . . .' " But, he insisted, it was also good for show business because it was popular, it stimulated business, and it earned money for performers. Furthermore, he pointed out, that it " 'opened the way for a lot of colored and white songwriters. Finding the rhythm so great, they stuck to it changing the lyrics, and now you get song hits from my creations without the word "coon." ' " Hogan believed that he had made ragtime possible. " 'The *ragtime* players were the boys who played just by ear their own creations of music which would have been lost to the world if I had not put it on paper.' " [27] According to Fletcher's report of the conversation, Hogan emphasized the commercial matter over that of racial self-esteem.

Black performers helped to perpetuate the "darky" tradition

in other ways. From the beginning, the blackface characters wanted nothing more than to get back to "dear ole' massa." Indeed, the minstrels contributed greatly to the myth of the Old South and the nostalgia that sentimentalized much American literature and drama. Notably, this sentiment antedates the Civil War and the "Lost Cause"; Dan Emmett's "Dixie," for instance, was first performed in New York City on April 4, 1859.[28] Apparently, northern whites (perhaps more than southern) found some genuine satisfaction in the myth. Black performers were as eager to capitalize on that commercial possibility as any other.

Probably no one went to the lengths that the black promoter Billy McClain did to exploit the idea of the sentimental South. His first effort was a minstrel review called *The South Before the War*. But far the most remarkable was *In Black America*, which opened in Brooklyn's Ambrose Park in the summer of 1896. With the support of a white producer, Nate Saulsbury, McClain reproduced a southern plantation into which he worked a Negro show. In the end he used five hundred people. Cotton plants (with buds) were transplanted, bales of cotton and a real cotton gin were set up. There was livestock and cabins for the "field workers"; some of the cast actually lived in the cabins for the summer. This property was arranged throughout the park to provide "atmosphere," and the patrons could wander through, watching the black actors pretend to be slaves in the South. At a signal, all would assemble under a tent for a standard musical review in the minstrel tradition. The success of *In Black America* might have been due to the novelty, to the lack of theatrical entertainment during the summer's off-season, to the circus atmosphere; nevertheless, it is remarkable that New Yorkers would make the rather difficult trip to Brooklyn to watch a mock-up of a mythical plantation. *In Black America* was just an extreme example of a rather general phenoenon: black performers perpetuating rather than changing the theatrical stereotype.

Some Negro performers, however, did make conscious efforts to bring about substantive as well as formal changes in the racial proscriptions of the American stage. Their efforts may appear slight to us today, but they are significant nonetheless. The struggles of the famous team of Bert Williams and George Walker will illustrate the narrow limits within which black entertainers had to work and the meager innovations that would seem victories.

A veteran of the stage, Leigh Whipper, claimed that Egbert A. Williams was born March 11, 1875, in Riverside, California, of Bahamian immigrant parents. Little is known of Bert Williams' early life, but he was eighteen when he teamed up with George Walker in San Francisco. Walker described him as "a gaunt fellow over six feet, of orange hue; leaning on a banjo, haggling with a manager." That was in 1893. The two stage-struck youngsters formed a vaudeville team which was to bedazzle Broadway and, after Walker's death, to make Bert Williams the first Negro star of the *Ziegfeld Follies*.

George Walker could not remember a time when he was not a part of the theater. As a boy, he joined a company of amateur colored minstrels in his native Lawrence, Kansas. He left Lawrence for the West, going bit by bit, joining one circus, musical show, or medicine show after another. As Walker remembered it, in the West there were many "quack doctors" who traveled from town to town and used entertainers to attract large crowds in order to sell their medicines. "When a boy," Walker recalled, "I was quite an entertainer. I could sing and dance, and was good at face-making, beating the tambourine, and rattling the bones." These were the talents that would draw crowds in the sundry western towns through which the medicine wagons passed. Walker learned two lessons from this experience: "white people are always interested in what they call 'darky' singing and dancing; and the fact that I could entertain in that way as no white boy could, made me valuable to the quack doctors as an advertising card." For whatever reason, common ordinary white people would pay money to see antic blacks on stage. And Walker asked himself the most natural medicine-show question, why should the public settle for less than a genuine fraud? [29]

The public was paying well to see many teams of white performers doing blackface vaudeville. McIntire and Heath, George Primrose, Al G. Fields, Lew Dockstadter, Press Eldridge, and Neil Moore were some of the most popular of the numerous vaudervillians who made their reputation as blackface comedians. Walker saw these white men who "blacked up" as a barrier to Negro performers. "We finally decided," Walker recalled, that "as white men with black faces were billing themselves 'coons,' Williams and Walker would do well to bill themselves the 'Two Real Coons,' and so we did." It was in this way that the team got the attention of managers and achieved success in the West Coast vaudeville houses. They were called out of the West in 1896 to play in a New York production, *The Gold Bug*, which was unsuccessful. But they were engaged by Koster and Bials in what turned out to be a record run of forty weeks. Not only was the team successful, their performance created the Cakewalk fad. Everyone began to do this dance that had been associated with Negro shows; Williams and Walker, with a great flair and sense of publicity, were largely responsible for making it the vogue.[30]

Williams and Walker struggled with several shows until, combining talents with Jesse Shipp and Will Marion Cook, they produced three substantial musical comedies. Each had original music, a reasonably strong plot line, and very elaborate scenery and properties. Two of the productions were placed in Africa, with Williams and Walker playing American

Negroes wandering through exotic lands. The African scenes greatly expanded the possibilities of black theatrical performances, since they broke the minstrel stereotypes, the productions that mounted these shows were also larger in scope and richer than any Negro shows had been before.

In Dahomey (1902) was the first of these musical comedies. In that play two private detectives from Boston, Shylock Homestead and Rareback Pinkerton (Williams and Walker) are called by the president of the Dahomey Colonization Society, Cicero Lightfoot, to find a silver casket which he has lost. The whole company has to search in Dahomey, where they encounter African royalty, fall into difficulties and are sentenced to be executed, but they are saved by the fact that the two detectives have made friends with the King.[31] *Abyssinia* (1906) is only slightly different. This time the comedians lead a group of Negro pilgrims from Kansas to Jersualem through Addis Ababa, where they fall in and out of trouble. Both of these plays anticipate the "road" films of Bing Crosby and Bob Hope. *Bandanna Land* (1908), the last appearance of the Williams and Walker team, was the story of a minstrel comic, heir to a fortune in a southern town, turning the tables on shrewd and conniving white and black townspeople and tricking them to his own advantage. All three of these productions were outstanding commercial and critical successes. They each proved, in their limited ways, that Negro shows could deviate from the minstrel formula. George Walker fell ill during the run of *Bandanna Land*, and he never recovered.

While these productions did not make radical departures from the conventional Negro comedies, they served to shift focus from the arid and artificial minstrel stereotypes and to give the Negro a context in which to work that was more culturally and historically rich. The characters were still African stereotypes, true enough, and to a large extent they were white determined, yet Negroes could, through them, deal with a

black royalty, a black power, a black elegance, and a black
beauty even as they continued to hold themselves up for ridicule. That was George Walker's thought about it anyway. The
inspiration about Africa first came to him in 1893. San Francisco's midwinter fair of that year planned to use some Africans
from Dahomey. They were late to arrive for the Fair's opening
and, to use George Walker's language, "Afro-Americans were
employed and exhibited for native Dahomians." Williams and
Walker were among the sham Africans. But it was there that
Walker was first to see real Africans when they finally arrived.
He and Williams studied them very closely and "were not long
in deciding that if we ever reached the point of having a show
of our own, we would delineate and feature native African
characters as far as we could, and still remain American, and
make our acting interesting and entertaining to American audiences." Walker saw the addition of African themes to be a
real freedom for the black performer. Managers, he claimed,
were unwilling to accept the notion that Negroes could act.
"All that was expected of a colored performer was singing and
dancing and a little story telling. . . ." He recognized the immediate cause of the problem. White performers in blackface
"used to make themselves look as ridiculous as they could
when portraying a 'darky' character. In their 'make-up' they always had tremendously big red lips and their costumes were
frightfully exaggerated. The one fatal result of this to the colored performers was that they imitated the white performers in
their make-up as 'darkies.' Nothing seemed more absurd than
to see a colored man making himself ridiculous in order to por-
tray himself." [32]

Walker's word is a good one, "absurd." Here is a reiteration
of W. E. B. DuBois's observation that the American Negro's
predicament "yields him no true self-consciousness, but only
lets him see himself through the revelation of the other world
. . . . a world that looks on in amused contempt and pity."

Walker thought that African themes were a way out. Yet, they too had to be adapted to the American stage and made "interesting and entertaining to American audiences." That was a "catch" that made real escape impossible.

Bert Williams waited in vain for George Walker to recover from his illness. The team had developed a modern expression of the classical "darky" comics—George Walker as the sleek, smiling, prancing dandy, and Bert Williams as the slow-witted, good-natured, shuffling Negro—heirs to the Dandy Jims and the Jim Crows of the mid-nineteenth century. Without Walker, Williams drifted. He went out alone in *Mr. Lode of Kole* (1909), which was to be his last Negro show. He joined the *Ziegfeld Follies* in 1910 and remained with that show for ten years. In 1920, Williams was the star of the review, *Broadway Brevities,* and in 1922, suffering from what was to prove a fatal illness, he took the star's role in *The Pink Slip* (later *Under the Bamboo Tree*). Falling ill on the road trip of this last production, he was returned to New York City, where he died, March 4, 1922. During this time as a single performer, Williams reflected continuously on his dead partner and the team which had been reaching for a perfection of the blackface comedy. Walker had not only been entertaining, but he had also been a very intelligent and purposeful man. He had seen unerringly into the racial implications of traditional blackface comedy, and he saw the team as moving black performers out of the narrow, racist restraints of conventional theater. It may have been an illusion, but the team shared it. Williams could find no partner to take Walker's place, and it seems that he lost a sense of his own purpose in the years following Walker's death.

Yet, it was in this period, when Williams was performing as a single in the *Ziegfeld Follies,* that he achieved the greatest popular acclaim; the Bert Williams of this period is most remembered. Nor should it be surprising, for he brought his style of loose-limbed dance and pantomime and plaintive-voiced patter song to its perfection. He moved on stage in the most casual way—arms, hips, legs, feet, all parts of his body, seemingly indifferent to the whole—his burnt-cork clown mask with wide, innocent eyes or sad-cynical mouth. And, so, he would perhaps do his famous pantomime skit of a terribly unfortunate poker player, and surely he would go into one of his patter songs accompanied by the most liquid and subtle dance.

And the songs, themselves, gave Williams the means of providing a distinctive dimension to "darky" humor. They were in dialect, but never as gross as some black and all white performers used. His songs could be light in their humor, "Bon Bon Buddy, The Chocolate Drop"; often they were cynical, "I May Be Crazy, but I Ain't No Fool" and "The Darktown Poker Club." [33] Bert Williams' voice was plaintive; his songs were heavy with pathos. Yet, it was a pathos that asked for and expected no pity. He simply told of the isolated and vulnerable condition of men; he spoke for his audience as well as himself. The song, "My Landlady," told the universal story of the tenant in the ruthless and impersonal clutches of the female manager of the house. Could she be mother and wife as well? As in the song, "Nobody," [34] he sang those words—land-laid-DEE and no-bud-DEE—so that those frail final syllables were almost tears. The art, however, was in the complete lack of sentiment, the absence of self-pity. In "Nobody," after each verse describing his frailty, hunger, or hurt, he would ask who would help, and his answer was always "no-bud-DEE." Then he would sing the refrain:

> I ain't never done *nuh*-thin for *no*-bud-DEE
> I ain't never got *nuh*-thin, from *no*-bud-DEE—*no* time
> Until I *can* get sum-thin from—sum-bud-dee sum-time
> I don't *intend*—to do *nuh*-thin for *no*-bud-DEE—*no time.*

Or, again, Bert Williams would sing "Why Adam Sinned." [35]

I heeard da ole folks talkin' in our house da other night
'Bout Adam in da scripchuh long ago
Da lady folks all 'bused him, sed, "He knowned it was'n right."
An' 'cose da men folks dey all sed, "Dat's so."
I felt sorry fuh Mistah Adam, an' I felt like puttin' in,
'Cause I knows mo' dan de do, all 'bout what made Adam sin:

Adam nevuh had no Mammy, fuh to take him on her knee
An' teach him right fum wrong an' show him
Things he ought to see.
I knows down in my heart—he'd-a let dat apple be
But Adam nevuh had no dear old Ma-am-my.

He nevuh knowed no chilehood roun' da ole log cabin do',
He nevuh knowed no pickaninny life.
He started in a great big grown up man, an' whut is mo',
He nevuh had da right kind uf a wife.
Jes s'pose he'd had a Mammy when dat temptin' did begin,
An' she'd a come an' tole him,
"Son, don' eat dat—dat's a sin."

But, Adam nevuh had no Mammy fuh to take him on her knee
An' teach him right fum wrong an' show him
Things he ought to see.
I knows down in my heart he'd a let dat apple be,
But Adam nevuh had no dear old Ma-am-my.

This song is achingly funny when one thinks beyond the surface theology. For, the lyrics satirize the sentiment of mother-
hood and southern nostalgia. But they also evoke the game of
ridicule among Negroes, "The Dozens," in which the ultimate
"put-down" is to tell a man, "you don't have no momma."

George Walker's death and Bert Williams' defection from
the all-black productions seem to have halted an apparent development toward a genuine black, sophisticated musical theater. For in the years that Williams and Walker were doing
their Africa-inspired productions, another promising team was
writing the material for their own shows. Bob Cole had joined
J. Rosamond Johnson (the musician brother of James Weldon)

in what proved to be a fruitful partnership. Cole and Johnson wrote the book and music and played in *The Shoofly Regiment* (1906) and *The Red Moon* (1908). James Weldon Johnson describes these plays as operettas "with a well-constructed book and a tuneful, well-written score." He believed that Williams and Walker and Cole and Johnson had been making distinctive steps away from the grotesque blackface of the minstrel tradition. The greatest taboo on the white stage, he noted, was against a black male and female in truly romantic roles. He believed that *Red Moon* made a slight step toward Negro romance.[36] But, alas, Bob Cole too fell ill and ended that promising association.

Present-day readers will doubtless find the modest innovations of the Williams and Walker and the Cole and Johnson teams feeble change indeed. They were still in blackface, and they still performed what has to be called "darky" material. Yet, in each instance, these teams tried to give the conventional forms greater variety and sophistication. At least, they wanted to create a Negro humor that was not dependent on self-ridicule. In small ways they were successful.

Little wonder that the Negro did not develop a recognizable ethnic theater in the twentieth century. As this rather long digression on the minstrel tradition demonstrates, the Negro (at least a representation of him) had a very substantial place in the American theatrical tradition, a characterization that could not be displaced by whim or will. The theater that was most authentic to the American ethos was largely Negro albeit distorted and grotesque; thus unlike the immigrant, in trying to establish ethnic theater the Afro-Americans had a tradition to contend with. Whatever the advantages in and the justification for finding a genuine black theatrical voice and form, the overwhelming pressure of tradition (not to mention national character) was against it. Needless to say, commercial success—

always a powerful lure—pulled black performers away from their furtive efforts at truly ethnic drama. And even the small theater groups that developed, abandoning the standard musical review and comedy, tended to mimic the white "serious" theater.

There is one very important exception to this failure of Afro-American drama. At least one person, James Weldon Johnson, has pointed to the dramatic character of the Negro church.[37] Johnson described a rural "big meeting" where the preacher developed and extemporized a sermon on Old Testament texts, creating a "primitive" poetry as he went along—providing visual and dramatic experience for an audience which participated in song and spoken word. Aside from the preacher, there was a leader of the gospel songs, who knew the songs, created them as he went along, and chose the right dramatic moment to break the service with the *right* song, leading the congregation as a chorus to punctuate and heighten the dramatic effect. The Negro churches (the unsophisticated and unpretentious ones) embodied a living drama. Throughout black New York City, and other cities and towns where black men and women met to worship, this most essential theater could be seen, and it was purely ethnic. Black men had taken the orthodox theology and the Old Testament stories and transformed them into vivid, powerful, and exciting literary statements—it was part of their oral tradition. And the congregations were welded into the dramatic performance—as actors, audience, Greek chorus—their bodies, voices, and spirits fused into the most emotional, demanding experience. So valid were these dramatic events (weekly, sometimes nightly) that, for many, the images and characters that they witnessed and "played" were more real than the often sordid lives that interrupted their glory.[38]

Harlem, however, made several efforts to produce uptown drama with black performers. There were several companies.

The Anita Bush Players used the Lincoln Theater at 135th and Lenox, but the most notable group was the Lafayette Players, which began in 1914. Similar groups started in other cities. The Pekin Theater managed to perform serious dramatic productions from about 1901 to 1909 on 30th and State Streets in Chicago.[39] And most notably, the Karamu Theater of Cleveland has promoted Negroes into drama since its founding in 1916. Important as they were in providing theatrical experience for black technicians and actors, these theaters were hardly ethnic. For the most part, they managed to do uptown performances of white melodrama: *Madame X, Dr. Jekyll and Mr. Hyde, The Count of Monte Cristo,* Shakespearean plays, and even grand opera.[40]

However much one may regret the lack of a theater of Negro writers, producers, directors, actors, and technicians orienting their talents to the service of a Negro audience, these small theater groups had their value. There was no other place for Negroes to get theatrical experience. Those who were to find fame in white commercial drama generally gained their initial experience in these theaters: Charles Gilpin, Abbie Mitchell, Inez Clough, to name a few. Downtown theater always expropriated uptown talent whenever it had need of it, but of course white commercial theater saw no need to train and develop black performers.[41]

By all odds, the most important theatrical Negro enterprise in the 1920s was *Shuffle Along* (1921), the black extravaganza that Langston Hughes remembered to have symbolized Harlem to him and to have been a greater attraction to him than Columbia University. After a hiatus of Negro musical reviews, spanning the war years, Flournoy Miller and Aubrey Lyles (who had begun writing plays together at Fisk University) did the book for Eubie Blake's and Noble Sissle's music. *Shuffle Along* was to reintroduce to New York the popular Negro review. Updated, and with fresh material, this theater was little different from the older Williams and Walker and Cole and Johnson productions. It had a thin plot about an election for mayor in the all-black Jimtown, Mississippi. But neither was the plot of consequence, nor the comic routines, which included a pantomimed boxing bout between Miller and Lyles, and a grocery store scene in which a customer with no money wanted to buy goods from a proprietor who could not count to make change. By all reports, the real power of the production was in the music and the dancing. "And how they all danced," said the reporter in the New York *Sun,* "especially the chorus, which is full of dash and ginger." The world needed cheering up in 1921, and it appeared that *Shuffle Along* was just the right tonic. So, at least, thought the writer in the New York *Herald:* "But it is when the chorus and the principals of a company that is said to contain the best negro troupers in these parts gets going in the dances that the world seems a brighter place to live in. They wriggle and shimmy in a fashion to outdo a congress of eels, and they fling their limbs about without stopping to make sure that they are securely fastened on." 42

The Jazz Age had arrived. The postwar hangover that encouraged a generation of Americans to lose themselves in cabarets, rhythms, dances, and exotica could not help but approve this lively Negro musical. The jazz-hungry public was ecstatic about *Shuffle Along,* which was produced on a shoe-string, and which thrived at a makeshift theater on 63rd Street. It was, like Harlem itself, infectious; it made everyone want to forget his troubles and do it, like the chorus of dancers. "Talk about pep!" wrote Alan Dale in the *American,* "these people made pep seem something different to [*sic*] the tame thing we know further downtown." That, after all, was what Harlem and Negroes were all about. Perhaps no one put it more simply than Dale: "They revelled in their work; they simply pulsed with it, and there was no let-up at all. And gradually any tired feeling

that you might have been nursing vanished in the sun of their
good humor and you didn't mind how long they 'shuffled
along.' You even felt like shuffling a bit with them." Yet, it
would take some doing for white men to duplicate the black
rhythm and abandon. "How they enjoyed themselves! How
they jigged and pranced and cavorted, and wriggled and
laughed. . . . Every sinew in their bodies danced; every ten-
don in their frames responded to their extreme energy." [43] The
Negro musical theater was tuned in to help jazz up the American scene.

   Shuffle Along produced some good original songs; "I'm Just
Wild About Harry" is the only one that the present generation
would recognize. The show also launched some important theatrical careers. Josephine Baker started in its chorus, and Florence Mills's short but spectacular career really began in this
show. Notably, too, *Shuffle Along* ushered in a vogue of Negro
singing and dancing that lasted until the Great Depression. No
year seemed complete without its Negro show. In 1922 came
Strut Miss Lizzie and *Seven-Eleven*. Maceo Pinkard wrote the
score for *Liza,* which was a hit in 1923. Florence Mills starred
in *Dixie to Broadway* in 1924, and in the same year Miller and
Lyles opened with *Runnin' Wild,* which became a sensation
partly because it introduced the Charleston. Sissle and Blake's
Chocolate Dandies began a long run in 1925. Florence Mills
made a great hit in *Blackbirds* in 1926, and in 1927 Ethel Waters starred in *Africana.* Bill "Bojangles" Robinson starred in
518 Broadway performances of *Blackbirds* in 1928, and in the
same year, riding the crest of a wave they had started, Miller
and Lyles tried again with *Keep Shuffling.* This vogue, like
most others of the time, ended in 1929; but in that year *Hot
Chocolates* made a hit of Fats Waller's "Ain't Misbehavin'." [44]
The Negro vogue of the twenties served to bring to commercial
success many Negroes of talent. Yet, as in art and letters, little
that was original and permanent was added. Of course, each

musical brought ragtime, jazz, and blues to the public; and the shows brought new dances—from the Cakewalk, Charleston, Black Bottom to the Lindy Hop. But except for music and dance, which was after all, the real substance of these performances, the Negro shows failed to refine black theatrical arts; they mainly continued to exploit a corrupt tradition.

Nor was this exploitation restricted to the downtown shows. The 1920s were the heyday of the black reviews at the Apollo and Lafayette Theaters. These Negro shows were little different from those downtown, except they were a little more raucous, broad, and dirty; therefore they were probably funnier. Midnight shows at the Lafayette were really community social events; the real drama was in the audience. Wallace Thurman described the scene: "There was much noise . . . much passing to and fro, much stumbling down dark aisles. . . . Then people were always looking for some one or for something, always peering into the darkness, emiting code whistles, and calling Jane or Jim or Pete or Bill. At the head of each aisle . . . people were packed in a solid mass, a grumbling, garrulous mass, elbowing their neighbors, cursing the management, and standing on tiptoe trying to find an empty intact seat—intact because every other seat . . . seemed to be broken." That was the Lafayette, according to Thurman, "the Jew's gift to Harlem colored folks." [45] While it is probably true that the Yiddish theaters were just as disorderly, Jews did not have Thurman's sense that they were being exploited by others for profit. This exploitation was perceived by some in Harlem to be that of white men using black talent for their own gain; so it was downtown, but uptown Negroes felt doubly used because they were the audience as well as the performers. And while the white promoters made money, they were doing very little to contribute to the development of black theatrical arts. Such a complaint was a strong undercurrent in what was essentially a labor dispute of Negro operators at the Lafayette Theater in

1926 and 1927.[46] While the great majority of Harlem residents seemed perfectly content to be entertained at the Apollo and Lafayette with the typical review, some Negro intellectuals wanted this commercial exploitation of Harlem by whites to at least result in some permanent cultural development.

Those who were closest in spirit to the "New Negro" movement felt an urgent need for an authentic Negro theater—a "folk theater" some called it. For a brief time, the Krigwa Players Little Negro Theater tried to serve that end. W. E. B. DuBois was one of its strongest promoters. He believed that real Negro drama had not been called for in American history. Such could only be "evoked by a Negro audience desiring to see its own life depicted by its own writers and actors." This let out of consideration those "excellent groups of colored amateurs" who adapted Shakespeare or Synge or successful Broadway plays for Negro audiences. As DuBois saw it, the Negro theater movement had four fundamental principles. "Negro theater," he wrote, "must be: I. *About us.* That is, they must have plots which reveal Negro life as it is. II. *By us.* That is, they must be written by Negro authors who understand from birth and continual association just what it means to be a Negro today. III. *For us.* That is, the theatre must cater primarily to Negro audiences and be supported and sustained by their entertainment and approval. IV. *Near us.* The theatre must be in a Negro neighborhood near the mass of ordinary Negro people." [47] The first main problem was to get plays. The Krigwa group managed remarkably well. In 1925, it put on several short plays which were written, acted, directed, and viewed by Negroes. One of those plays has survived in *The New Negro;* Willis Richardson's one-act tragedy, "Compromise," was published in that volume.

Of course, there was more to it than plays and actors and audience. The real threat to Negro theater was success. That was, after all, the name of the American game, and it was im-

possible for people who had always had very little to resist the
temptation to make it big. This worked in two ways to undermine efforts to sustain an ethnic theater. First, since plays
which were written by Negroes were scarce, it was always a
temptation to borrow or adapt white plays. Conditions did not
encourage the suffering through on thin or limited material
with the hope of forcing the development of playwrights in the
long run. Also, the audience would have to be educated into
being supporters of such a theater. After all, they were Americans and affected by the good and bad taste of their countrymen. Like other Americans, blacks knew a commercial success
—even when they might not know whether or not it was good
—and their entertainment was tailored to the standards of
mass culture. No one, not even DuBois, was willing to hold
ethnic theater efforts as superior or preferable to Gilpin or
Robeson in *The Emperor Jones*. There was something to be
proud of when a black person made it big in any field; the
theater was no exception. As long as that was so, it was futile
to talk of folk theater. And finally, Negro performers were ultimately pulled into the commercial star system. Success was
tangible and important; it was acclaim, and it was money. It is
unreasonable, if not unfair, to expect men or women of talent
to pass up their "chance" in order to sustain an ethnic theater
which was problematic at best. Such tensions were a constant
pull and explain why Krigwa and later efforts at ethnic (or
"community" as it was sometimes called) theater have foundered.[48]

White interest in the Negro was evidenced in the theater as
well as in literature and night life. Beginning just before America's entry into World War I, downtown plays about Negro
subjects became standard fare, and continued throughout the
decade of the 1920s. The poet Ridgely Torrence brought three
plays—*The Rider of Dreams, Granny Maumee,* and *Simon the
Cyrenian*—to the Garden Theater in April 1917. James Wel-

don Johnson thought the event the most important in the entire history of the Negro in the American theater,[49] because they were serious drama, and as he saw them, smashed the historical stereotypes. While the plays were critical successes, the entry of the United States into the European war seemed to cast a pall on theater for the season. But following the war, dramatic productions with important Negro characters and with Negro subjects increased.

This was not so much a wave of liberalism in the theater's attitude toward race as it was the development of theatrical realism in the United States. Until about 1915, the genteel restraints on American theater were almost total. Respectable drama was European or melodramatic. Realism and naturalism entered cautiously through Europeans such as Ibsen.[50] American realism in the theater, however, was a more difficult matter. It appears that the Negro subject permitted an easier entry for Americans into sordid and "realistic" subjects than could any possible white counterpart. The kinds of subjects that European playwrights had long treated—crime, passion (lust), human limitation—could more comfortably be given to Negro characters than to white in these years. One might say that the treatment of tragedy was impossible in an American mythology which insisted that moral and energetic men and women always triumphed—spiritually, if not materially. The dogma of the American Dream denied true dramatic tragedy, because it held that humanity was perfectible. The very arrogance of such a conception converted hubris into simple personal fault or error. The Negro, on the other hand, as he was traditionally conceived, fitted perfectly into pathos, if not tragedy. His efforts at manhood had necessarily to fall short; the tradition offered no other possibility. So, when American dramatists wanted to come close to reality—human limitation—the Negro was more readily available as a subject than whites. In this respect, the theater followed along behind general American lit erature. Many writers—Hawthorne, Melville, Twain, Dreiser —had struggled against the American euphoria to reach true human experience. But even in the novel the Negro's presumed inability was given considerable mileage in "realistic" themes like the tragic mulatto.

James Weldon Johnson was applauding the advent of the popular theater's doing what the more pedestrian novels had been doing for some time, treating the Negro as a serious subject although in stereotyped ways. Whatever else may be said about plays like Torrence's *Granny Maumee* and DuBose Heyward's *Mamba's Daughters* (1927), they were variations on the tragic mulatoo theme. Paul Green's *Abraham's Bosom,* which won the Pulitzer Prize in 1926, was produced by the Provincetown Players, and came as close to dramatic realism as anything in the decade. Yet the power of the play (and the terror of it) relied on the audience's recognition that the Negro's plight was impossible. For the tragedy rested on the disparity between the Negro's limited circumstances and his unlimited dignity. The more sentimental, and the ultimately more popular, *Porgy* manipulated stereotypes of Negro primitivism and impotence to great emotional effect. This morality play was seen as beautiful by countless American audiences (in its original dramatic presentation as well as the musical adaptation, *Porgy and Bess*). The beauty was in the simple, ingenuous folk of Catfish Row—indifferent to their poverty and simplicity— struggling toward a natural goodness against raw, pure evil. Bess's hold on virtue (and self-respect) is always frail and wholly dependent on Porgy's protection and love. And that is the selfless love of a cripple, who could not corrupt her if he would. Although Porgy's strength is sufficient to overcome the evil of Crown (to kill him), it is not enough to make him a man. It is his superstition and irrational fear of white law that causes his arrest (ironically, for contempt of court) and his final loss of Bess. And Bess, without her Porgy, could not with-

stand the one gulp of liquor and her ultimate abandon to sail-
ors who take her away. The Negroes in *Porgy* are treated with
sympathy (as they are in many of the plays of the decade), but
it is a sympathy for mythical figures—stereotypes. This was realistic theater only in so far as the "black mask" permitted portrayal of dimensions of human life not likely in other guise.

Eugene O'Neill attempted something different. His early
plays should not be considered part of the popular drama of
the time. They were more special, *avant garde*. O'Neill's interest was something other than realism. August Strindberg's naturalism was the great influence on him, "super-naturalism" as
the American chose to call it. His effort was to look beneath
the surface realisms to the quick of human experience. "Yet it
is only by means of some form of 'supernaturalism,'" O'Neill
wrote, "that we may express in the theatre what we compre-
hend intuitively of that self-defeating self-obsession which is
the discount we moderns have to pay for the loan of life."
Realism (or naturalism, as that term had come to be used in
the theater) was inadequate. "It represents our fathers' daring
aspiration toward self-recognition by holding the family kodak
up to ill-nature. But to us their old audacity is blague; we have
taken too many snap-shots of each other in every graceless position; we have endured too much from the banality of sur-
faces." O'Neill proclaimed himself, and the new theater, to be
breaking with the old habits of keyhole peeping realism,
"squinting always at heavy, uninspired bodies—the fat facts—
with not a nude spirit among them; we have been sick with
appearances. . . ." Strindberg showed how to peel away the
facile realities and to expose the quivering spirit-flesh which
was living essence.[51] In O'Neill's hands this "super-naturalism"
sometimes appeared to be primitivism.

The Emperor Jones, first produced in 1921 with Charles Gilpin in the title role (revived in 1925 with Paul Robeson), must
be understood in this context. For here was no stereotype of

Negro character. Emperor Jones's ultimate fall, although superstition is involved, occurs because the artifices that have propped him up have been removed. So, exposed and defenseless, Jones—like any other man—falls victim to his fear and his essential, primitive nature. In certain ways, therefore, this is only incidentally a Negro play; it could well have used any man. O'Neill's insight into the human condition is, if anything, marred by the play having a Negro subject. The analogies to *Othello* were too tempting for the reviewers to miss, and few of them understood the play as more than an artful and powerful treatment of travesty of Negro pretense. *The Hairy Ape* (1922) treats the same insight in a different way, this time with a white subject. And on this occasion, the reviewers revealed that they had missed the original point entirely. Lawrence Remner, writing in the New York *Herald* (March 10, 1922), felt that *The Hairy Ape* lacked convincing motivation. He noted a "dramatic form" similar to *The Emperor Jones,* but confessed, "it was a much more exciting game to see the negro usurper beaten by fate. He was a clever rascal in his way. The hairy ape is only a feeble giant who is bowled over by the first blow of fate." Seen as conventional tragedy, the Negro was more convincing because of this "clever" pretense. But the hairy ape was assuming to be a man and civilized, and once the props that sustained him had been challenged—taken away—he was reduced to his essential animal. Perhaps Remner's failure was that he could not see that for a white man humanity might be a pretense. Notably, no critics complained about *The Emperor Jones* for its reduction of the Negro to primitivism; that, of course, was not strange. But J. Rankin Towse, writing in the New York *Post* (March 10, 1922), was offended by *The Hairy Ape;* he saw it as an attack on the working class. It was a "crude realism," he said, "a travesty which one would think would be more displeasing to labor than it is libelous on capital." O'Neill used Negro characters in *The Emperor Jones* (and in a more confused way in *All God's Chillun Got Wings*) to make general statements about humanity through them. The fact that the critical audience did not always perceive that (and the fact that the statements were sometimes confused) is a testimony to the deep and unshakable tradition of Negro stereotype in the theater.

Whatever the intention and quality of the white plays in the 1920s, the remarkable thing was that Negro performers were getting an unprecedented chance to do respectable, serious drama in downtown theaters. Inez Clough, Opal Cooper, Frank Wilson, Rose McClendon, Paul Robeson, Charles Gilpin, Jules Bledsoe, Clarence Muse, Leigh Whipper, and many others had their moment in the Broadway bright lights after long drudgery in stock companies like the Lafayette. However much one might regret the failure of an authentic ethnic theater, it is impossible to challenge their right to grasp the chance to contribute to the American stage.

Appropriately, the decade of the 1920s ended with the greatest commercial success and the most perfect charade of them all, *The Green Pastures* (1930). Marc Connelly's allegory (or fantasy or dream) was a simple translation of orthodox Protestant theology into the imagined dream-fantasy of southern Negro children. A black Sunday school class, unable to understand its Bible lesson, is told a series of parables which use local folk as heavenly creatures—the old preacher is "De Lawd," Heaven becomes a familiar neighborhood that is filled with pleasures: fish-frys, conviviality, joy. The biblical story— Genesis, the creation, the fall, the flood, the decision to save man through Christ—is transformed into the assumed southern Negro idiom and image and (further still) into the imaginations of little black children.

The Green Pastures was a remarkable success; only *Abie's Irish Rose* surpassed it in those years. Doubtless, part of its popularity was due to the high quality of performers; the Hall

Johnson Choir made it a stirring musical production. There was a cast of hundreds of black performers. Richard B. Harrison was perfect as De Lawd. He was over 65 when he got the role; his only theatrical experience had been as a dramatic reader for Negro clubs, schools, and churches. He learned the dialect from a white coach and stepped right into the role that he was to play for 1,568 straight performances. Harrison had become so much identified with the role that when some of the cast, protesting the National Theater's (Washington, D.C.) policy of excluding Negroes from the audience, were fired from the show after having gone on strike, De Lawd played on. Playing God was not to be taken lightly. He could not go on strike.

The Green Pastures was not just a play, it was a phenomenon. Its success, of course, was in the white Americans' acceptance of it. And whites seemed unable to see enough. Why? It was beautiful and moving, everybody said. It was the most beautiful, simple, and innocent play around (except, perhaps, for *Abie's Irish Rose*). There must have been something more to it. Would they have been equally moved by *Paradise Lost* done in chorus with white performers? Surely not. The religious element was very important, but so was the minstrel tradition and the black masks through which the white audience projected itself.

Notably, the postwar years were marked by a deep American awareness of religious crisis. Many signs were pointing to the irrelevancy of traditional faith. The Protestantism that had sustained most Americans throughout their history had been shaken. It was both liberating and frightening. Everywhere there were signs of it. The Scopes Trial, for instance, demonstrated where the sophisticated stood on the matter of Genesis and faith (now sometimes called superstition). Who dared not be sophisticated in the 1920s? But on a deeper level there was evidence that the crisis of faith was troubling. Theologians and social commentators wrote and worried. Walter Lippmann's *Preface to Morals* (1929) was the most concise discussion to appear in these years which explored the troubling question of what moral order could exist where traditional religion had become a victim of science and skepticism. The cornerstone of traditional American culture seemed undermined. In the twentieth century and especially since World War I, science, Freud, and the realities of human experience had made religious belief seem a luxury of innocence. While it might have been difficult, if not impossible, to believe in the old way, people desperately wanted to. The failure of faith carried a heavy burden of guilt and anxiety.

The beauty of *The Green Pastures* was that, for a moment, it made faith possible and vicariously experienced. The production made it the faith of those who had no pretense of sophistication and who, therefore, could believe in an uncluttered and simple way. Doubt seemed impossible in the black child's fantasy. In this, the play relied on the standard and theatrical stereotype of the Negro, child-like and credulous. De Lawd, after all, was merely a transmuted Uncle Tom. And like white audiences that had watched blackface ministrels throughout the history of the American stage, these found in the black surrogate the possibility of being transported into black innocence. Through the supposed fantasies of black children it was possible to experience the beauty of a fading faith, to be credulous again. The stage Negro served to provide white audiences with occasions to play roles through projection behind the Negro mask that seemed impossible for whites to manage in their own right. Here, again, it was the qualities that whites had invested the Negro with, qualities that they had insisted on through the perpetuation of the stereotype, that made the emotional and religious experience possible. The black mask again was a way to psychic peace. Harlem, as we have seen, also served such ends. That, too, is what the history of the black mask in American theater seems to tell us.

W. E. B. DuBois saw the matter keenly. Black identity has been, too often, the projection of white vision and white needs. The men (who by traditional assessment would have been called ordinary), who created a society out of a wilderness, experienced a crisis of civilization. The cultural doubt of provincialism, the fluidity and impermanence of status in a democracy, the phantom of identity where institutions and order were always in flux, the anxiety of an achievement ethic, the possible terror in some views of change itself, these have been the traumas of American life. Reality has been the more shadowlike and doubtful the more landmarks and all that is familiar change within one's view. In these contexts, identity has been a desperate issue for white and black Americans. One view of the white man's Negro is to see him as a manufactured point of reference in a scene of radical flux and change, the one permanent and unchanging thing. The black myth, like that of the Old South, was a created tradition. William Faulkner has been quite explicit in asserting that the Negro, like the land, was permanency and order (that author thought it a compliment to blacks, though it deprived them of hope in American life). Faulkner was not alone. So many whites have genuinely "loved" their Negroes because they have been the only selves they know. The persistence of the Negro stereotype has tended to make the Negro the one constant, through all change and various guises. It has been a great convenience for those who have wanted to find or lose themselves behind the mask.

Epilogue

Taken all in all, it becomes easy to dismiss as mere vainglory the celebration of Harlem culture following World War I. On balance it appears that Wallace Thurman was more correct in his cynicism than Alain Locke was in his eager optimism. But such a cold view ignores what those Harlem literati left to the generation that followed. Such rude rejection also fails to see the phenomenon as natural, given the perplexing paradoxes of American, particularly Afro-American, life. More than this, the episode in the 1920s placed the black experience clearly within general American cultural history. It had been a remarkable conspiracy of events that caused Harlem to blossom at the close of World War I. Rare luck ceded to Negroes a prime portion of Manhattan real estate so that there could be a black enclave in the heart of the biggest, best, and busiest American city. The Negro migration into cities like New York dramatically shifted the Afro-American image from rural to urban, from peasant to sophisticate. And the urban crossroads acquainted black Americans with their international brotherhood of blood and color. And everything was pollenated by the spirit of self-determination which pervaded the world at that time. Little wonder Harlemites anticipated the flowering of Negro culture into a racial renaissance.

Dreams aside, they could not escape their history and culture in their attempt to create a new one. Whatever its exoticism, the "renaissance" echoed American progressivism in its faith in democratic reform, in its extraordinarily high evaluation of art and literature as agents of change, and in its almost uncritical belief in itself and its future. The creation of the "New Negro" failed, but it was an American failure, having its counterpart in countless similar frustrated promotions. Harlemites could believe in the future of the "New Negro" because they accepted the system without question. Just like their contemporary white intellectuals who, though often grudgingly, took the American economic and industrial apparatus for granted, these black intellectuals seemed unprepared for that rude shock which was to make their paeans to black art and identity echo false. Nobody could have anticipated the Great Depression, but the Negro renaissance was shattered by it because of naïve assumptions about the centrality of culture, unrelated to economic and social realities. They were comrades in this innocence with many white intellectuals of the time. When the decade of the 1930s opened, the innocent Harlem Renaissance ended.

Yet, the experience of Harlem in the 1920s was not for naught. It left its mark as a symbol and a point of reference for everyone to recall. Of course the place remained—a part of a city—but it was still more than that. The very name continued to connote a special spirit, new vitality, black urbanity, and black militancy. Through the activities, the writings, the promotion of Negroes in the 1920s, Harlem had become a racial focal point for knowledgeable black men the world over. To them, Harlem had come to mean what no other place-name could. And so it remained, for a time, a race capital. What

Claude McKay had learned in his travels was that Senegalese
and Haitians, Cameroons and Martiniquais could come together in their common awareness of the "Black Metropolis."
That was one of the important things that McKay wanted the
Marseilles docks to illustrate in *Banjo*. McKay himself had
needed no novel or travel to tell him that. After all, Harlem
was that very magnet which had pulled him out of the West
Indies, as it had Marcus Garvey. And that same force was to
draw Africans, West Indians, and Afro-Americans from the
South and West of the United States for some time to come. So
many and so varied were those who came and wrote about it
that Harlem continued to attract black men long after the renaissance aborted.

Alain Locke had been right in a way, seeing Harlem as a
necessary stage in race-building. To him, the key was urban
pluralism, you will recall. "The peasant, the student, the businessman, the professional man, artist, poet, musician, adventurer and worker, preacher and criminal, exploiter and social
outcast," he had observed, "each group has come with its own
special motives . . . but their greatest experience has been the
finding of one another." For it required the complexity of the
urban setting for black men to truly appreciate the variety of
black life. The race consciousness that Locke and his generation hoped for required that shared experience.

Doubtless, Harlem contributed to a maturity of racial
concept—a new sense among black people that they had
something of value in common. It surely encouraged the new
appreciation of folk roots and culture that was part of the
spirit of the renaissance. The exploitation of peasant folk materials and spirituals provided not only a rich source for racial
imagination, but it also attested to a sophistication that was at
least partly freed from embarrassment of past condition. Harlem thus bequeathed a new self-appreciation to blacks as well

as its too naïve faith in the possibility of creating an ethnic culture.

It was not to black men alone that Harlem was to continue to symbolize a new freedom. White men and women continued for a while to find, as Carl Van Vechten had, the same emotional release in Harlem that earlier whites had discovered in the fantasy-become-reality of the minstrel personality. While the end of prohibition dulled much of the excitement and "sin" of Harlem, white women (sometimes in "ermines and pearls") and their escorts continued to enjoy uptown nightlife until poverty made it too drab and the poverty-induced violence made it too dangerous. Increases in violence and crime, however, are not the only reasons for changes in the entertainment patterns of affluent whites. Harlem has been replaced. The exotic island paradises in the Caribbean are too close and too cheap for Harlem to compete with, even if peace were to return to its streets. No longer serving the exotic fantasies of whites, Harlem has been reduced to the stone-cold realities which had earlier been obscured by dream gossamer.

Harlem's legacy to our time is necessarily limited by the character of the renaissance. For, regardless of its rhetoric, the whole moment and place had been imprisoned in its innocence. Despite claims to the contrary, it had been very much bound to an emulation of whites. Political spokesmen who had prided themselves on their militant and forceful language had echoed the values and the conceptual limitations of American progressives. Their techniques of exposé and demand for democratic reform had denied both the realities of American urban politics and the implications of racism that have made practical reform irrelevant to Negro life. Even the exception, Marcus Garvey, while correctly finding reform within the system to be unreal, had been forced to champion an alternative which had rapidly become escapism and fantasy. And the social mimicry of whites had been equally pronounced. The Harlem intellectuals had been anxious to make those class distinctions which would mark them as different from their black brothers further down. So while proclaiming a new race consciousness, they had been wearing the clothes and using the manners of sophisticated whites, thereby earning the epithet "dicty niggers" from the very people they were supposed to be championing. When, for instance, W. E. B. DuBois's daughter, Yolande, had married Countee Cullen, it had been billed as the marriage of the age. No expense had been spared to make it that, even to the doves that had been released to fly through the church at the proper nuptual moment. It was a parody or travesty of ceremony, no less striking in its mimicry than the pomp-filled parades of Marcus Garvey. The marriage itself had been a sad pretense. It had not been made in heaven, as their contemporaries wanted to think, but it had been made up by the same imaginations that had promoted the renaissance. As we have seen, this enslavement to white forms and values had been most pronounced in that art which was to have been the real evidence of the Negro's coming of age. At a time when some American literature and art was truly innovative and fresh, men like Countee Cullen and Claude McKay were bound to a literary past which had little to say for their own experience and their own vision. The great innocence of the renaissance is most clearly seen in the irony that, where its proponents had wanted to develop a distinctive Negro voice, they had been of necessity most derivative.

It is hard to imagine that it could have been otherwise. Seen through black men's eyes—whether in acceptance or rejection —the white eminence had been overwhelming. A white commerce had determined what was to be considered success in business, industry, and art. A white establishment had really defined art and culture. As long as the white norms remained unchallenged, no matter what the Negro's reaction to them, he always needed to return to the white judge to measure his achievement. It would have required a much more profound rejection of white values than was likely in the 1920s for Negroes to have freed themselves for creating the desired self-generating and self-confident Negro art. I am not suggesting that blacks needed to acquire a race hatred; there was evidence of that already. I mean merely that Negroes had to see whites—without the awe of love or the awe of hate—and themselves truly, without myth or fantasy, in order that they could be themselves in life and in art.

So it was an encumbered legacy that the renaissance left to the following decades of Afro-American culture. Of course, it was a symbol, that is clear enough. At least until World War II, it was the claimed "golden age" of Negro literati. Actually, however, nothing that was produced then can compare with the fruits of recent years. Some black writers and artists have since that time become less provincial, more masterful of craft, less tied to the white patron. Recent black artists have enjoyed a far wider audience than could have been expected in the 1920s. There is a sizable black audience; but also many whites are interested in the Negro experience, and they are willing to learn whatever is necessary to understand the black artist. For these reasons the best black craftsmen have been freed from the weight of the didactic which had so crippled the art of the 1920s. While many of the issues and problems are the same now as then, these circumstances along with the greater sophistication and cynicism that have resulted from his own frustrations and the clear perception of the general American cultural malaise have made it possible for the American Negro to produce a more genuine art than ever occurred in the renaissance. Writers as different as Melvin Tolson and Eldridge Cleaver have exploded into the American mind. They shape thought, image, and language. That is something that the Harlem literati could not have dared. Nevertheless, as one looks today, there is a similar race promotion and self-conscious search for identity which cannot help but perpetuate the ethnic province. Whatever that provincialism may contribute to identity and sociology, it will constrict the vision, limiting the possibilities of personality. Needless to say, that will produce a crippled art.

It is in the paradox of ethnic provincialism that we discover the most important gift that the renaissance has left to us: a lesson from its failures. The dilemma is a tough one: the race consciousness that is so necessary for identity most likely leads to a provincialism which forever limits possibility of achieving good art; but without it the perplexities of identity are exacerbated by confusion of legitimate heritage. Nowhere is this problem better illustrated than in the strange separation of the Negro from American culture. Except for a few blacks, then and now, the most striking thing about them is that they are native American. The negative implications of that fact have been easily grasped by most Negroes: they, unlike the immigrants, had no immediate past and history and culture to celebrate. But the positive implications of American nativity have never been fully appreciated by Afro-Americans. It seems too simple: the Afro-American's history and culture is American, more completely so than most others in this country. Why has that not been enough to say? Of course, few Americans have been content to rest on that alone. Most have sought cultural validity in older traditions. Not only have Negroes failed to exploit the truth of their birth, they have voiced a strange alienation from that culture. They wrote about it as if they were not a part of it, or it a part of them. American culture—their native culture—was a pronoun, *it*. Sometimes black intellectuals made claims for the Negro contribution to *it*. Sometimes they tried to fashion their work in *its* image. Occasionally, they attempted to deny *it* and to adopt some other culture and tradition to work within. Whatever, it was something that was not them. What a perverse conception! The truth was (and is) that black men and American culture have been one—such a seamless web that it is impossible to calibrate the Negro within it or to ravel him from it. To know that is one thing, but to feel it and to assert it is something else. At least the decade of the 1920s seems to have been too early for Negroes to have felt the certainty about native culture that would have freed them from crippling self-doubt. I think that is why the art of the renaissance was so problematic, feckless, not fresh, not real. The lesson it leaves us is that the true Negro renaissance awaits Afro-Americans' claiming their *patria,* their nativity.

Notes

INTRODUCTION

1. James Weldon Johnson, *Black Manhattan*, New York, Knopf, 1930, pp. 156–59. But even the most enthusiastic champion of the renaissance was sobered by the depression. See Alain Locke, "Harlem: Dark Weather-Vane," *Survey Graphic*, XXV (August 1936), pp. 457–58. I am indebted to Mr. John Samuel Jordan, a graduate student at Columbia Teacher's College, for bringing this article to my attention.

CHAPTER 1

1. James Weldon Johnson, *Autobiography of an Ex-Coloured Man*, New York, Hill and Wang, 1960, pp. 103–9, describes the early Negro cabarets in New York City. See also, Johnson, *Black Manhattan*, pp. 75–77.
2. There are several descriptions of the emergence of black Harlem. Johnson, *Black Manhattan*, chap. 13; Seth M. Scheiner, *Negro Mecca: A History of the Negro in New York City, 1865–1920*, New York, New York University Press, 1965, passim; Gilbert Osofsky, *Harlem: The Making of a Ghetto, Negro New York, 1890–1930*, New York, Harper and Row, 1966, especially pp. 81–123.

3. James Weldon Johnson, *Along This Way*, New York, Viking, 1961.

4. W. E. B. DuBois, *Dusk of Dawn: An Essay Toward an Autobiography of a Race Concept*, New York, Harcourt, Brace and World, 1940; W. E. B. DuBois, *Souls of Black Folk*, New York, Fawcett, 1965; Francis L. Broderick, *W. E. B. DuBois: Negro Leader in Time of Crisis*, Stanford, Calif., Stanford University Press, 1959; Elliot N. Rudwick, *W. E. B. DuBois: A Study in Minority Group Leadership*, Philadelphia, University of Pennsylvania Press, 1960.

5. Charles Flint Kellogg, *NAACP*, Vol. I (1909–20), Baltimore, Johns Hopkins University Press, 1967, is the official history of the Association. Of course, the story of its origins is quite familiar and appears in several of the books cited in the previous footnote.

6. Edmund David Cronon, *Black Moses: The Story of Marcus Garvey and the Universal Negro Improvement Association*, Madison, University of Wisconsin Press, 1955, is still the most scholarly study of this intriguing figure. See also Amy Jacques-Garvey, *Garvey and Garveyism*, Kingston, A. Jacques-Garvey, 1963; Amy Jacques-Garvey, ed., *Philosophy and Opinions of Marcus Garvey*, New York, Atheneum, 1969. For interesting judgments by Garvey's contemporaries see: Johnson, *Black Manhattan;* Claude McKay, *Harlem: Negro Metropolis*, New York, Dutton, 1940; and E. Franklin Frazier, "The Garvey Movement," *Opportunity*, IV (November 1926), pp. 346–48, reprinted in August Meier and Elliott Rudwick, eds., *The Making of Black America*, Vol. II, New York, Atheneum, 1969, pp. 204–8.

7. Observations from an interview with Mrs. Louise Thompson Patterson.

8. Langston Hughes, *The Big Sea*, New York, Hill and Wang, 1963, pp. 72–89.

9. Claude McKay, *A Long Way from Home*, New York, Harcourt, Brace and World, 1970, chap. 1.

10. From an interview with Mrs. Regina Andrews.

11. DuBois, *Dusk of Dawn*, pp. 234–35.

12. Ibid., p. 235.

13. Johnson, *Along This Way*, pp. 300–301.

14. Stephen R. Fox, *The Guardian of Boston: William Monroe Trot-*

ter, New York, Atheneum, 1970, pp. 179–85; DuBois, *Dusk of Dawn*, p. 236; *Crisis*, IX (1914–15), pp. 119–20.

15. DuBois, *Dusk of Dawn*, pp. 233–38. See also Martin L. Kilson, Jr., "Political Change in the Negro Ghetto, 1900–1940s," in Nathan I. Huggins, Martin L. Kilson, Jr., and Daniel M. Fox, eds., *Key Issues of the Afro-American Experience*, Vol. II, New York, Harcourt Brace Jovanovich, 1971.

16. *Crisis*, XV (January 1918), p. 114.

17. *Crisis*, XVI (July 1918), p. 111; DuBois, *Dusk of Dawn*, pp. 253–55.

18. From an interview with A. Philip Randolph.

19. DuBois implies as much in *Dusk of Dawn*, p. 255; DuBois cites Newton Baker's indifference on p. 251.

20. Frederick Douglass, *The Life and Times of Frederick Douglass*, New York, Collier, 1962, chap. 11.

21. W. E. B. DuBois, "My Evolving Program for Negro Freedom," in Rayford W. Logan, ed., *What the Negro Wants*, Chapel Hill, University of North Carolina Press, 1944, pp. 31–70, quoted pp. 58–59. For American army violence against Afro-American combat troops see Arthur W. Little, *From Harlem to the Rhine*, New York, Covici-Friede, 1936, chap. 46 and passim.

22. See Cronon, *Black Moses*, passim; and McKay, *Harlem: Negro Metropolis*, pp. 143–80, for descriptions of Garvey's style.

23. There is evidence that Garvey tried to make common cause with the Ku Klux Klan. Cronon, *Black Moses*, pp. 103–9, 189–90; McKay, *Harlem: Negro Metropolis*, pp. 159–60.

24. *Crisis*, XL (April 1933), p. 93.

CHAPTER 2

1. Henry F. May, *The End of American Innocence: A Study of the First Years of Our Own Time, 1912–1917*, New York, Knopf, 1959, for an excellent interpretation of assumptions of the generation of Americans who went into World War I.

2. W. A. Domingo's article appears in *Messenger*, III (August 1920), pp. 73–74.

3. Arthur W. Little, *From Harlem to the Rhine*, chaps. 47 and 48; John Hope Franklin, *From Slavery to Freedom*, New York, Knopf, 2nd ed., 1960, pp. 453–62, for the experience of Negro military in Europe.

4. Alain Locke, ed., *The New Negro: An Interpretation,* New York, Albert and Charles Boni, 1925, for the clarion of the Harlem Renaissance. See Locke's attempt at definition, "The New Negro," pp. 3–16.

5. Malcolm Cowley, *Exile's Return,* New York, Viking, 1962, pp. 3–36.

6. Hughes, *The Big Sea,* pp. 53–56; "The Negro Speaks of Rivers," first appeared in *Crisis,* XXII (June 1921), p. 71, and was published in Langston Hughes, *Weary Blues,* New York, Knopf, 1926, p. 51.

7. Hughes, *Weary Blues,* p. 43.

8. Countee Cullen, *Color,* New York, Harper, 1925, p. 3.

9. Cullen assumes here that the art of the poet is ideally neutral (he would say universal) and not bound to *culture* (i.e. the sum of personal-group-human experience). Thus, in Cullen's eyes, the perplexity is not in the making of a *black poet,* but in the making of a poet *black.*

10. McKay's poem was first published in Max Eastman's *Liberator,* II (July 1919), p. 21, and later appeared in *Messenger,* II (September 1919), p. 4, and in McKay, *Harlem Shadows,* New York, Harcourt, Brace and World, 1922, p. 53.

11. McKay's introductory remarks to his reading of "If We Must Die," for Arna Bontemps, ed., *Anthology of Negro Poets,* Folkways Record, FP91.

12. Locke, ed., *The New Negro,* pp. 231–67.

13. Zora Neale Hurston, *Dust Tracks in the Road,* Philadelphia, Lippincott, 1942, passim. The basis for this judgment will be discussed in Chapter 3, below.

14. Locke, "The Negro Spirituals," in Locke, ed., *The New Negro,* pp. 199–210; see also, James Weldon Johnson, *The Book of American Negro Poetry,* New York, Harcourt, Brace and World, 1922; see his Preface, as well as his Preface in James Weldon Johnson and J. Rosamund Johnson, *The Books of American Negro Spirituals,* New York, Viking, 1925–26.

15. Locke, "The Legacy of Ancestral Arts," in *The New Negro,* pp. 254–67.

16. "Heritage," from Cullen, *Color,* p. 36.

17. First appeared in *Crisis,* XXXVII (July 1930), p. 235.

CHAPTER 3

1. May, *End of American Innocence*, p. 86.
2. Oscar Handlin, *The Americans*, Boston, Little, Brown, 1963, chap. 17, for an interesting discussion of these questions.
3. May, *End of American Innocence*, pp. 232–36.
4. Paul Morand, *New York*, New York, H. Holt and Co., 1930, pp. 269–70.
5. Carl G. Jung, "Your Negroid and Indian Behavior," *Forum*, LXXXIII (April 1930), pp. 193–99.
6. Seymour Krim, *Views of a Nearsighted Cannoneer*, New York, Excelsior, 1961, pp. 44–58; Milton "Mezz" Mezzrow, *Really the Blues*, New York, New American Library, 1964; see a more recent account in Norman Mailer, *The White Negro*, San Francisco, City Lights, 1969. Originally in *Dissent*, IV (Summer 1957), pp. 276–93.
7. Hughes, *The Big Sea*, pp. 268–72. Edward Lueders, *Carl Van Vechten*, New York, Twayne, 1964, is a good literary biography and less academic than that author's *Carl Van Vechten and the Twenties*, Albuquerque, University of New Mexico Press, 1955. By far the best biography of Van Vechten and his times is Bruce Kellner, *Carl Van Vechten and the Irreverent Decades*, Norman, University of Oklahoma Press, 1968. I have used Van Vechten's interview for the Columbia University, *Columbia Oral History* in 1960.
8. Harold Cruse, *The Crisis of the Negro Intellectual*, New York, Morrow, 1967, p. 35. Cruse thinks that Harlem ultimately paid the greater price. Hughes, James Weldon Johnson, and Van Vechten's biographers think he gave more than he got.
9. Van Vechten's judgments about art and culture are very well treated in the biographies previously cited.
10. *New York Evening Post*, December 31, 1921; Carl Van Vechten, *Excavations*, New York, Knopf, 1926, pp. 57–80; Lueders, *Carl Van Vechten*, pp. 55–57; Kellner, *Carl Van Vechten*, pp. 180–82.
11. Edmund Wilson, "Violets from the Nineties," in *Shores of Light*, New York, Vintage, 1961, pp. 68–72.
12. David Daiches, *Some Late Victorian Attitudes*, New York, Norton, 1969.

13. See Lueders, *Carl Van Vechten and the Twenties,* for a full discussion of the relationship between *Peter Whiffle* and the decadent novels, J. K. Huysmans' *Á Rebours* and Oscar Wilde's *The Picture of Dorian Gray.* I think, however, that *Peter Whiffle* lacks the strong moral charge of *Dorian Gray.* It is the absence of real moral tension that makes Van Vechten's decadence a feeble echo of London's *fin de siècle.* If comparison must be made, the character of Peter Whiffle comes close to Ernest Pontifex in Samuel Butler's *The Way of All Flesh.*

14. Mable Dodge Luhan, *Intimate Memories,* Vol. III, New York, Harcourt, Brace and World, 1936, pp. 79–80.

15. Morand, *New York,* pp. 269–70.

16. Lueders, *Carl Van Vechten,* p. 103.

17. Hughes, *The Big Sea,* pp. 168–72; James Weldon Johnson, "Romance and Tragedy in Harlem—A Review," *Opportunity,* III (October 1926), pp. 316–18, 330.

18. D. H. Lawrence, *Phoenix, The Posthumous Papers of D. H. Lawrence,* New York, Viking, 1936, pp. 361–63.

19. W. E. B. DuBois, "Books," *Crisis,* XXIV (December 1926), pp. 31–32.

20. Henry Nash Smith in *Virgin Land,* New York, Vintage, 1950, chap. 6, discusses the problem of the heroine in James Fenimore Cooper's novels.

21. From Max Eastman's introduction to *Selected Poems of Claude McKay,* New York, Bookman Associates, 1953, p. 110, later comments from an interview with Max Eastman.

22. Claude McKay, "A Prayer," in *Harlem Shadows,* p. 58. Max Eastman asked that the printed dedication be dropped because he thought it inappropriate to dedicate a *prayer* to a man, and to an atheist at that. From an interview with Max Eastman. See also, McKay, *A Long Way from Home,* Part I, for McKay's attachments to white patrons.

23. Wallace Thurman, *Infants of the Spring,* New York, Macaulay, 1932, pp. 229–30.

24. Hughes, *The Big Sea,* p. 239.

25. Zora Neale Hurston, *Dust Tracks in the Road,* pp. 183–85. When I interviewed Langston Hughes (only a few weeks before his death) he was still quite upset by the memory of his experience with this lady patron; he still honored his trust not to divulge her name. Zora Hurston, however, tells us that she was

Mrs. R. Osgood Mason. Mrs. Louise Thompson Patterson confirms her identity and these impressions.

26. Hughes, *The Big Sea*, pp. 324–30.

CHAPTER 4

1. Robert A. Bone, *The Negro Novel in America*, New Haven, Yale University Press, 1965, however, attempts to evaluate black writers in terms of this dichotomy. See also Irving Howe, "Black Boys and Native Sons," *Dissent*, X (Autumn 1963), pp. 353–68, and *The New Leader*, XLVII (February 3, 1964), pp. 12–22, which attempts to answer Ralph Ellison's criticism. Ellison's critical essay and final rejoinder appear in his *Shadow and Act*, New York, Signet, 1964, as "The World in a Jug," pp. 115–47.

2. Edwin S. Redkey, *Black Exodus: Black Nationalist and Back-to-Africa Movements, 1890–1910*, New Haven, Yale University Press, 1969; as well as that author's "The Flowering of Black Nationalism: Henry M. Turner and Marcus Garvey," in Huggins, Kilson, and Fox, eds., *Key Issues*, Vol. II, pp. 107–24; Cronon, *Black Moses; E. U. Essien-Udom, *Black Nationalism: A Search for an Identity in America*, New York, Dell, 1964; Theodore Draper, *The Rediscovery of Black Nationalism*, New York, Viking, 1970.

3. See May, *End of American Innocence*, pp. 9–51, but especially p. 51, for definition.

4. Paul H. Buck, *Road to Reunion*, Boston, Little, Brown, 1937; see also William R. Taylor, *Cavalier and Yankee: The Old South and American National Character*, New York, Braziller, 1961. Men like George Washington Cable were as much stifled by northern indifference and publishers' hostility as by southern anger.

5. See the brilliant description and analysis of Uncle Tom as Mrs. Stowe's "Black Christ" in Kenneth S. Lynn, *Mark Twain and Southwestern Humor*, Boston, Little, Brown, 1959, pp. 107–11; also Ellen Moers, "Mrs. Stowe's Vengeance," *The New York Review of Books*, XV (September 3, 1970), pp. 25–32.

6. Johnson, *Autobiography of an Ex-Coloured Man*, p. 190.

7. Bone, *The Negro Novel*, wrongly stresses that the protagonist was plagued with guilt for his cowardice. This clearly was not

Johnson's meaning. It rather reflects Bone's consistent sense of revulsion at what he thinks to be race rejection.

8. Theodore Dreiser's *Sister Carrie* had been suppressed, remember, because of the portrayal of the disintegration of Hurstwood and the corruption of Carrie without redeeming moral uplift.

9. From *Color*, p. 14.

10. From *Weary Blues*, p. 107.

11. From *Harlem Shadows*, p. 6.

12. Again Bone, *The Negro Novel*, pp. 76–77, misses the point and thinks Aunt Hager has lost joy.

13. Henry May's phrase to define the conservative establishment that defended the genteel tradition.

14. May, *End of American Innocence*, p. 248.

15. Johnson, *The First Book of American Negro Poetry*, Preface.

16. George Schuyler's thinking and writing style showed the influence of H. L. Mencken; they shared a fascination for H. G. Wells as well as a cynical, feisty attitude. Hart Crane was a close friend of Jean Toomer's, who was more closely related to Greenwich Village than to Harlem.

17. From *Color*, p. 36.

18. Ibid., p. 24.

19. I am grateful to Mr. Wendell Wray for having arranged for my viewing of Douglas' murals when they were still hidden away. Mr. Wray, who is librarian at the Countee Cullen Branch of the New York Public Library, is largely responsible for having saved these works for present viewing. Much of my comment about Aaron Douglas' work is based on interviews with that artist. I was also blessed by the opportunity to talk with the late Meta Warrick Fuller when she was in her ninetieth year.

20. McKay denied any influence from Van Vechten's novel. *A Long Way from Home*, pp. 282–83.

21. Lilyan Kesteloot, *Les Écrivains noirs de langue française: naissance d'une littérature*, Bruxelles, Université Libre de Bruxelles (2me éd.), 1965, pp. 63–82.

22. Claude McKay, "On Becoming a Roman Catholic," *The Epistle*, XI (Spring 1945), pp. 21–22.

23. From Jean Toomer, *Cane*, New York, Boni-Liveright, 1923, p. 21.

24. In fact these qualities and spirit, which came to be summed up as "negritude" and sometimes "soul," since they laud non-in-

dustrial and non-commercial characteristics, were making the best out of postwar African reality and white racism. "So we are not industrious and frugal," they were saying, "we are better; we are natural; we are human." In the 1970s, however, many Africans are impatient with Senghor's "negritude" because they see it as denying the possibility of African industrial, economic development. Primitivism has its price.

25. Cowley, *Exile's Return*, chap. 3.
26. Max Eastman said it was for medical care.

CHAPTER 5

1. This attitude persists, strangely in the minds of white critics of Negro writers. It is at the bottom of Irving Howe's exchange with Ralph Ellison (see Chapter 4, footnote 1). See also Robert Bone's treatment of this question; note especially his assessment of Frank Yerby.

2. Although different in many ways, it is interesting to compare *The Rise of David Levinsky*, 1917, with *The Autobiography of an Ex-Coloured Man*. In both novels acceptance and success in American society come at the cost of a rich cultural heritage.

3. Alain Locke, "Art or Propaganda?" *Harlem*, I (November 1928), p. 12.

4. Langston Hughes, "Negro Artist and the Racial Mountain," *Nation*, CXXII (June 23, 1926), pp. 692–94.

5. George S. Schuyler, "Negro-Art Hokum," *Nation*, CXXII (June 16, 1926), pp. 662–63. Schuyler resented that the editor, Freda Kirchway, solicited Negro opinion about his article before she printed it. "I think an editor ought to be able to make up his mind, or her mind, about what they're going to carry without questioning everybody in town." George S. Schuyler's interview for the *Columbia Oral History*, pp. 76–77 of typescript.

6. From *Color*, p. 68.

7. Ibid., p. 106.

8. Ibid., p. 78.

9. McKay, *Harlem Shadows*, pp. xx–xxi.

10. Ibid., p. 20.

11. McKay, *A Long Way From Home*, pp. 18–19.

12. From *Selected Poems of Claude McKay*, p. 38.

13. From *Harlem Shadows*, p. 52.

14. Arna Bontemps, ed., *Anthology of Negro Poets.*
15. From *Cane*, p. 6.
16. Hughes, *The Big Sea*, p. 56.
17. Ibid., p. 56. An interview with Langston Hughes. In the last years of his life, Hughes very successfully combined the religious format, gospel singers, and modern dance into effective theater: *Tambourines to Glory, The Nativity*, and *The Prodigal Son* are the most notable.
18. From *Selected Poems of Langston Hughes*, New York, Knopf, 1966, p. 118.
19. Ibid., p. 35.
20. Ibid., p. 237.
21. From *Fine Clothes to the Jew*, New York, Knopf, 1927, p. 75.
22. From Sterling Brown, *Southern Road*, New York, Harcourt, Brace and World, 1932, p. 59.
23. Johnson, *The Book of American Negro Poetry*, p. 9. Strangely, Johnson goes on to argue that it could be done, that the Negro could produce the art and literature that would place him on a par with whites. Indeed, he points out that Negroes have already produced all that could be considered distinctively American, especially in music and dance. But his preference for *high* culture and *serious* art tied him to scales of value which were not in the determination of Afro-Americans. Curiously, he did not wonder that despite a creative history in the New World, the Negro's race image had not improved. He might also have asked if American whites, themselves, had a criterion which was distinctive enough (not European) to recognize excellence and originality when they found it.
24. See Roger D. Abrahams, *Deep Down in the Jungle*, Philadelphia, Aldine, 1970, for an excellent discussion of street language of Negro boys. Bruce A. Rosenberg, *The Art of the American Folk Preacher*, New York, Oxford University Press, 1970, is an excellent and scholarly treatment of the oral tradition as manifested in Negro folk sermons. There are several works on the blues and its tradition, but see Charles Keil, *Urban Blues*, Chicago, University of Chicago Press, 1966; Leroi Jones, *Blues People*, New York, Morrow, 1968; and Paul Oliver, *The Meaning of the Blues*, New York, Collier, 1963.
25. Abrahams, *Deep Down in the Jungle.*
26. Johnson, *The Book of American Negro Poetry*, p. 6.

27. Henry James, *Hawthorne*, Ithaca, Cornell University Press, 1956, p. 11.
28. See Warner Berthoff, *American Literature: Traditions and Talents*, Oberlin, Ohio, Press of the Times 1960, for an interesting discussion of this question. I am grateful to David and Margery Guillet for bringing this pamphlet to my attention.
29. Bone, *The Negro Novel*, p. 93.
30. Hughes, *The Big Sea*, pp. 233–41.

CHAPTER 6

1. Hutchins Hapgood, *The Spirit of the Ghetto*, New York, Schocken, 1966, pp. 118–75. Although first published in 1902, this remains the best description of the Yiddish stage.
2. This backface parallel to traditional American comic types seems obvious, but no one to my knowledge has observed it and accepted the implications. For the standard interpretation see Carl Wittke, *Tambo and Bones*, New York, Greenwood, 1968. For the best discussion see Hans Nathan, *Dan Emmett and the Rise of Early Negro Ministrelsy*, Norman, Oklahoma, University of Oklahoma Press, 1962. For discussions of the traditional comic types see: Kenneth S. Lynn, *Mark Twain and Southwestern Humor;* and Constance Rourke, *American Humor*, New York, Doubleday, 1953.
3. Tom Fletcher, *The Tom Fletcher Story: 100 Years of the Negro in Show Business*, New York, Burdge, 1954; Johnson, *Black Manhattan;* Johnson, *Along this Way;* Loften Mitchell, *Black Drama, The Story of the American Negro in the Theatre*, New York, Hawthorne, 1967; all include good general discussions of the history of the Negro in the theater.
4. Oscar Handlin, *The Americans*, chap. 17 is suggestive.
5. Nathan, *Dan Emmett*, passim, gives detailed descriptions which makes this point. Notice, here, the animalistic and savage characteristizations and the use of animal bones for instruments. See also, the numerous "How to put on a Minstrel" books like that of Frank Dumont, *The Witmark Amateur Minstrel Guide*, Chicago, Witmark and Co., 1899.
6. Frances Trollope, *Domestic Manners of the Americans*, New York, Vintage, 1960 was first published in 1832. Mark Twain pointed out that she had been taken in by just the kind of back-

woods humor that made up minstrelsy, Mark Twain, *Life on the Mississippi*, Hill and Wang, 1963, p. 219.

7. Dixon Wecter, *The Saga of American Society*, New York, Scribner's, 1937, p. 160. The event occurred in September 1832; Wecter quotes from the New York *Evening Post*.

8. Kenneth S. Lynn, *Mark Twain and Southwestern Humor;* William R. Taylor, *Cavalier and Yankee.*

9. Oscar Handlin, however, mentions the elaborate promotion of a lunatic white boy named Daniel Pratt by socially prominent New Englanders for the humor of it: *The Americans,* pp. 238–39. A number of luminaries indulged themselves at the expense of the eccentric or feebleminded; San Francisco's Emperor Norton is another example.

10. Fletcher, *The Tom Fletcher Story,* p. 58.

11. Ibid., p. 141.

12. Ibid., p. 322.

13. I mean by this, American humor that uses the Negro and in which Negroes may participate. This is probably different from an indigenous Negro humor.

14. Rourke, *American Humor,* chaps. 1–3; and Lynn, *Mark Twain and Southwestern Humor,* passim.

15. From a stump speech, "Any Other Man" written and delivered by Byron Christy. Printed in Byron Christy, *Christy's New Songster and Black Joker,* New York, Dick & Fitzgerald, pp. 9–11.

16. Several studies have demonstrated that the western frontier, as it became organized, coupled democratic fervor with intense racism: Leon Litwack, *North of Slavery,* Chicago, University of Chicago Press, 1961; Eugene Berwanger, *The Frontier Against Slavery,* Chicago, University of Chicago Press, 1969; V. Jacque Voegeli, *Free But Not Equal,* Chicago, University of Chicago Press, 1969; Forrest G. Wood, *Black Scare,* Berkeley, University of California Press, 1968.

17. There is an argument whether or not Garvey's middle name was "Aurelius." It was used widely by contemporaries without apparent complaint from him. Claude McKay used it in *Harlem, Negro Metropolis.* Mrs. Amy Jacques-Garvey, however, insists that his middle name was "Mosiah." Nevertheless, the common use of Marcus Aurelius illustrates my point about travesty.

18. Lady Emmeline Stuary Wortley, *Travels in the United States . . . During 1849–1850,* New York, 1885, chap. 12.

19. Dumont, *The Witmark Amateur Minstrel Guide*, p. 15.

20. Wecter, *The Saga of American Society*, especially chap. 9; Handlin, *The Americans*, pp. 285–91.

21. New York *Tribune*, March 25, 1888.

22. My description of the Bradley Martin ball is taken from Wecter, *The Saga of American Society*, pp. 368–70.

23. Johnson, *Black Manhattan*, p. 105, the letter is quoted.

24. Ibid., gives an excellent summary of this theatrical history. The quote is from page 103. Langston Hughes and Milton Meltzer, *Back Magic: A Pictorial History of the Negro in American Entertainment*, Englewood Cliffs, New Jersey, Prentice-Hall, 1967, contains more written description and analysis than the title implies. Mitchell, *Black Drama*, has a brief discussion of the same period but focuses on mid-twentieth-century theater; Ann Charters, *Nobody, The Story of Bert Williams*, London, Macmillan, 1970, gives some special insight into that performer's life.

25. Johnson, *Black Manhattan*, p. 103.

26. Fletcher, *The Tom Fletcher Story*, pp. 139–40.

27. Ibid., pp. 142–43.

28. Nathan, *Dan Emmett*, pp. 265–66; Kenneth Lynn observes that the southern nostalgia began early and had significant power in the North, *Mark Twain and Southwestern Humor*, passim; also, Taylor, *Cavalier and Yankee*.

29. George W. Walker, "The Real 'Coon' on the American Stage," *The Theatre Magazine*, VI (1908), pp. i–ii, 180.

30. There was a series of dances that became fads for whites and blacks: the Black Bottom, the Charleston, the Lindy Hop, and Truckin' are notable. Each came from the Negro stage and swept white and black societies.

31. This account of *In Dahomey*, which I have taken from contemporary playbills and newspaper clippings, differs in an important way from descriptions in Charters, *Nobody*, p. 70. Mrs. Charters gives no comment about African scenes in this show and in *Abyssinia* whereas contemporary accounts make Africa the focus of the shows.

32. Walker, "The Real 'Coon' on the American Stage," pp. i–ii.

33. The last song was revived by the white orchestra leader, Phil Harris, in the 1940s.

34. "Nobody," words by Alex Rogers, music by Bert Williams, copyright 1905 by the Attucks Music Publishing Co., copyright 1932 by Lavinia Rogers, and assigned to Edward B. Marks Music Co.

35. "Why Adam Sinned," was first sung in *In Dahomey* (March 21, 1905), copyright 1904 the Attucks Music Publishing Co. While this song was first sung by Mrs. George (Ada Overton) Walker, Bert Williams sang it as well. Alex Rogers' lyrics are printed in Johnson, *The Book of American Negro Poetry*, pp. 158–59. Rogers also wrote the lyrics to "The Jonah Man," "Bon Bon Buddy, the Chocolate Drop," "I May be Crazy, But I Ain't No Fool" among other songs that Bert Williams sang.

36. Significantly, this taboo has persisted into our own time, for it is only with *For the Love of Ivy* (1968) that a major dramatic or cinematic production permitted sexual or romantic love between black couples.

37. Johnson, *Autobiography of an Ex-Coloured Man*, pp. 174–81.

38. Langston Hughes was successful in transforming this insight into effective commercial theater.

39. I am grateful to Mrs. Katherine Gerhardt Pinelo whose research, while an undergraduate at Lake Forest College in Illinois, discovered many old playbills of the Pekin Theater and some of the still living performers as well.

40. Hughes and Meltzer, *Black Magic*, pp. 121–22 for the Lafayette Theater and pp. 189–91 for the Karamu Theater.

41. Cruse, *The Crisis of the Negro Intellectual* treats the white expropriation of Afro-American theater throughout the book.

42. New York *Sun*, May 23, 1921; New York *Herald*, May 24, 1921.

43. Alan Dale, New York *American*, May 25, 1921.

44. Hughes and Meltzer, *Black Magic*, pp. 97–105.

45. Wallace Thurman, *The Blacker the Berry*, New York, Macauley, 1928, pp. 200–201.

46. Cruse, *The Crisis of the Negro Intellectual*, pp. 73–82; *The Amsterdam News*, September 1926 through April 1927.

47. *Crisis*, XXXII (July 1926), p. 134.

48. Harold Cruse feels strongly that this failure through success has been very self-defeating for black ethnic theater. Present-day efforts at community theater probably have a greater chance of

surviving. There are more black playwrights and an audience potential that did not exist in the 1920s.

49. Johnson, *Black Manhattan*, pp. 175–77.

50. May, *End of American Innocence*, pp. 185–87.

51. Eugene O'Neill, "Strindberg and Our Theatre," *Provincetown Playbill* (1923–24 Season), No. I, pp. 1 and 3.

Index

1-800 852-2200

_____

(201) 752 - 1000

1 800 525 0280
Continental

1800 EASTERN
327-8 3 7 6

Monday

— Eastern

#340 5^{45} – 7^{00} Atlanta
5^{45} – 4^{45}
7^{00} – 268^{00} #150 8^{00} – 10^{22}

Continental

Monday   3pm → 5^{33}

"368

685
5194